THE LITERATURES OF
THE BRITISH COMMONWEALTH

THE LITERATURES OF
THE BRITISH COMMONWEALTH

EDITOR: A. L. McLEOD

Australia and New Zealand

G. A. WILKES and J. C. REID

A Rider College Publication
THE PENNSYLVANIA STATE UNIVERSITY PRESS
University Park and London

Standard Book Number 271-00128-3
Library of Congress Catalogue Card Number 71-121856

Printed in the United States of America

CONTENTS

The Muse, disgusted at an age and clime
  Barren of every glorious theme,
In distant lands now waits a better time,
  Producing subjects worthy fame:

In happy climes where from the genial sun
  And virgin earth such scenes ensue,
The force of art by nature seems outdone,
  And fancied beauties by the true:

In happy climes, the seat of innocence,
  Where nature guides and virtue rules,
Where men shall not impose for truth and sense
  The pedantry of courts and schools:

There shall be sung another golden age,
  The rise of empire and of arts,
The good and great inspiring epic rage,
  The wisest heads and noblest hearts.

Not such as Europe breeds in her decay;
  Such as she bred when fresh and young,
When heavenly flame did animate her clay,
  By future poets shall be sung.

Westward the course of empire takes its way;
  The four first acts already past,
A fifth shall close the drama with the day;
  Time's noblest offspring is the last.

—George Berkeley (1752)

PREFACE

In the past decade there has been a tremendous growth of interest in the literature emanating from the countries of the Commonwealth. This interest has been both general and academic, and has resulted in the introduction of university courses of study based on the poetry and fiction of non-British, non-American writers in English; in the sponsoring of international conferences on Commonwealth literature; in the founding of the first journal devoted exclusively to the subject; in the inauguration—in Sweden—of a monograph series; in the publication of national or regional anthologies and of anthologies of Commonwealth verse; and in the publication, both in Britain and the United States, of an impressive number of books by Commonwealth authors.

An earlier era was familiar, in a distant and indulgent way, with the names and occasionally the works of some of the writers in the colonies: with Sarah Gertrude Millin or Olive Schreiner; with Henry Lawson and Henry Kendall; with Katherine Mansfield and Claude McKay; with Thomas Pringle and Rabindranath Tagore. And it was assumed that these writers and their small coteries of anonymous associates were rare and frail outcroppings in inhospitable surroundings, destined to a brief and stunted existence and unlikely ever to produce progeny of consequence or elegance. Today, a new generation has become familiar with such names as Nadine Gordimer, Patrick White, Hugh MacLennan, V. S. Naipaul, and Mulk Raj Anand, and it has likewise assumed that these writers are *sui generis* in their several countries.

These assumptions, in the absence of a history of Commonwealth writing, are not unreasonable, for the standard histories of English literature have never given more than passing mention—if any—of what was being produced beyond the shores of Britain or the United States. It was not until 1961 that a first, modest introduction to Commonwealth literature, *The Commonwealth Pen*, was published. That book made no pretense to being more than a general survey of a vast and largely unsurveyed domain, and the rapid development of interest in Commonwealth literature—resulting, among other things, in the issuance of an entire series of books by contemporary African writers—has frequently and urgently pointed to the need for a substantial account of the development of literature in the various regions of the former British Empire.

There have long been, it is true, excellent histories of Australian and Canadian literature, though within just a matter of four or five years the earlier "standard" accounts have been superseded. The other countries are either wholly without literary histories or still dependent on what are now seriously dated and hence unreliable ones. H. M. Green's monumental two-volume *History of Australian Literature* is too prolix for readers who are not concerned with minute details and literary minimi; "Han Suyin's" two-page article on Malaysian literature hardly begins to indicate the present extent of the topic. Neither of these accounts suffices for the reader who is interested in the whole range of Commonwealth literature or in learning about the several countries' creative writing in reasonable compass, and for whom the present series is intended.

Because Canada, Australia, and New Zealand have developed discrete national literatures of considerable quantity and sophistication, these have been discussed in individual chapters. But from a literary viewpoint the writing that has come out of India, Pakistan, and Ceylon has emanated from a single, common experience unrelated to recent political subdivisions, and is therefore to be considered an entity. To most people outside the countries themselves, this is all "Indian" writing; but in recognition of the sentiments that prevail in these countries, their contributions to Commonwealth literature will be described and assessed in separate sections of the volume devoted to Africa and Asia. By tacit consensus the literature of the Republic of Ireland is excluded, while that of the Republic of South Africa is included. And in considering the literature that has been produced in Africa or by Africans it is hardly possible and seldom helpful to speak in terms of national rather than regional achievement, for while politicians are likely to think and act in terms of political boundaries newly or recently described, the English-language writers appear to have accepted instead a wider, more defensible concept of regionalism—something akin to the *négritude* that was shared by the writers of the former French colonies in Africa. Likewise, the present political structures of the former British West Indies have been disregarded so that the literature in English of the entire Caribbean region has been considered as a whole, for it is hardly to be contested that there is no identifiable national quality to discriminate between the fiction produced in Tobago and that written in Jamaica. Conversely, it is demonstrable that fiction produced anywhere in the Caribbean is not likely to be mistaken for Indian—or New Zealand, or Canadian—writing. Because it has more in common with the literature of Africa than any other, the minuscule literature of Malta has been treated in the same chapter, though separately.

Since biographical and bibliographical studies have not been as fully developed in Asia and Africa as in the other areas, it has occasionally been impossible to ascertain dates of birth and death of authors or dates of publication of books; where internal evidence or informed speculation suggests a date, one has been provided. The assistance of Mrs. Mildred Scarpati, who typed the manuscript, is gratefully acknowledged.

A. L. McL.

Rider College
TRENTON, NEW JERSEY

NOTES ON CONTRIBUTORS

A. L. McLeod: Professor of English and Speech and Dean of the School of Liberal Arts and Sciences in Rider College. He holds the B.A., M.A., and Diploma in Education from the University of Sydney, the B.Ed. from the University of Melbourne, and the Ph.D. from The Pennsylvania State University. He is the author of *Rex Warner: Writer* (1960) and editor of *The Commonwealth Pen* (1961), *The Pattern of Australian Culture* (1963), *Walt Whitman in Australia and New Zealand* (1964), *The Pattern of New Zealand Culture* (1968), and *Australia Speaks* (1969).

J. C. Reid: Professor of English in the University of Auckland, from which he obtained the B.A., M.A., and D. Litt. degrees. In 1952–53 he was Fulbright Research Fellow at the University of Wisconsin, and in 1968 was Visiting Professor of English in the University of Aarhus, Denmark. His principal publications include *Creative Writing in New Zealand* (1946), *The Mind and Art of Coventry Patmore* (1957), *Francis Thompson: Man and Poet* (1959), *Thomas Hood* (1963), *Dickens's "Little Dorrit"* (1967), and *Non-Fiction in New Zealand* (1968). In addition, he has collected and edited several anthologies of New Zealand writing and edited *The Tempest.*

G. A. Wilkes: Challis Professor of English and head of the department in the University of Sydney, was appointed Lecturer in English in 1949, after having graduated with First Class honors and the University Medal in English. He was subsequently appointed Professor of Australian Literature, the first such appointment, before assuming his present position. After obtaining the M.A. at Sydney University, he took the D. Phil. at Oxford. Professor Wilkes has published widely on Henry Handel Richardson and Christopher Brennan. His major publications include *New Perspectives on Brennan's Poetry* (1954) and *The Thesis of "Paradise Lost"* (1961).

INTRODUCTION

FIFTY years ago, on the publication of the *Cambridge History of English Literature,* the existence of small yet identifiable literatures in India, Canada, Australia, and New Zealand was acknowledged by the inclusion of short chapters on them. (Sir Herbert Warner declared that there was, at that time, still no literature in South Africa except the poetry of Thomas Pringle, Southey's friend, and so devoted the chapter on "South African Poetry" almost wholly to a consideration of that poet's work.) The assumption then was that to write in the English language was simply to contribute to the great treasury of English literature. And before the First World War there were still some traditionalists who (if they saw merit at all in anything that had been written in the United States) regarded American literature, too, as an integral part of the same treasury, denying the possibility of the existence of American literature as a separate, homogeneous, organic body of writing. But the very fact that separate chapters of the *Cambridge History* were devoted to the literatures of former colonies was an indication that they did not, with ease and reason, fit into the neat compartments of periods and genres that had so commodiously accommodated the growth of English literature and its criticism in the past.

In 1916 no one writing in English outside Britain and America could reasonably be compared in achievement to, say, Henry James, Joseph Conrad, or Theodore Dreiser. Yet there were writers whose work was hardly inferior to that of Bret Harte, Edith Wharton, George Gissing, and Rudyard Kipling: in fact, for fifty years books of definite literary merit had been appearing in or from the older colonies, only to be reviewed condescendingly or ignored completely. From the end of the Edwardian era there was a change in attitude, it seems, to the literature developing in the further outposts of empire. There was, perhaps, an awareness that from the roots of nationalism new branches of literature had developed, branches that might, with the passage of time and under propitious circumstances, flourish like the branch in the United States which, partly because it was almost a century older, was already worthy of the attention and scrutiny of scholars and critics.

Since the First World War—and especially since the 1930's—

there has been a remarkable increase in the literary productivity of the older Commonwealth countries and an unprecedented maturation; at the same time has occurred the initial growth of identifiable regional literatures in the smaller former British possessions. As each colony has moved inexorably towards Independence or Federation, there has been a quickening of written expression and a growing consciousness of the close relationship—if not the singleness of purpose—of literature and political, or national, aspiration.

Though regional literatures develop at rates determined by numerous factors, some literary or intellectual, others political or social, there is apparently a close connection between the movement towards national sovereignty and the evolution of an independent, national literature. Of the Commonwealth countries, Canada attained Dominion status first, at Confederation, and developed its own literature soon afterwards; Australia witnessed its first great literary florescence almost a generation before Federation; New Zealand took almost a generation after attaining Dominion status to produce any true literature; and in the Caribbean a literature was in the making during the 1930's, if not even a little earlier, though Federation (and subsequently dissolution and reorganization) did not occur until thirty years later. In Africa, Malta, and Malaysia, nationalism and regional literatures have been almost contemporary in origin and development.

The literature now being produced in the Commonwealth countries is so sophisticated (in a critical sense) that William Barrett, writing in *The Atlantic Monthly* recently, could open a review with the previously almost indefensible statement that "It can be argued, although not palatably in London, that the best writing in English is now coming from the colonials." Of course, the "colonials" would be quick to point out that they are now Commonwealth authors (or New Zealanders, Australians, Pakistanis, Jamaicans, or Malaysians, as the case may be), and that while "colonial" may have been a useful term in the past, it is now useful as a meaningful literary term only in so far as it describes the essentially historical phenomenon of the transplanting of the English language and its attendant literary traditions outside the British Isles. In all contexts except this last-mentioned, the term "colonial" today carries only that pejorative connotation that it gained when used by British civil service administrators, most of whom are now comfortably retired in Surrey or Kent. So strong has been the reaction to the term, in fact, that a poet writing in Suva maintains with some justification that though he lives in the Colony of Fiji he is helping to establish a Fijian national literature.

Today increasing numbers of scholars and literary historians recognise the validity and utility of making a tripartite division of the literature produced in English into British, American, and Commonwealth. It is not to be expected that this will come about without demur: academic innovations gain ground slowly. The present "modern languages"—English, German, French, Spanish—date only from the mid-nineteenth century as university subjects, and American Literature was without a professor until the 1920's.

The triune division of English literature into British, American, and Commonwealth is appropriate as well as convenient. A writer in Tobago has little in common with another in Connecticut or one in Cornwall, but he shares the same "Commonwealth" experience—colonial settlement, British cultural heritage, emergent national ethos—as a writer in Kuala Lumpur or Lagos, just as the New England poet shares the same "American" heritage as a Southern novelist. The New Englander and the Southerner are identifiably regional, but they are even more clearly American and neither British nor Commonwealth. That is, the characteristics that they share are much more noticeable than their differences; and in essence these traits are the result of a common cultural heritage. Even though a Commonwealth author lives and writes in London, he can rarely hope to become a British writer: he must be content to remain an expatriate Australian, Jamaican, or whatever the case may be, just as Gertrude Stein and Ezra Pound, among the most familiar expatriate writers, must always be considered as having contributed to American literature. Inspiration and culture are involved, but it is more: it amounts to a matter of identity.

It is difficult to explain the empathy that exists between members of the Commonwealth, yet it exists. Perhaps it is the result of a common feeling of discrimination: as "colonials" they were collectively the recipients of a certain British condescension. Perhaps it is the result of sharing a similar heritage and an educational system that was immutable and lacked local variation. But there is an intangible, ineffable feeling of "community": individuals from the Commonwealth recognize it immediately, others seldom sense it.

Today fifty million people in Britain produce one "regional" literature in English, two hundred million produce another in America, and fifty million English-speaking members of the Commonwealth produce a third. The third group has been excluded from both the *Oxford Companion to English Literature* and the *Oxford Companion to American Literature*—with the exception of "Banjo" Paterson and a few intrusive Canadians. This, argues Professor R. T. Robertson, amounts to a general recognition that all writing in English other than British and American must be Commonwealth. His viewpoint receives tacit support from the Modern Language Association which, in its *Annual Bibliography*, lists all references to the literatures of the Commonwealth countries under a separate rubric. Of Commonwealth literature Professor Robertson has written:

> This literature is best understood as that which exhibits a common movement of the human spirit in undergoing a roughly similar historical process in different parts of the world at different times. The most obvious bonds which hold together this human experience are the English language and the English tradition; other literatures in a common language reflect a similar process.
>
> The literature of the Commonwealth is properly defined by the common vision and intention of the colonial writers. This "colonial principle," comparatively deduced, has a certain value in pulling together the early writing of a colony, in unifying a certain amount of all writing in English at different times, and in throwing fresh light on the relationship between what are now often regarded as separate branches of English literature, although its value correspondingly decreases as the regional literature attains what may be roughly spoken of as independence. It is similar to the conceptualizing of any part of literature in English as a period or movement.

Classification becomes a matter of concern to some readers and critics. They wonder whether Roy Campbell is properly considered a South African, or whether he should be regarded as an Englishman: but they allow that he should not be thought of as a Spanish author. They are uncertain, too, whether Christina Stead (who left Australia some forty years ago, has only now returned, and whose novels make almost no use of Australia for setting or incident) can any longer be considered an Australian novelist. The question does not, of course, lend itself to any single, universally acceptable and dogmatic answer. When Conrad totally identified himself with England, he became a British author. (And though he used Malayan and African locales, he was never a Commonwealth author. He used exotic backgrounds merely for artistic purposes.) T. S. Eliot is claimed by both British and American literary historians, and he seemed quite content with that.

But classification, in the end, becomes a matter of consensus, though it should be guided by the author's identification, either for a number of years or substantially throughout his writing career, with one country rather than another. Whether he actually lived there permanently, spasmodically, or not at all, is not always relevant. Douglas Stewart, born and raised in New Zealand, is by choice considered an Australian writer; Nevil Shute, who retired to Australia, was ever a British writer, since he did not regard himself as an Australian, did not share its ethos, nor help to develop its national culture and identity: he was, like D. H. Lawrence before him, merely a transient so far as literature is concerned. Maxwell Hall, for over thirty years a resident of Sabah, and deeply associated with it both politically and culturally, is a Malaysian author, as is Katherine Sim, a former resident now living and writing in England, though using her Malayan experience for the very substance of her writing. There will always be difficult cases: one wonders how to categorize Peter Abrahams. Should he be considered South African, or Caribbean?

Commonwealth literature was first taught as a separate subject at university level by Professor A. Bruce Sutherland at The Pennsylvania State University in 1941. Because of library limitations and the compression required in a course that lasted only one semester, the instruction was necessarily restricted to Canadian, Australian, and New Zealand authors. Since then, however, the course has included writers from other parts of the Commonwealth. Soon after the Second World War Professor S. B. Liljegren of the University of Upsala extended the range of his teaching in English literature by discussing the work of Australian, Canadian, and Irish writers, and established two monograph series, devoted to Canadian and Australian literatures. By so doing he became the principal Commonwealth literature advocate and scholar in the European universities and attracted German students, two of whom presented theses on Australian subjects for graduate degrees.

By 1957 there was sufficient interest in United States academic circles to justify the founding within the Modern Language Association of a Conference on Commonwealth Literature. Since then the *Annual Bibliography* of the M.L.A. has included a Commonwealth literature section, and the Conference has published a *Newsletter*, edited by Professor Joseph Jones of the University of Texas. An invitational conference, restricted to Commonwealth citizens, was held at the University of Leeds, under the sponsorship of Professor A. N. Jeffares, in 1964 to consider the general subject of Commonwealth literature; an international convention of writers, critics, and teachers on the same theme is now being planned in the United States.

In Canada, Commonwealth literature has received considerable support. Upwards of half a dozen universities offer courses in the subject and have specialists teaching it. At Queen's University Dr. John P. Matthews has been appointed Director of an Institute of Commonwealth and Comparative Studies, which initially is concentrating on literature. (The Commonwealth Studies Center at Duke University has, in the many years of its existence, wholly excluded literary studies from its domain.) Dr. Matthews' own *Tradition in Exile,* which examines the poetry of Canada and Australia in the nineteenth century, suggests the direction in which studies in the Institute will probably proceed.

In Australia and New Zealand, isolated culturally almost as wholly as geographically from the remainder of the Commonwealth, there is still a greater concern for the national literature than for the literature of the Commonwealth at large. Perhaps this indicates an essentially parochial outlook; certainly it is unfortunate. While students and teachers in Nigeria and Trinidad reveal an enviable first-hand acquaintance with the work of South African, Canadian, and Indian writers, few Australian university graduates, with good degrees in English, are familiar with even New Zealand authors—with the exception of Katherine Mansfield. Within the past few years, in Australia, courses in Australian literature have been introduced in the larger universities and brief series of lectures on the subject have been part of the curriculum in the other institutions for some time; British, American, and Australian writers are studied to the exclusion of the remainder of Commonwealth writers. Unfortunately, there is a feeling that is too widespread in Australia, that the local literature is superior in quality and greater in quantity than that produced elsewhere in the Commonwealth.

Today, however, without reference to the whole body of Commonwealth writing, it is far more difficult to consider a national literature adequately than it might have been some years ago. Further, it is hardly more enlightening than to study, say, Queensland literature without seeing it in its proper perspective as part of Australian literature, or than to study Nigerian literature without regard to the rest of the English literature of West Africa.

There is much to be gained from the comparative view which a reader or critic of one Commonwealth country's literature can take of a novel, play, or poem written in another; but local studies of an indigenous literature are the most difficult of all to assess dispassionately, and hence validly. Chauvinism, or criticism based on personal or political friendships and animosities rather than on intrinsic flaws and merits, too frequently jaundices judgments. As Professor A. N. Jeffares has observed,

There is a danger, where a local audience may be small, of overpraise from a coterie or underpraise from the jealous. . . . To praise a writer in an emergent country because he writes at all, or because he writes in English, or because he writes in an unusual English about unusual things is, in effect, to insult him, to display an insularity both archaic and arrogant. The overseas writer in English, no less than the local writer, must be judged by the best, most rigorous standards. . . . What he needs, therefore, is to be read outside as well as inside his own country.

Perhaps the person best qualified to judge the work of Commonwealth authors is one who shares the same general heritage, is properly informed about the mainstreams of British and American writing, and (though sympathetic) is yet sufficiently removed in place and relationship, if not in time, to render discriminating and sound evaluations. The publication of anthologies of Commonwealth literature in both Britain and the United States has done a great deal towards the establishment of a critical overseas readership—much more than the vociferous protestations of patriots and partisans in distant "outposts of Empire."

The future of literature in English in some of the Commonwealth countries is far from certain: though Afrikaans is now the official language of the Republic of South Africa, it is unlikely in the forseeable future to produce any literature of lasting significance, since there is no reading public beyond the boundaries of the country and an Afrikaans-speaking population of two million is unlikely ever to be able to support the publication of even modest numbers of novels and volumes of poetry. Government subvention may overcome the economics of commercial publication, but few writers of ambition or stature are likely to be content with writing in a literary vacuum and to pass unnoticed—except in a possible translation—outside South Africa.

In India, Pakistan, Ceylon, Malta, Malaysia, and some of the African nations, the situation is no more clear, since English has been relegated to "associate" status in India and has been superseded by Malay as the official language of Malaysia, while in the other countries it remains a minority language. In discussing the use of English as a medium of expression for essentially non-British sentiments, however, Dr. C. D. Narasimhaiah, Professor of English in the University of Mysore, has written:

Two of our best and most successful novelists writing in English—R. K. Narayan and Raja Rao—have found English quite adequate for their purposes. Indeed, they have baffled translators in our own languages. For it all sounds to our ears better in English than in our languages. I have no doubt that this would be true of some other successful writers in different parts of the English-speaking world.

And so long as the language of higher education, of international intercourse, and of the more influential newspapers and journals within the Commonwealth continues to be English, those writers with literary aspirations of the highest order will surely elect to write in English and to seek publication in Britain or the United States. Throughout the Commonwealth, Westernization and the English language are synonymous: it is as natural for the British-educated Indian or African to think and write in English as in any local language. That it can be done with great grace, fluency, and distinction is attested by the achievement of Jawaharlal Nehru, Chinua Achebe, Gabriel Okara, and Chin Kee Onn, among numerous others.

In the development of the indigenous literatures of the older Commonwealth countries, certain rather clearly-defined stages can be recognized, though it is uncertain that the newer nations, whose independence or federation has been achieved at what might seem an artificially accelerated pace, will necessarily follow the same schedule. In fact, because their independence as political states has come somewhat before they were able to establish a national (as distinct from tribal or local) culture, it may well be that they will continue in the first, or Colonial, stage of literary development while we would normally have expected them to have progressed to the National stage. Alternatively, they may by-pass the National stage entirely. Time alone will tell. The older literatures, however, have gone through the following stages of development:

1) *The Colonial Period: An Historical Concept.* In this period are produced works of general prose—letters, diaries, journals, descriptive and statistical accounts—by settlers and explorers anxious to make their new situation known to those who have remained in the homeland; with the passage of time, histories and biographies recording the development of the new settlement and the achievement of the first generations of settlers; later still, odes and similar commemorative verses, written in imitation of the literary styles that prevailed with popular authors when the settlers left their homeland, and introducing local argot, flora and fauna, customs and values. All these are written, Professor Arlin Turner suggests, "with the deliberate intention of bringing literature, written according to established and honored rules, from the old home to the new." After lyric verse comes narrative, and

even pseudo-epic; adventure fiction of commercial standards exploiting the novelties of geography and botany and having, to subsequent generations, no literary value except historic; tracts and treatises; epideictic speeches and hortatory sermons.

In a paper entitled "Colonialism and Regionalism: Twin Concepts in Literary History and Criticism," Professor R. T. Robertson observed that

> The colonial period, however roughly defined in each literary history, has two obvious features: it does not begin in literature until some time after the colony has been planted, and it continues after the colony has achieved political independence. These facts are reflected in an intermediate stage noted by the Canadian scholars, Leon Edel, A. J. N. Smith, and E. K. Brown, as two conflicting themes in colonial literature: (1) the backward glance at the "good old days," unrecorded in their time, and (2) the premature assertion that "Jack's better than his father." To the literature of the backward glance we give the name "local color," generally a nostalgic celebration of a disappearing and now apparently attractive stage of society. On the whole, this theme produces better writing than the other, which is possibly why it can be more easily identified in literature.

There is no *point* at which this early literature of a colony ceases to be Colonial and becomes National, notwithstanding the insistence of some politicians and chauvinists; there is, rather, a period during which the transformation takes place gradually, even imperceptibly, until one writer or work of literature incontrovertibly heralds the arrival of the second stage. Though the change is organic, it can usually be noted, in retrospect, to have taken place within a certain span of years; perhaps a decade, perhaps a generation. This transitional era has been called the period of "local color" (Edel), of "regionalism" (Brown), and of "local realism" (Smith). Each of the terms has merit, and none is better than another: the concept is the significant thing.

Whereas the early colonial literature is the product of adult settlers of at least modest educational accomplishment and moderate affluence and leisure, the transitional literature is increasingly the work of the native-born, including women, some of whose poetry, especially, reaches commendable levels of lyricism.

2) *The National Period: A Political Concept.* In this second period, during which Federation or Independence is achieved, there is a conscious, overt attempt to produce a literature that is appropriate to the new national status. By superseding parochial and regional imagery, subject matter, and appeal with the more general and national, there is a conscious effort on the part of writers

to develop a literature that will provide cultural or national cohesion. In a fashion, literature at this stage of development becomes the handmaiden of politics. In the United States, for example, the literature of the early nineteenth century was consciously American rather than New England or Midwestern as it had been earlier and was to become again. Writers of the National period try to change and improve upon the modes and criteria of their regional, colonial predecessors. As E. H. Dewart wrote in the Preface to his *Selections from Canadian Poets* (1864), "A national literature is an essential element in the formation of a national character. It is not merely the record of a nation's mental progress: it is the expression of its intellectual life, the bond of national unity, and the guide of national energy."

Because of the urge—compulsion, even, in some writers—to stress the national rather than the universal elements and themes, the literature of this period is peopled by atypical characters—those who are so far removed from other "national types" that they would immediately stand out in any cosmopolitan gathering. In trying to draw the "typical" representative of his country, the nationalistic author all too often draws, instead, a caricature. The resultant caricature is then sometimes accepted as a national archetype and is enshrined in the national ethos. Recently Professor Russel Ward has demonstrated that this is what happened in Australian literature when a fictitious "average Australian" was created in the image of the shearer or drover battling the hardships of the "outback." In fact, the drover was as uncharacteristic of the urban and farming population of nineteenth-century Australia as was the fur trapper of early Canada.

In the National period the novel and short story mature swiftly. There is usually a growing literacy, and this helps to support the publishing industry upon which the fiction writer is dependent. Subject matter is found in national rather than regional situations: shearing and droving; fur trapping or railroading; Japanese Occupation or communist emergency; racial segregation or social discrimination based on color. Almost all of this literature is produced by second- and third-generation authors, some of whom leave their native land in protest against the emergent and strident nationalism of the scene to pursue their craft in the more sophisticated literary centers of the English-speaking world. The literature of Nationalism is not great, nor is all of it even good, but it has the attractiveness of vitality and youth. As the reviewer of *The Commonwealth Pen* wrote in the *Times Literary Supplement*:

> Comparisons forgotten, this literature stands a chance. The New Zealand or South African novelist may not have excelled in characterization or style or

plot, in so far as these may be judged by the supposedly immutable rules of fiction, but as he cannot but have reflected and commented upon the character and experience of his countrymen, they are at least brought face to face with themselves in his work; and as they are historically in search of an identity which they sense as existing but cannot yet define, they must find this more invigorating than the contemplation of an alien life, however plausibly rendered by a more commanding art.

3) *The Commonwealth Period: A Geographical Concept.* Writers using the English language, who are neither American nor British, reach the acme of their achievement when their work is unmarred by national self-consciousness and they write in full certainty of their purpose—when they are emancipated from the necessity to use local idiom, local episodes or situations, local character-types and all the other paraphernalia of the National period, bringing the minds of writer and reader into a direct communion and treating of universal problems, emotions, and aspirations while only incidentally and for wholly artistic reasons (and then unobtrusively) using local color. Local settings are not used for their exotic, different, or startling effect, but only because some setting must be used and the local one is the one best known by the writer.

Some of the harbingers of the arrival of national literatures at the Commonwealth level of development were C. J. Brennan, Henry Handel Richardson, Rabindranath Tagore, Sri Aurobindo, Roy Campbell, Claude McKay, and Katherine Mansfield.

The quotidian themes of this final stage in the development of Commonwealth literature, through which authors universalize their particular experiences, are six in number:

(1) *Political Disillusionment.* No longer much used, it seems, in serious fiction in the older Commonwealth countries, this is popular in the newer ones where Lord Acton's *bon mot* that power corrupts has been accepted without demur. Malfeasance, hypocrisy, opportunism, manipulation, duplicity—all the traits that are anathema to idealists—are the substance of African writing by authors just becoming aware of the reality of political machination. Politics, they seem to say, is the bane of society. Cyprian Ekwensi's demagogue, Jacob, in *Beautiful Feathers* (1963), and his venal, contriving Uncle Taiwo in *Jagua Nana* (1961) remind us of counterparts in all our countries; but his novels are not simply *romans à clef*—they are dissertations, often comic and ironic, on the tragic consequences of the acquisition by small men of largely unrestrained power. This same disillusionment is seen in T. M.

Aluko's *One Man, One Machet* (1964), the very title of which parodies the Western political concept.

In southern Africa the white writers (almost all opposed to the government policy of *apartheid*) assert the intellectual proposition that blackness does not preclude a man's being human, while the black writers protest physical separation, violence, detention, humiliation and inequality under the law, and perpetual disenfranchisement. Together, black and white writers present an anti-Establishment front: their goal, the elimination of oppression; their faith, the perfectability of man's political institutions.

(2) *Social Disillusionment.* Sometimes this is presented as a classical Hobbesian drama of the individual pitted against a Leviathan system, as in the short stories of the Malayan, Patrick Onn, whose typical, Kafkaesque character is merely trying to get through the labyrinthine bureaucracy of a falsely decent and intensely stupid Civil Service. In many ways, this is Christian *en route* to the Celestial City; it is also a sad colloquy on the ineluctable disillusionment of a young, educated person kept from ameliorating the malaise of his country which cannot progress without the proffered and rejected assistance. Variations on this theme are explored by V. S. Naipaul and Edgar Mittelholzer, who utilize Caribbean mercantile situations; and by Mulk Raj Anand, who depicts the stoicism of ordinary people leading lives of quiet desperation. Readers in any country—and especially underdeveloped ones—will see the allegorical theme in such stories. Essentially, this is the theme that pervades C. P. Snow's works; but while few of us can identify with Snow's awesome corridors of power, most can appreciate subtler nuances of the same theme when restated in less extraordinary terms.

(3) *Cultural Conflict.* This theme is hardly to be found in Australia and New Zealand writers, whose countries are culturally homogeneous, and it is not common in Canada; but where (as in the West Indies, South Asia, and Africa in particular) there are at least two cultural traditions, writers find material in the counterclaims of their natal or tribal culture (which they see as largely irrelevant to social progress) and the Western white culture to which they can never make full claim, *négritude* having become *passé*. In Canadian literature this theme is slightly modified, as in Hugh MacLennan's *Two Solitudes* (1945), where he explores with consummate dexterity the quest for unity of two antagonistic, contiguous cultures, the French-Catholic and the English-Protestant (which may be a parable for South Asia); and *The Precipice*

(1948), in which he explores the cultural conflict that results from a simple Canadian girl's marriage to an American businessman.

Quite recently the Pakistani novelist, Zulfikar Ghose, in *The Murder of Aziz Khan* (1969), has written a morality tale on the conflict between the Old Order of Muslim society (of which Aziz Khan is the symbol) and the new secular business-and-success-oriented culture (symbolized by the Shah brothers). Overseas critical response suggests that Ghose has managed to transform a Bengali real estate problem into a human tragedy of significant dimension.

(4) *Race.* Perhaps no theme is more widely used in the Commonwealth now, and is more universally relevant, than race. In South Africa it pervades everything, and has become obsessive since Jan Hofmeyer's famous "Herrenvolk" speech of 1946, in which he delivered a passionate plea for a fifth freedom—freedom from racial prejudice. There the problem is most variously posed: it is not simply White versus Black, but each of these *vis-à-vis* Colored, Indian, and Oriental. And there it has been presented lugubriously, provocatively, but never more movingly than by Peter Abrahams, who protests, "But inside I'm not black."

Whereas, in the United States, race seems to imply miscegenation, in Africa it implies misanthropy: one nation sees the problem in sexual terms, the other views it in terms of human love and dignity.

While race has not become a common theme in Canada, Australia, or New Zealand, it is important in Malaysia, where Malays, Chinese, Dasuns, and Indians have to maintain a *modus vivendi.* In the West Indies—and especially in Guyana—more literary material is certain to focus on race as the Afro-Indian-White roles change.

(5) *Isolation.* This can be presented as the voluntary insularity of the individual within the context of his own environment—alienation—or as an involuntary experience—loneliness—and is explored at several levels of intensity. At one level we get trenchant criticism and febrile denunciation, as in West African novels; at another, a melancholic withdrawal amid plaintive jeremiads, as in some Malaysian short stories whose authors, like Wordsworth, apparently find the world too much with them; but unlike Browning, they deny that all's right with the world and are uncertain that the best is yet to be. Chinua Achebe, in *Things Fall Apart* (1958) and *No Longer at Ease* (1960), has captured the ambience of Nigerian society and made good use of alienation as a

theme. His characters, like those of Cyprian Ekwensi, see themselves in a world they never made, never expected, and feel unable to join; one that at its most crass represents the worst of both Africa and Europe. Their response is uniform: they withdraw. Present effects of this response are a propensity to satire (not yet elevated to allegory), a penchant for melodrama, an unexercised sense of the comic, and an absence of romantic love, most notably from poetry.

Loneliness has held a special significance for Australian writers, and Ray Lawler's play, *The Summer of the Seventeenth Doll* (1955), makes pellucid the thesis that in love, not sex, is the surcease of loneliness, the source of meaning in life. So well is this done, that the Negro Ensemble Company in New York, by changing only the locale from Australia to the Deep South, saw in the play a parable for modern man. Janet Frame, in New Zealand, has worked with the same theme, pursuing it to its ultimate consequence—the disintegration of personality and the victory of illusion over reality. At a much more percipient level Patrick White, the Australian novelist, dramatist, and short-story writer, has explored through his entire *oeuvre* this concept of human loneliness, developing the Gandhian thesis that love, faith, simplicity, and humility are the true virtues; that smugly militant virtue is ultimately disintegrated by the evil power of pride; and that though men are self-destructive, suffering is redemptive. White's novels have an architectonic complexity of structure and employ tenuous symbolic equations, but he is indubitably preeminent as a novelist of ideas—perhaps the only contemporary Commonwealth author who can, without ridicule, be compared to Melville, say, in achievement and importance. And he is no longer unique in Australian fiction: Randolph Stow, a generation younger than White, is depicting in allegorical novels of considerable magnitude man's confrontation with the vicissitudes, the loneliness, the paradox of life, salvation being found only in the ineffable mysteries of human and divine love.

(6) *Exile.* This variation of the Grail or Wanderer theme is also found seminally in some Colonial immigrant novels, but has not been notably utilized in recent American or British fiction. It has become a pandemic theme of South African poetry, having been iterated from Roy Campbell to the young and hardly known poets of today. In some, it evokes a petulant, ululant note; in others, self-pity and nostalgia for their rejected heritage combined with truculent self-condemnation—a love-hate response. Campbell's splenetic, sardonic intensity precluded maudlin sentimental-

ism, but he never found true inner peace, being torn continually by his rootlessness. In "Tristan de Cunha" he wrote:

> Exiled like you and severed from my race
> By the cold ocean of my own disdain,
> Do I not freeze in such a watery space?

A few African exiles, such as William Plomer, have been agreeably assimilated in England; but most of them—such as David Wright and Roy McNab—fail to find their elusive goal of an ideal social milieu. They remain taunted, mobile, ambivalent, depressed, disillusioned.

These six themes collectively can be viewed as variations on what Professor Northrop Frye calls the "Thermopylae Theme"—the individual pitted against incredible odds—which he observes to have largely vanished from British writing. In the Colonial period it was stated in terms of the settler against an overwhelming, hostile environment; in the National period, as the new country and its culture against the rest of the world.

Claude McKay, having left Jamaica and exiled himself first in the Soviet Union then Harlem, brought all these themes to clear focus in his mordant lines; and R. K. Narayan attempts, it seems, the same thematic amalgam as he develops Malgudi into an Indian paradigm of the universal microcosm, comparable to Barchester, Wessex, and Yoknapatawpha.

Many of these themes are not now prominent in British and American literature; and conversely, it should be observed that the *carpe diem, ubi sunt,* and metaphysical aesthetic themes have almost no currency in Commonwealth literature—for the forward look rather than the backward glance is its characteristic motif.

In a special issue of the *Times Literary Supplement* devoted to the literature of the Commonwealth, the editorial writer put the case for the recognition of that literature as a single body of work rather than as a congeries of territorial literatures, and as being worthy of study:

> If Commonwealth literature—even understood only in the most basic geographic sense—has established anything during recent years, it is that writers are emerging from Canada, the West Indies, Australia, Africa, and elsewhere, who can stand on their own feet, be judged by international standards and take acceptance or rejection by these standards with equal equanimity. If the various literatures of the Commonwealth have not been unfairly regarded up to now as the children of that universal mother, "English Literature,"

it is rapidly becoming clear that the children have, almost without our noticing, grown up.

In the interim, Commonwealth authors have continued to produce works of the highest quality, so that Nadine Gordimer, Judith Wright, Patrick White, Chin Kee Onn, R. K. Narayan, Chinua Achebe, V. S. Naipaul, Hugh MacLennan, Frank Sargeson—to be highly selective yet representative—have been judged by the most taxing criteria and found not wanting. Collectively they have established the legitimacy of Commonwealth literature as the "third force" in English literature beside British and American, and made it, in the words of the *Times*, "the most interesting literary phenomenon of our time."

A. L. McLeod

AUSTRALIAN LITERATURE

THE view of Australian literary history offered in this essay was sketched out in a series of lectures at the University College of Townsville, under the auspices of the Foundation for Australian Studies, in May–June 1967. Although the lectures attempted a survey of literary development from the beginnings to the present, the illustration of this development was necessarily limited, apart from some closer consideration of the work of Joseph Furphy, Henry Handel Richardson, and Patrick White. In meeting the condition that lectures under the Foundation should be published, I have taken the opportunity to add some tissue to the outline, while still proceeding by the study of individual authors and keeping within the limits that a "conspectus" allows.

I express my thanks to the University College of Townsville and its Foundation for Australian Studies for the invitation to deliver the lectures, and for their kindness during my stay.

University of Sydney G. A. WILKES

I

THE COLONIAL PERIOD (TO 1880)

THE DEVELOPMENT of Australian literature is the history on one hand of the extension of European civilization to the south, and on the other of the growth of an indigenous culture in Australia itself. There are three broad stages to be distinguished. The first was the colonial phase, extending from the beginnings to the mid and later nineteenth century, in which native writing was shaped mainly by overseas patterns. The second stage was the achievement of an independent and consciously "Australian" literature in the 1880s and 1890s, a movement that extended beyond the turn of the century to the First World War. In the third phase, from the 1920s to the present, the two streams have come together, to produce a literature that is both distinctive and mature. This pattern has a schematic value only, and the role of the 1890s in the evolution is more complex than it might suggest. It would be a distortion, moreover, to read the development simply in terms of the emergence of a new and vigorous literature from the repudiation of effete European conventions. At every stage the two processes have been operating—the extension of European civilization, and the assertion of an indigenous culture—and though at times one has been hostile to the other, each has remained a source of enrichment and advance.

As the legendary continent of the south, Australia had an existence in imagination and in literature even before its discovery by European navigators. The contacts of the early voyagers with *terra australis* are recorded in the sixteenth and seventeenth centuries, although it was not until 1770 that the east coast was discovered by Cook and formally claimed for the crown. It was settled as a penal colony by Governor Phillip in 1788. In this decade Thomas Warton had become Poet Laureate, and Cowper published *The Task*; the oratory of Burke was heard in the impeachment of Warren Hastings, and Gibbon reached the last volume of *The Decline and Fall.* The influence of the eighteenth century is therefore strong on the first literary attempts made in Australia.

Not surprisingly, in this age of Boswell and Gibbon, and in the circumstances of the Colony's foundation, the first literary form to become established was the journal. Joseph Banks, who had sailed with Cook, has left the finest example of the journal as it was conceived in this period—as a means for the writer to record his observations, commune with himself, speculate on the ways of providence, and offer reflections on such topics as the Noble Savage and the simple life. No later journal has the combination of Banks's gifts. The virtues of the annalist, carefully gathering and recording information, distinguished David Collins's *Account of the English Colony in New South Wales* (1798–1802). To follow the movement of a lively, enquiring mind, and catch the atmosphere of living, we look rather to Watkin Tench's *Narrative of the Expedition to Botany Bay* (1789) and *A Complete Account of the Settlement at Port Jackson* (1793)—reprinted together in a modern edition as *Sydney's First Four Years*. The tradition of generalizing from the particular, and offering the reflections of an educated man for the polite reader, is upheld in James Tuckey's *Account of a Voyage to . . . Port Philip* (1805). The population of New South Wales in 1800 was slightly below five thousand, the majority with no leisure for literary pursuits: writing in this genre exceeded all others in volume. There are a number of "foundation journals" still in manuscript.

The impression made on eighteenth-century sensibilities by the primitive cultures of the Pacific has been traced in the visual arts by Bernard Smith in *European Vision and the South Pacific 1768–1850* (1960). Professor Smith has shown how educated observers brought their civilized ideas of the primitive with them, the early artists representing the aboriginal according to the established ideal of the Noble Savage, or the new terrain according to received ideas of "picturesque" landscape. The transfer of eighteenth-century conventions is equally conspicuous in literature, especially in its more formal manifestations. The striking characteristic of the first poetry written in Australia is the effort at elegance and correctness, in forms like the ode, the pastoral, the elegy—and occasionally the epigram or lampoon. The series of odes by Michael Massey Robinson, written each year from 1810 onward to celebrate the birthdays of George III (4 June) and Queen Charlotte (18 January), subdue the local scenery and its inhabitants to Augustan convention, presenting the aborigines as "yon sable race" and the Blue Mountains as "the craggy Cliffs that guard the ling'ring Waste". The consistent theme of Robinson's odes—stamina is his chief attribute as a poet—is praise of Albion, and of the propagation of her virtues in the south by those "sturdy Swains" who have adventured into these latitudes:

Time was, when o'er this dread expanse of land
No trait appear'd of Culture's fost'ring hand:
And, as the wild Woods yielded to the Blast,
Nature scarce own'd the unproductive Waste.
O'er rugged Cliffs fantastic Branches hung,
'Round whose hoar Trunks the slender Scions clung,
Imperious Mountains met the ling'ring Eye,
Whose cloud-capt Summits brav'd the Sky.
Rocks, whose repulsive Frown access defied,
And Bays, where idly ebb'd the slumb'ring Tide—
Unless some straggler of the NATIVE RACE,
In crude Canoe expos'd his sooty Face;
With lazy Motion paddled o'er the Flood,
Snatch'd at the spear-struck Fish—and hugged his Food.

But when BRITANNIA's Sons came forth, to brave
The dreary Perils of the length'ning Wave;
When her bold Barks, with swelling Sails unfurled,
Trac'd these rude Coasts, and hail'd a new-found World;
Soon as their Footsteps press'd the yielding sand,
A sun more genial brighten'd on the land:
Commerce and Arts enrich'd the social Soil,
Burst through the gloom and bade all Nature smile.

(*Sydney Gazette*, 8th June 1811)

Robinson was an Englishman by birth, educated at Oxford, and, as the unofficial poet laureate of the Colony, naturally pledged to the literary fashions of the day. They are equally dominant, however, in the first volumes of poetry published by native-born Australians, W. C. Wentworth's *Australasia* (1823) and Charles Tompson's *Wild Notes, from the Lyre of a Native Minstrel* (1826). Wentworth had earlier written imitations of Horace and engaged in verse satire; "Australasia" was the subject set for the Chancellor's Medal when he was at Cambridge in 1823, and his poem gained second place. Wentworth's account of the progress visible in the Colony after "seven revolving lustres scarce have run" since Phillip established it, shows his firm control of the style of the "public" poem in the Augustan manner:

Lo! thickly planted o'er the glassy bay,
Where Sydney loves her beauties to survey,
And every morn delighted sees the beam
Of some fresh pennant dancing in her stream,
A masty forest, stranger vessels moor,
Charged with the fruits of every foreign shore;
While, landward,—the thronged quay, the creaking crane,
The noisy workman and the loaded wain,
The lengthened street, wide square, and column'd front

Of stately mansions, and the gushing font,
The solemn church, and busy market throng,
And idle loungers saunt'ring slow among—
The lofty windmills that with outspread sail
Thick line the hills, and court the rising gale,
Show that the mournful genius of the plain,
Driv'n from his primal solitary reign,
Has backward fled and fix'd his drowsy throne
In untrod wilds to muse and brood alone.

Charles Tompson's surviving verse has a wider range than Wentworth's. He wrote pastorals in imitation of Pope, Pindaric odes after the fashion of Gray and others, and some shorter poems "In the Style of Cowper" or "In Imitation of Cowper". The long pastoral "Retrospect" recalls Tompson's schooldays at the Rev. Henry Fulton's seminary, presenting the scenery of the Castlereagh as it might have figured in Pope's *Windsor Forest*:

The myrtle grove that skirts thy sloping sides,
And the tall summit from the plain divides,
The rich acacias waving o'er the rill
That pours its scanty stream beneath the hill;

with the contemplative passages that decorum also prescribed:

Here let Reflection cast her sober eye
O'er the sad trophies of mortality!
Life is a sandy base, which if we trust,
Our minds, our spirits, centre in the dust;
We feel no monitor—no heavenly thrill—
Prompt us to good, or bid us shrink from ill,
But all the soul, by worldly frenzy tost
Trusts in itself, and is for ever lost.

Tompson has the most marked lyrical talent of the early poets, insecure in such hectic forms as the Pindaric and slack and nerveless in his poems to Sylvia, but at his best in passages of melancholy reverie, as at the conclusion to "Retrospect".

The decorum of eighteenth-century verse extended from stately forms like the ode and the pastoral to others like the lampoon, and this tradition was perpetuated too in the "pipes" that circulated in manuscript in the early years of the Colony. Generally aimed at someone in authority, like Governor King or the Rev. Samuel Marsden, they were written on sheets of paper and passed from hand to hand, or dropped in some public place. It could be claimed that the first literary work published in Australia was a volume containing pipes—"published" by being dropped in the Parramatta Road in 1818. Dr William Bland was sentenced to twelve months' imprisonment as a result.[1] Wentworth could well have received a similar sentence for his satire on Colonel Molle, but he left the Colony in 1816 before his authorship became known. Very few texts of "pipes" have survived—some are known only through references given in the proceedings against the suspected authors—though Edward Kemp pilloried in print a number of contemporary officials and politicians in *A Voice from Tasmania* (1846).

Other light forms of verse, including epigrams and acrostics, appeared from time to time in the *Sydney Gazette* from 1803 onward, under the editorship of George Howe. It was Howe who in 1819 published the divertisement of Judge Barron Field, *First Fruits of Australian Poetry.* Field's claim on the title-page to be the first "Austral Harmonist" has led historians to take his verses more seriously than they were intended.[2] *First Fruits* contained two poems only: "Botany Bay Flowers", a light-hearted celebration of *epacris grandiflora,* likened to "a Fairy's parasol", and the second a sportive account of the kangaroo, seen as an engaging freak of Nature:

> She had made the squirrel fragile,
> She had made the bounding hart,
> But a third so strong and agile,
> Was beyond ev'n Nature's art;
> So she joined the former two
> In thee, Kangaroo!
> Thy fore half, it would appear,
> Had belonged to "some small deer",
> Such as liveth in a tree;
> By thy hinder, thou should'st be
> A large animal of chase,
> Bounding o'er the forest's space;—
> Joined by some divine mistake,
> None but Nature's hand can make —
> Nature, in her wisdom's play,
> On Creation's holiday.

Barron Field had been a contemporary of Leigh Hunt's at Christ's Hospital, and was the author of a biography of Wordsworth (still unpublished): his *First Fruits* was reviewed by Lamb in *The Examiner* in 1820. But to see Field as inaugurating a romantic movement in Australian poetry would be to make a claim that his verse

[1] See John V. Byrnes, "Our First Book", *Biblionews* (August 1962) and "William Charles Wentworth—and the Continuity of Australian Literature", *Australian Letters,* V, iii (1963), 15-16.

[2] The claim itself was playful, echoing Joseph Hall's assertion in *Virgidemiarum* (1597):

> I first adventure: follow me who list
> And be the second English Satyrist.

could not possibly support. *First Fruits* has the character of a gentlemanly diversion, in which the Australian scenery is used to supply material for the exercise of wit. The later poem, "New South Wales", published in *Bentley's Miscellany* in 1846, shows Field pursuing the same playful vein.[3]

From 1770, when the journal of Banks on the *Endeavour* described New South Wales as it appeared to a scientist of birth and breeding, to the publication of Wentworth's *Australasia* in 1823 and Tompson's *Wild Notes* in 1826, Australian literature had a more cultivated temper than it was ever to possess again, and an elegance of form that it would be long in recovering. The libraries of educated colonists at this time typically included the works of Pope, Cowper and Goldsmith, with Thomson's *Seasons*, Young's *Night Thoughts*, and Blair's *The Grave*.[4] It was completely natural for local writers to follow these literary modes, as it had been for the Colony's first play to be a performance of Farquhar's *The Recruiting Officer*, with prologue and epilogue improvised for the occasion (4 June 1789).

The first performance given in a playhouse was of Edward Young's *The Revenge* (16 January 1796), and it is unfortunate that there should be no positive evidence to connect this with the prologue (of still uncertain authorship, despite the attribution to George Carter) which begins

> From distant climes, o'er wide-spread seas we come,
> Though not with much *éclat*, or beat of drum;
> True patriots all, for, be it understood,
> We left our country for our country's good:
> No private views disgraced our generous zeal,
> What urged our travels was our country's weal:
> And none will doubt but that our emigration
> Has proved most useful to the British nation.

No local playwright emerged until the 1820s, when David Burn wrote his melodrama, *The Bushrangers*, and in his collected *Plays and Fugitive Pieces* (1842) the influence of English fashions is still plainly discernible.

In Australian fiction, on the other hand, the nineteenth century was not so long delayed. *Pickwick Papers* was being published in weekly parts in Van Diemen's Land in 1838. The "beginnings" of Australian fiction are not easy to determine. There are early convict

[3] See Clive Hamer, "An Unknown Poem by Barron Field?", *Southerly*, XIV (1952), 62-65.

[4] See Elizabeth Webby, "English Literature in Early Australia: 1820-1829", *Southerly*, XXVII (1967), 266-285. In prose the popular authors were Johnson, Smollett, Fielding, Le Sage (*Gil Blas*), and especially Scott.

journals—like some of those published over the name of George Barrington—that may be considered largely fictional, while on the other hand the *Memoirs* (1819) of James Hardy Vaux, for long regarded as an offshoot of the picaresque tradition, is in the main authentic.[5] The first novel published in Australia was Henry Savery's *Quintus Servinton* (Hobart, 1830–31), the history of an educated and well-to-do merchant transported for forgery, in which the autobiographical element is still strong. Although little more than one fifth of the story is set in Australia, and the descriptions given there are quite perfunctory, *Quintus Servinton* indicates the pattern that came to dominate Australian fiction in the earlier nineteenth century. The authors are in the main English by birth and education, and they write to report on their colonial experiences for a public overseas. There was a demand in England for information on life and prospects in New South Wales, which grew stronger with the programme of assisted immigration in the 1840s and after the discovery of gold in 1851. The emigrant's manual was a popular form, and a host of novels appeared with such titles as *Tales of the Colonies; or The Adventures of an Emigrant, Gertrude the Emigrant: A Tale of Colonial Life*, and *Tallangatta, the Squatter's Home*. Novels and stories of this class naturally fixed on the distinctive features of Australian life—the convict system, the depredations of the blacks, station life, bushranging, the gold rushes—nevertheless presenting them mainly from the outside. The typical novel also exhibited a colonial society to which the English class system had been transferred, and in its literary conventions—intrigue, heroines and villains, the happy ending to crown all—it conformed to the practices of the day. These features of colonial fiction were to draw the scorn of later Australian writers, especially those touched by the democratic sentiment of the 1890s.

The representative Anglo-Australian novel is *The Recollections of Geoffry Hamlyn* (1859). It was written by Henry Kingsley, the brother of Charles, as a consequence of five years spent in Australia in 1853–58, though the novel itself purports to be set in the 1830s. The narrative begins in England, and returns there at the end. The main characters are Englishmen transplanted, drawn from the governing class—landowners, military officers, clergy—who read *Waverley* and *Pickwick* in their leisure time. The Australian experiences of the Buckleys and the Brentwoods provide the romantic episodes of their lives, and the adventures befalling them have since become a stereotype of the Australian bush novel: the taking-up of land in the wilderness, the activities of mustering and branding, the

[5] See the edition of *The Memoirs of James Hardy Vaux* by Noel McLachlan (London: Heinemann, 1964).

encounter with bushrangers, the child straying into the bush who is found dead with flowers in his hand.

Yet later criticism has misrepresented *Geoffry Hamlyn* in regarding it as a novel of "pioneering". The process by which the emigrant families become established is apt to be summarily described, as when the narrative rejoins Hamlyn and Stockbridge in Australia in Chapter XVIII:

> At this time Stockbridge and I had been settled in our new home about two years, and were beginning to get comfortable and contented. We had had but little trouble with the blacks, and having taken possession of a fine piece of country, were flourishing and well to do.[6]

The narrator deliberately curtails the "pioneering" features of the story, with the explanation "I am writing a history of the people themselves, not of their property" (p. 104). The narrative depends for its interest on whether Alice will marry Sam Buckley or Cecil Mayford, when Desborough will have his final reckoning with George Hawker, whether Tom Troubridge will finally win Mary. Kingsley relies on the romantic conventions of the Victorian novel in working out the history, as in the coincidence that brings Frank Maberly to Australia, or in the revelation that Dr Mulhaus is the Baron von Landstein.

The use of the Australian environment as no more than a background to the "history of the people themselves", and the literary conventions by which the history is sustained, fix the special place of the colonial novel in Australian fiction. Australia is a land of sunshine and wide horizons where hardy adventures may be encountered but prosperity and happiness are to be won; for the enterprising it will yield a prolongation of the aristocratic life they had led in England; any scoundrel finding his way there will receive his just deserts, while the young and upright will be preserved through adversity to the happy ending. This colonial aristocracy of English gentleman-farmers and retired army officers, however much writers of the nineties may later have resented it, was a genuine aspect of the Australian society of the time. The ordering of events to a providential design, and the fictional patterns used in the process, are likewise "period" features. When Joseph Furphy complained later of "the slender-witted, virgin-souled, overgrown schoolboys who fill Henry Kingsley's exceedingly trashy and misleading novel with their insufferable twaddle",[7] he was voicing a protest against the conven-

[6] Henry Kingsley, *The Recollections of Geoffry Hamlyn* (London: Dent, 1924), p. 149. Page references are to this edition.

[7] Joseph Furphy, *Such is Life*, 1903 (Sydney: Angus and Robertson, 1945), p. 205.

tional hero of Victorian fiction, as Meredith had against the Victorian heroine. It is amusing, however, that the narrative method adopted by Kingsley—the telling of the story by Hamlyn, using letters as evidence, pleading uncertainty about some incidents beyond his knowledge—should have anticipated Furphy's own rejection of "romance" for the sterner virtues of "chronicle" in *Such is Life*. Kingsley has his own comments to make on the "romances" of the day, ascribing Mary Thornton's protestations to Hawker to her reading of them: "What though the words in which she spoke were borrowed from the trashy novels she was always reading—they were true enough for all that" (p. 68).

Geoffry Hamlyn is still the most attractive of the emigrant novels, possibly because it shows Australia as a more romantic and adventurous place than the realist school of the 1890s was to find it: here the Arcadian atmosphere still lingers. But it cannot of itself suggest the range of writing in this class. The "emigrant" bias is stronger in Charles Rowcroft's *Tales of the Colonies* (1843), where the narrative of Thornley's experiences is interspersed with advice on procuring land grants, felling timber and milking wild cows. A decade before the appearance of *Geoffry Hamlyn*, Alexander Harris had made the transition from the "documentary" *Settlers and Convicts* (1847) to *The Emigrant Family* (1849), in some later editions renamed *Martin Beck*. For Lieutenant Bracton and his family Arcady is disturbed by a cattle-duffing overseer, who evenually turns outlaw, after inciting a raid on the homestead by the blacks. *The Emigrant Family* is unusual in having among its leading characters an Australian, Reuben Kable, who—lean, tanned and nonchalant—already has the attributes that become part of a stereotype in later ninteenth-century fiction. The harsher aspects of colonial life are exposed in James Tucker's *Ralph Rashleigh*, the experiences of a convict and assigned servant. At a higher level of accomplishment is Catherine Spence's *Clara Morison: A Tale of South Australia during the Gold Fever* (1854), the history of a gentlewoman sent to Australia as a governess, but obliged to go into service instead. *Clara Morison* gives a more detailed picture of Australian domestic life than any other novel of the time—the goldfields are described only in letters back to Adelaide—and the management of dialogue and social situations (in Clara's interview with Mrs Denfield, for example) show the author's study of Jane Austen and George Eliot.

The Anglo-Australian novel found its fulfilment in the later nineteenth century in "Rolf Boldrewood" and Marcus Clarke. Boldrewood (T. A. Browne, 1826–1915) had come to Australia as a child and had gained a wide experience of Australian pastoral life by the time he was appointed goldfields commissioner in 1871. Of the dozen or so novels he published from 1878 onward, *Robbery Under Arms* (serialized in 1882–3) most deserves the reputation it has acquired. Boldrewood's gift as a story-teller finds most freedom in this narrative of the adventures of Dick and Jim Marston, who decide by the toss of a coin to join Captain Starlight in cattle-duffing, and then (after Dick's escape from Berrima gaol) in the bushranging exploits that end in Starlight's death. Though the women in the story, like Gracey Storefield and Aileen Marston, are pallid versions of the Victorian heroine, the less conventional characters are memorably portrayed—the half-caste Warrigal with his glittering teeth, Ben Marston and his dog Crib—and the description of Terrible Hollow shows Boldrewood's flair for the picturesque features of the Australian scene. The secret of the book's attraction is the use of Dick Marston as narrator, so that all the scenes and adventures come to us as they appear to a young Australian, chafing at the routine of ordinary work, his blood roused by the jingle of a horse's bit, or at the prospect of a night ride with the wind in his face.

Marcus Clarke (1846–81) gives a much more sombre, if no less romantic, view of colonial life. Educated at Highgate School with Gerard Manley Hopkins, and sent to Australia at the age of sixteen, Clarke threw himself into Bohemian life in Melbourne in the 1860s, finding an outlet for his literary talents in journalism. *His Natural Life*, written to give some basis to his finances in 1870, appeared in instalments in *The Australian Journal* in 1870–72, and was then published in revised form as a book in 1874. (The title *For the Term of His Natural Life* was adopted after Clarke's death in 1885.) It is an historical novel, based on Clarke's research into convict records of Van Diemen's Land in the 1830s and 1840s.

Richard Devine, to save his mother's honour, submits to being charged with a murder he did not commit, and is transported to Van Diemen's Land as Rufus Dawes. His history reflects something of the pattern of *Les Misérables*, Cosette finding an equivalent in Sylvia Vickers, the child who befriends Dawes on the *Malabar* and whom Dawes saves when they are marooned at Macquarie Harbour; the Javert of Hugo's novel corresponds to Maurice Frere, who takes from Dawes the credit of preserving the marooned party, and then pursues and oppresses him from prison to prison, so that the truth cannot come out. The end of the story—in the revised version—is tragic, with Richard Devine and Sylvia drowning in each other's arms.

The crudities of *For the Term of His Natural Life* are emphatic and obtrusive. The story survives the melodramatic absurdities leading to Dawes's conviction in England, only to run into the greater improbability of Sylvia's loss of memory of all the events at Macquarie Harbour, and of her marriage to Frere. The account of the brutalities of the convict system verges on the sensational, and Clarke is constantly being betrayed by the excesses or ineptitude of his prose ("it seemed to him that he was in the presence of some strange tropical flower, which exhaled a heavy and intoxicating perfume"). Yet the book has an intensity which no other Australian novel of the time achieved. It comes partly from the involvement of the story in the convict system, of which Clarke shirks no unpalatable feature, from flogging to cannibalism and sodomy: as most of the episodes can be documented, it is only the aggregation of them that produces a melodramatic effect. But Clarke's melodrama is in the strain of Edgar Allan Poe, where the horrors are reflected in a human consciousness, and the writer is able to explore excited or neurotic states of mind. Clarke shows the condition of numbness which his sufferings produce in Dawes, and the indifference that passes into bravado at Norfolk Island, as he is careless whether he lives or dies; he shows the strange complexity of Maurice Frere, by nature coarse and brutal, yet when he walks unarmed in an enclosure of convicts who hate him above all men, surviving because of their respect for a personality stronger than theirs. Clarke is as equal to the spiritual agonies of the Rev. Mr North as to the patient, scheming mind of John Rex or the brutishness of Gabbett: no other novel of the period has the same psychological penetration or grasp.

Catherine Spence, describing genteel society in Adelaide in the 1850s in *Clara Morison,* showed her heroine discussing the merits of Byron with Mr Reginald, and reading Tennyson to the invalid Minnie Hodges. By this time the poetry written in Australia was itself reflecting similar influences. In the earlier nineteenth century, as we have seen, the persistence of Augustan modes had been more conspicuous than any incipient Romanticism, and although Scott and Byron were to be found in colonists' libraries in the 1820s, a copy of Wordsworth was a rarity.[8] The main exemplars of the Romantic movement in Australian verse were to be Charles Harpur (1813–68), Henry Kendall (1839–82), and Adam Lindsay Gordon (1833–70).

Harpur, the son of ex-convict parents, is regarded as the first native-born poet to write from a consciousness of his literary role and mission: a radical in politics, he also anticipated in some of his poems the Utopian dream that has been taken as an invention of the 1890s. No less influential in his work, however, is the Romantic conception of the poet. Harpur saw himself as one dedicated to the Muse, revering his art, persisting despite slights and disappointments —all faithful enough to the circumstances of his life, but at the same

[8] See further Elizabeth Webby, "English Literature in Early Australia: 1820-1829", *Southerly,* XXVII (1967), 266-85.

time evidence of his fealty to a Romantic principle. He wrote feelingly on the nature of the poet, with tributes to Shakespeare, Chatterton, Shelley, and Coleridge, but in the more subjective of these poems his hero is himself, and the recurring mood is a mournful self-congratulation with his lot.

Harpur's poems first found their way into print in the 1830s, in the Sydney press, and *The Tragedy of Donohoe*, appearing in the *Monitor* in February 1835, was the first play by a native-born writer to be printed in Australia. *Thoughts: A Series of Sonnets* (1845) was followed by three other volumes in Harpur's lifetime, and a collected *Poems* (1883) fifteen years after his death. The early sonnets are the work of a consciously Romantic sensibility, and Harpur soon found a liking for the Romantic narrative and the long descriptive poem. Much of his work has no connection with the Australian scene: in *The Witch of Hebron* he joins the Romantic cult of legend and marvel, in an "atmospheric narrative" recalling *Christabel* and *The Eve of St Agnes*; *The Tower of the Dream* and the unpublished *Genius Lost* are philosophical excursions in the Romantic manner; other shorter pieces use the convention of the vision and the dream. Although the non-Australian poems have won little critical notice, without this dimension Harpur's work would be the poorer—as it would also be the poorer without his political satires.

Harpur is best known for the much-anthologized "A Midsummer Noon in the Australian Forest", and his literary importance has been taken to consist in bringing Australian landscape into Australian verse. It is already there, of course, in the work of Wentworth and Tompson: the difference is that Harpur adopts the manner of Wordsworth, so that the Australian scenery seems more recognizable in "A Storm in the Mountains" to a reader familiar with the Romantic tradition than in Tompson's more formal "Retrospect". The poem of Harpur's most praised by his contemporaries was "The Creek of the Four Graves", which begins with a party setting out to explore the Australian bush:

> So they went forth at dawn; at eve the sun,
> That rose behind them as they journeyed out,
> Was firing with his nether rim a range
> Of unknown mountains, that like ramparts towered
> Full in their front; and his last glances fell
> Into the gloomy forest's eastern glades
> In golden gleams, like to the Angel's sword,
> And flashed upon the windings of a creek
> That noiseless ran betwixt the pioneers
> And those new Apennines—ran, shaded o'er

> With boughs of the wild willow, hanging mixed
> From either bank, or duskily befringed
> With upward tapering feathery swamp-oaks,
> The sylvan eyelash always of remote
> Australian waters, whether gleaming still
> In lake or pool, or bickering along
> Between the marges of some eager stream.

Could it be claimed that the Australian landscape is rendered here with any particularity of vision? The shimmering, glaring quality of the Australian sun is suggested in the opening lines, but not captured there; the observation is blurred by the Romantic diction of "the gloomy forest's eastern glades" and the "duskily befringed" stream; there is some evocation of a prospect at evening with the sunset catching on leaves and water, but no scene is made present to the senses. The reader has generally to search hard in the vagueness of Harpur's landscapes for the particular observations that have been singled out for attention: the "rush of startled kangaroo", the "upland growths of wattles", "the steep-banked mountain creek".

Estimates of Harpur must be tentative while so much of his verse remains in manuscript, and while the text of 1883—still the only collected edition—represents his poems as mutilated and "improved" by H. M. Martin after their author's death. The editor's motives, so far as they may be gathered from his omissions and conflations, were partly to include as many pieces as possible, and partly to represent Harpur as a tame descriptive poet. Judith Wright has shown how the philosophical passages—some of them going beyond Wordsworth's views of the relation of the soul and nature—have unfailingly been excised.[9] One poem that has survived with only minor interference, *The Tower of the Dream*, indicates that while Harpur may have been an interesting and adventurous thinker, this has not conferred any striking merit on his verse. In all branches of his versatile work, it is possible to commend his aspiration but not find a commensurate distinction in his performance. Harpur is historically important for beginning to adapt the Wordsworthian tradition to the Australian scene, for suggesting the Utopian vision that was to animate later writers, and for acclimatizing the Romantic mystique of the poet. While his poetry offers more to engage the mind than the work of any other of his period, it marks him still as one of the labourers before the dawn.

Harpur became one of the influences on the poetry of Henry Kendall (1839–82), who came to know his work through W. G. Pennington. Pennington was a member of the literary circle in

[9] Judith Wright, *Charles Harpur* (Melbourne: Lansdowne Press, 1963), 16-17.

Sydney—other members were N. D. Stenhouse, D. H. Deniehy, Henry Halloran—who had given Harpur encouragement. Kendall wrote to the older poet on 8th January 1862:

> Your influence is beginning to be felt, and it is to be regretted that you have been so silent lately. I speak for the rising generation of Australians, who are far more intellectual than their predecessors, who *must* turn to you, as I have already done, with the love and reverence which is due to their national poet.[10]

Kendall was at this time in his early twenties: brought up on farms on the north and south coast of New South Wales (his father had died when Kendall was thirteen), he had already served as an apprentice on a whaler and as shop assistant in Sydney, and was shortly to become a clerk in the civil service. Kendall found in Sydney a better established literary milieu than had greeted Harpur, and when he moved to Melbourne in 1869, became a fellow-member of the Yorick Club with Marcus Clarke, G. G. McCrae and Adam Lindsay Gordon. But as in Sydney he had been brought close to ruin by family misfortunes, in Melbourne the decision to support himself by his pen quickly brought Kendall near to destitution, and despair and drink very soon brought on a mental collapse. He was admitted to the Gladesville Asylum in July 1871, and again in April 1873.[11] Kendall's later years, in the employment of a timber agency on the North Coast, were more serene; but his appointment as Inspector of Forests in 1880 involved him in work that exceeded his strength, and he died in 1882.

In the assimilation of the Australian environment to poetry—a process that tends to occupy historians of Australian verse in the nineteenth century—Kendall has always had a prominent place. In his earliest volume, *Poems and Songs* (1862), such pieces as "The Barcoo" and "Song of the Cattle Hunters" show that the hesitancy felt in some earlier treatments of the Australian scene has now disappeared:

> Good-bye to the Barwan and brigalow scrubs!
> Adieu to the Culgoa ranges!
> But look for the mulga and salt-bitten shrubs,
> Though the face of the forest-land changes.
>
> The leagues we may travel down beds of hot gravel,
> And clay-rusted reaches where moisture hath been,
> While searching for waters, may vex us and thwart us,
> Yet who would be quailing, or fainting, or failing?
> ("The Barcoo")

[10] The letter is preserved in the Mitchell Library MSS (item C 199).
[11] See Donovan Clarke, "New Light on Henry Kendall", *Australian Literary Studies*, II (1966), 211-13.

There are no longer any traces here of a "literature of exile". The particular quality of Kendall's treatment of landscape is made clearer, however, in *Leaves from Australian Forests* (1869). The successive anthologists who have chosen to represent Kendall by "Bell Birds" or "September in Australia" have indicated where his talent lies. These poems are memorable not for his observation of the bush, for the imagery is too general and the language too conventionally poetic for that: they are memorable rather as expressing Kendall's *feeling* for the bush. He was especially sensitive to the ferns and cascades of the coastal fringe, and conveys this beauty in a poem like "Mountain Moss":

It lies amongst the sleeping stones,
  Far down the hidden mountain-glade;
And past its brink the torrent moans
  For ever in a dreamy shade:

A little patch of dark-green moss,
  Whose softness grew of quiet ways,
(With all its deep, delicious floss,)
  In slumb'rous suns of summer days.

You know the place? With pleasant tints
  The broken sunset lights the bowers;
And then the woods are full with hints
  Of distant, dear, voluptuous flowers!

These three stanzas give an impression of a soft and verdant scene, but it is an impression and no more. The dissipation of the poem's effect in the idly poetic phrase "slumb'rous suns", "distant, dear, voluptuous flowers") shows that Kendall was too much the servant of the fashions of his period, and too little their master.

It would be unjust, however, to judge Kendall's nature poetry by standards not applicable to its genre. If he cannot be acquitted of lapses in execution, his method remains one in which exactness of observation is not especially aimed at. It is a method that becomes most effective in poems where the bush scenery figures vaguely in his recollections or supplies a background to his melancholy ("Rose Lorraine"). This is the distinction of his third volume, *Songs from the Mountains* (1880), where in "Mooni", "The Voice of the Wild Oak", and "Orara", the bush comes to evoke that melancholy that the nineteenth-century Romantics came to associate with it—the melancholy that Marcus Clarke fixed upon as "the dominant note of Australian scenery".[12] Although *Songs from the Mountains* con-

[12] In his preface to the *Poems of the Late Adam Lindsay Gordon* (1880), reprinted in the introduction to the Oxford edition of Gordon by F. M. Robb (1912), pp. cxxi-cxxiii.

tains "Beyond Kerguelen", with its rapid Swinburnian rhythms, and the political satire, "Ninian Melville", that was quickly suppressed, it is rather in the wistful, elegiac poem with a woodland setting that Kendall finds his characteristic vein:

> The air if full of mellow sounds;
> The wet hill-heads are bright;
> And, down the fall of fragrant grounds,
> The deep ways flame with light.
>
> A rose-red space of stream I see
> Past banks of tender fern:
> A radiant brook, unknown to me
> Beyond its upper turn.
>
> The singing silver life I hear,
> Whose home is in the green
> Far-folded woods of fountains clear
> Where I have never been . . . .
>
> ("Orara")

The evocative treatment of landscape here "places" Kendall in the development of Australian verse, as the sensibility revealed through it places him in the later Romantic tradition—a "placing" confirmed by Palgrave's choice of "Orara" and "After Many Years" for the *Golden Treasury*, and by Quiller-Couch's choice of "Mooni" for the *Oxford Book of English Verse*.

Kendall's picturesque contemporary, Adam Lindsay Gordon (1833–70), is the only Australian poet represented by a memorial in Westminster Abbey. Apparently expelled from at least one English public school, failing to gain a commission in the army, and rejected by a farmer's daughter with whom he had fallen in love at nineteen, Gordon came to Australia in 1853, to become a mounted trooper and horsebreaker, noted for his recklessness and daring in the saddle. Some verses published in the sporting journal, *Bell's Life*, led to Gordon's introduction to the Melbourne côterie of Shillinglaw, G. G. McCrae, and Frank Madden, and also to Marcus Clarke, then editor of the *Colonial Monthly*. Gordon's three volumes of verse, *Sea Spray and Smoke Drift* (1867), *Ashtaroth* (1867), and *Bush Ballads and Galloping Rhymes* (1870) testify again to the vitality of the Romantic tradition in the Australian verse of the time. The example of Scott lies behind the ballad "Fauconshawe" and "The Romance of Britomarte"; Swinburne's influence is palpable in "Bellona" and "The Swimmer"; "The Rhyme of Joyous Garde" is in the line of descent from Tennyson's *Idylls of the King*; the Browning of "Childe Roland" and "How we brought the good news" is more pervasively felt, extending to the "dramatic lyric" *Ashtaroth,* peopled with Byronic figures.

The Byronic melancholy in Gordon, the despondent streak that led him to shoot himself at the age of thirty-seven, has often been commented upon. Gordon's more important affinity with Byron, however, is that his work shares in the quality which Gordon's editor has claimed for the English poet, the capacity to bring relief to circumscribed lives. Gordon's poetry survives because it celebrates a simple ideal of the heroic, as Gordon himself seemed to do in his daredevil horsemanship:

> And forcing the running, discarding all cunning,
>   A length to the front went the rider in green;
> A long strip of stubble, and then the big double,
>   Two stiff flights of rails with a quickset between.
>
> She raced at the rasper, I felt my knees grasp her,
>   I found my hands give to her strain on the bit;
> She rose when The Clown did—our silks as we bounded
>   Brush'd lightly, our stirrups clash'd loud as we lit.
>
> A rise steeply sloping, a fence with stone coping—
>   The last—we diverged round the base of the hill;
> His path was the nearer, his leap was the clearer,
>   I flogg'd up the straight and he led sitting still.
>
> ("How We Beat the Favourite")

The action and movement in Gordon's verse is often dramatizing a kind of reckless fatalism, which finds expression also in world-weariness and languor. The blending of these two strains in Gordon is responsible for the appeal of the most popular poem in *Bush Ballads and Galloping Rhymes,* "The Sick Stockrider". There is first the recollection of adventurous days now past:

> 'Twas merry in the glowing morn, among the gleaming grass,
>   To wander as we've wandered many a mile,
> And blow the cool tobacco cloud, and watch the white wreaths pass,
>   Sitting loosely in the saddle all the while.
>
> 'Twas merry 'mid the blackwoods, when we spied the station roofs,
>   To wheel the wild scrub cattle at the yard,
> With a running fire of stockwhips and a fiery run of hoofs;
>   Oh! the hardest day was never then too hard!

and then the fatalistic reflection:

> I've had my share of pastime, and I've done my share of toil,
>   And life is short—the longest life a span;
> I care not now to tarry for the corn or for the oil,
>   Or for the wine that maketh glad the heart of man.

For good undone and gifts misspent and resolutions vain,
'Tis somewhat late to trouble. This I know—
I should live the same life over, if I had to live again;
And the chances are I go where most men go.

The deep blue skies wax dusky, and the tall green trees grow dim,
The sward beneath me seems to heave and fall;
And sickly, smoky shadows through the sleepy sunlight swim,
And on the very sun's face weave their pall.

Let me slumber in the hollow where the wattle blossoms wave,
With never stone or rail to fence my bed;
Should the sturdy station children pull the bush flowers on my grave,
I may chance to hear them romping overhead.

Gordon looks forward to the poets of the nineties in his ability to celebrate simple heroic virtues, in verse that appeals to the common man.

To the writers of the nineties, nevertheless, he was classified along with Kingsley and others as belonging to the generation of "Anglo-Australian" literature. Joseph Furphy so represented him in a discussion in the *Bulletin* on 9th February 1895, referring to Gordon as another Englishman in exile, his instinctive sympathies lying with "Sir John and His Grace, with baron and squire, and knight of the shire".[13] The nationalistic temper of the nineties has coloured critical attitudes towards the achievement of the Anglo-Australian period since that time. There has been a tendency to see the earlier writers as the heirs to a genteel and derivative literary tradition, which they sought to prolong in circumstances naturally resistant to it—an attempt as vain as that of any settler who ignored the Australian climate or regarded the bush as an English park. The "failure" of Tompson, Massey Robinson, and Barron Field is therefore satisfactorily attributed to their lack of any "genuine Australian vision". There is a tenuous line of advance (it is suggested) through the mid and later nineteenth century, as an authentic image or two ("Why roar the bullfrogs in the tea-tree marsh") appears through the Wordsworthian veil of Harpur and Kendall, and as the land itself—harsh but invincible—throws off the weak literary fashions that are used to clothe it. With the nineties, a genuinely Australian literature is achieved.

This is an overstatement of the legend, which in a milder form has a degree of validity. But as a critical formula for the evolution of the first hundred years of Australian writing, it obviously depends

[13] See further Leonie Kramer, "The Literary Reputation of Adam Lindsay Gordon", *Australian Literary Studies,* I (1963), 42-56.

on an appeal to extra-literary standards. That poetry is prized which faithfully reflects local characteristics; writing which is formal or elegant must be suspect; novels in which English aristocrats play a leading part are somehow false or spurious; the areas of a poet's work which are not concerned with his environment (like Harpur's *Witch of Hebron*) may be left out of account. These are some of the prejudices—rarely stated, but frequently operative—from which the writers of the Anglo-Australian period have suffered.

If "genuine Australian vision" were to be accepted as a test of literary merit, the rigorous application of it would yield results different from those usually reached. A novel set in the 1830s representing retired English army officers as a governing class may be a faithful representation of Australian life of the period. Nature verse in which the unusual Australian flora seem an embarrassment may have a fidelity of its own, in showing the reaction of a poet of English upbringing and tradition to a disturbing new environment. As a literary product, such a poem or novel is as "genuine" for its time, and as truthful a record of sensibility, as the ballads and short stories of a later period. It is not, however, the authenticity of this "Australian vision" that necessarily determines literary merit: so much depends on the effective translation of it into literary terms. Some poems, like Harpur's "The Emigrant's Vision", might be said to suffer not from the absence of an Australian sentiment, but from its presence. In certain novels in which the vision has been realized, on the other hand, its rendering may be in terms of which the nineties disapproved—as a Romantic response to the space and light and untouched beauty of Australia that many native writers seemed afterwards to miss. To much other writing, the criterion is simply immaterial. *For the Term of His Natural Life* has survived other novels of "the System" through its sheer intensity and psychological penetration; Kendall's poetry is sustained by his responsiveness to the bush, but it is sustained much more by the feelings for which the bush happens to supply a setting or frame of reference. When "failure" occurs in the poetry and fiction of this period, it can usually be assigned to the writer's paucity of talent.

Yet any general evaluation of the Anglo-Australian phase must remain tentative. No period is in need of such scholarly exploration and research as this one. Monographs such as Brian Elliott's *Marcus Clarke* (1958) and J. Normington Rawling's *Charles Harpur* (1962) are the exception rather than the rule; there is as yet no edition of Harpur giving his poems in any but the mutilated form of the 1883 text, and as may poems remain uncollected as have appeared in print. Charles Tompson's *Wild Notes, from the Lyre of a Native Minstrel*, is available only in the first edition of 1826, and Wentworth and Barron Field may be read only in libraries. The life of Kendall prepared by T. T. Reed still awaits publication; the most recent biography of A. L. Gordon belongs to 1934. Although Alexander Harris' *The Emigrant Family* has appeared in a modern edition, there are a half-dozen early novels of comparable literary merit to Kingsley's *Geoffry Hamlyn* which are out of print, such as Rowcroft's *Tales of the Colonies*, Boldrewood's *The Squatter's Dream*, and Catherine Spence's *Clara Morison*. The novel which Catherine Spence regarded as her best, *Gathered In*, has not been published except in serial form in *The Adelaide Observer* (1881–2), and another novel, *Handfasted*, is in manuscript. It is also hard to gauge how much of the achievement of Australian nineteenth-century prose may yet be found to lie in the unpretentious "documentary" writing of the time, samples of which have been recovered in forms so diverse as J. F. Mortlock's *Experiences of a Convict* (1965) and Annabella Boswell's *Journal* (1965).

2

THE NATIONALIST PERIOD (1880–1920)

THE *BULLETIN* SCHOOL: LAWSON, FURPHY, PATERSON

THE PERIOD from the nineties onward, the second general phase in the pattern we are tracing, is better documented. The 1890s have usually been regarded as a landmark in literary development, as fixing the stage at which Australian writing acquired a national consciousness. In the two dominant literary forms of the period, the ballad and the short story, Australian writers at last broke free from the English tradition, and created a new and buoyant literature from exploiting indigenous material. It was a literature which reflected the democratic temper of the times, the Australian hostility to privilege and social injustice, and the vision of a new Utopia in the south. (Mark Twain, returning from a visit to Australia in 1896, confided to his notebook: "The native Australian is as vain of his unpretty country as if it were the final masterpiece of God."[1]) In the vanguard of the movement was the new journal, *The Bulletin*, founded in 1880 by J. F. Archibald and John Haynes, supporting the radical cause in politics and appealing to readers in both Sydney and the bush. Most writers to emerge in the nineties were contributors to the *Bulletin,* or had the help of the editor of its Red Page of 1894–1906, A. G. Stephens, the first notable critic that Australia had produced.

The nationalist movement that began in the 1880s and 1890s lasted beyond the turn of the century, and beyond the First World War, and then had a second life in the anecdotes and recollections of those who had belonged to it. Figures like Stephens, "The Red Page Rhadamanthus", Brennan, and Lawson had become legends almost in their lifetime, and when Arthur Jose published his reminiscences of the period as *The Romantic Nineties*, or G. A. Taylor issued his under the title *Those Were the Days!*, the nineties began to have a glow and a radiance about them that even now is hard to dissipate. As Vance Palmer has shown in *The Legend of the Nineties* (1954), the period has become the embodiment of an Australian "myth". It set the tradition that dominated Australian writing

[1] See C. O. Parsons, "Mark Twain in Australia", *The Antioch Review*, XXI (1961-2), 455-68.

until the late 1920s and that is still influential.

The reputation of the writers of the nineties is only partly due to their exploitation of indigenous material, their conscious defiance of the English tradition, and their reformist political sentiment. It was based more firmly on the appeal of their work to the common man. Lawson's *While the Billy Boils* (1896) sold 32,000 copies in the twenty years after its publication, and his first collection of verse, *In the Days When the World Was Wide* (1896) had reached its "20th thousand" by 1914. On the other hand Kendall's *Poems and Songs* had been printed in an edition of 500 copies, his *Leaves from Australian Forests* in an edition of 1500 copies, and his *Songs from the Mountains* in an edition of some 1000 copies—and no title had found a ready sale. The writers of the nineties school were the mainstay of the first successful paperbacks in Australian publishing—the Commonwealth series from Angus and Robertson, which had sold over 140,000 copies by 1908, and the N.S.W. Bookstall series, advertised at the same time as "selling in thousands". The *Bulletin* itself was a magazine largely written by its own readers, and circulated in the backblocks until individual copies were read out of existence.

It is natural in these circumstances that many authors, like Edward Dyson and "Steele Rudd", should have won a greater reputation at the time than their work can support now. Yet to the nineties school belong the two most considerable figures that Australian literature had yet produced, Henry Lawson and Joseph Furphy. Lawson had been born on the goldfield at Grenfell in 1867, and spent his youth toiling on his father's selection at Eurunderee. His experience of the bush was limited to this period and to eighteen months spent back o' Bourke at the suggestion of Archibald of the *Bulletin* in 1892–3. The Australian writer who has become popularly identified with the outback was for most of his life a city-dweller.

In his unfinished autobiography, Lawson described the miserable life he led in Sydney in the 1880s, working in a factory and trying to educate himself at night-school. These experiences, together with his involvement in his mother's paper, *The Republican*, seem to have inspired the semi-political, humanitarian feeling that animates Lawson's early verse. "Faces in the Street" appeared in the *Bulletin* on 28th July 1888:

> They lie, the men who tell us in a loud decisive tone
> That want is here a stranger, and that misery's unknown;
> For where the nearest suburb and the city proper meet
> My window-sill is level with the faces in the street—
> Drifting past, drifting past,
> To the beat of weary feet —
> While I sorrow for the owners of those faces in the street.

And cause have I to sorrow, in a land so young and fair,
To see upon those faces stamped the marks of Want and Care;
I look in vain for traces of the fresh and fair and sweet
In sallow, sunken faces that are drifting through the street—
    Drifting on, drifting on,
    To the tread of restless feet;
I can sorrow for the owners of the faces in the street.

Lawson's rôle as spokesman for the underdog helped to give his verse a reputation that in his lifetime was equal to the reputation of his prose.

It is as a short-story writer, however, that Lawson will be remembered. In his boyhood he had fallen under the spell of Dickens, and also read Bret Harte and Mark Twain. But the stories that Lawson contributed to the *Bulletin* from 1888 onward, and collected in *Short Stories in Prose and Verse* (1894), *While the Billy Boils* (1896), *On the Track and Over the Sliprails* (1900) and later volumes, reveal an original and distinctive talent. The overseas visitor who wishes to discover as quickly as possible the distinguishing quality of Australian writing, the features that mark it off from literature written anywhere else, can still do no better than begin with Henry Lawson's short stories or Furphy's *Such is Life*. Even in the early collection of 1894, stories like "The Union Buries its Dead", "The Drover's Wife", "Rats", "The Bush Undertaker", and "The Mystery of Dave Regan" show the art and the insight that enabled Lawson to put on record forever the Australia of the track and the campfire, the shearing-shed and the shanty-keeper, the drover and the bush eccentric.

It is an Australia which is gaunt and arid, in contrast to the Arcady of the *Geoffry Hamlyn* school, and peopled by characters who are never aristocratic (unless they have fallen on evil days) and hardly ever heroic. It is not that Lawson has formulated any theory of the anti-hero; it is rather that his characters are sardonic and inarticulate, the gentler ones unassuming or withdrawn, and some of the most memorable "con" men or hard cases. He is already in full command of his method in the earliest volume, *Short Stories in Prose and Verse* (1894), in a story like "The Union Buries its Dead". The casualness of the opening is guided by a sure artistic instinct:

While out boating one Sunday afternoon on a billabong across the river, we saw a young man on horseback driving some horses along the bank. He said it was a fine day, and asked if the water was deep there. The joker of our party said it was deep enough to drown him, and he laughed and rode farther up. We didn't take much notice of him.

Next day a funeral gathered at a corner pub and asked each other in to have a drink while waiting for the hearse. They passed away some of the time dancing jigs to a piano in the bar parlour. They passed away the rest of the time skylarking and fighting.

The defunct was a young Union labourer, about twenty-five, who had been drowned the previous day while trying to swim some horses across a billabong of the Darling.

He was almost a stranger in town, and the fact of his having been a Union man accounted for the funeral. The police found some Union papers in his swag, and called at the General Labourers' Union Office for information about him. That's how we knew. The secretary had very little information to give. The departed was a "Roman", and the majority of the town were otherwise—but Unionism is stronger than creed. Liquor, however is stronger than Unionism; and, when the hearse presently arrived, more than two-thirds of the funeral were unable to follow.

Already the story is being controlled by the attitude of the narrator (not necessarily to be identified with "Lawson", here or anywhere else). From the first paragraph ("We didn't take much notice of him") the tone is that of a man to whom death is a fatalistic occurrence, and the skylarking of the mourners in the pub is accepted as almost routine. The narrator preserves this detachment as a procession of fourteen, all strangers to the corpse, follow the hearse, and receive sundry tokens of respect as they go along:

A horseman, who looked like a drover just returned from a big trip, dropped into our dusty wake and followed us a few hundred yards, dragging his packhorse behind him, but a friend made wild and demonstrative signals from an hotel veranda—hooking at the air in front with his right hand and jobbing his left thumb over his shoulder in the direction of the bar—so the drover hauled off and didn't catch up to us any more. He was a stranger to the entire show.

We walked in twos. There were three twos. It was very hot and dusty; the heat rushed in fierce dazzling rays across every iron roof and light-coloured wall that was turned to the sun. One or two pubs closed respectfully until we got past. They closed their bar doors and the patrons went in and out through some side or back entrance for a few minutes. Bushmen seldom grumble at an inconvenience of this sort, when it is caused by a funeral. They have too much respect for the dead.

On the way to the cemetery we passed three shearers sitting on the shady side of a fence. One was drunk—very drunk. The other two covered their right ears with their hats, out of respect for the departed—whoever he might have been—and one of them kicked the drunk and muttered something to him.

He straightened himself up, stared, and reached helplessly for his hat, which he shoved half off and then on again. Then he made a great effort to pull himself together—and succeeded. He stood up, braced his back against the fence, knocked off his hat, and remorsefully placed his foot on it—to keep it off his head till the funeral passed.

This is Lawson's "documentary" style at its best, sustained by the revealing detail: the horseman's friend on the hotel veranda "hooking at the air in front with his right hand and jobbing his left thumb over his shoulder in the direction of the bar"; the drunks who "covered their right ears with their hats". Lawson is like Furphy and Barbara Baynton in always being specific. We have left behind the vagueness of *Geoffry Hamlyn*, where a horseman dismounts "to set right some strap or another" (p. 149). While the narrator's attitude is still stoical, without illusion, yet—in the account of the fumbling attempts of the drunken shearers to show respect to the corpse—there is a hint that his sensibilities are not so much blunted as held in check.

We plodded on across the railway line and along the hot, dusty road which ran to the cemetery, some of us talking about the accident, and lying about the narrow escapes we had had ourselves. Presently someone said:

"There's the Devil."

I looked up and saw a priest standing in the shade of the tree by the cemetery gate.

The hearse was drawn up and the tail-boards were opened. The funeral extinguished its right ear with its hat as four men lifted the coffin out and laid it over the grave. The priest—a pale, quiet young fellow—stood under the shade of a sapling which grew at the head of the grave. He took off his hat, dropped it carelessly on the ground, and proceeded to business . . .

Just here man's ignorance and vanity made a farce of the funeral. A big, bull-necked publican, with heavy, blotchy features, and a supremely ignorant expression, picked up the priest's straw hat and held it about two inches over the head of his reverence during the whole of the service. The father, be it remembered, was standing in the shade. A few shoved their hats on and off uneasily, struggling between their disgust for the living and their respect for the dead. The hat had a conical crown and a brim sloping down all round like a sunshade, and the publican held it with his great red claw spread over the crown. To do the priest justice, perhaps he didn't notice the incident. . . .

The grave looked very narrow under the coffin, and I drew a breath of relief when the box slid easily down. I saw the coffin get stuck once, at Rookwood, and it had to be yanked out with difficulty, and laid on the sods at the feet of the heart-broken relations, who howled dismally while the grave-diggers widened the hole. But they don't cut contracts so fine in the West. Our grave-digger was not altogether bowelless, and, out of respect for that human quality described as "feelin's" he scraped up some light and dusty soil and threw it down to deaden the fall of the clay lumps on the coffin. He also tried to steer the first few shovelfuls gently down against the end of the grave with the back of the shovel turned outwards, but the hard dry Darling River clods rebounded and knocked all the same. It didn't matter much—nothing does. The fall of lumps of clay on a stranger's coffin doesn't sound any different from the fall of the same things on an ordinary wooden box—at least I didn't notice anything awesome or unusual in the sound; but, perhaps, one of us—the most sensitive—might have been impressed by being reminded of a burial of long ago, when the thump of every sod jolted his heart.

Here the story is at its most precarious stage. The narrator is revealed as a still sensitive man (how much of the basic humanity of Lawson's stories depends on this?) alert to the pathos of the situation he describes while rejecting any involvement in it. The story is to be moving and astringent at once. Lawson's control perhaps wavers in the reference to the heart-broken relations "who howled dismally while the grave-diggers widened the hole"; the comedy intended in "howled" does not succeed. The sentimentality that disfigures so many of his stories is approached in "a burial of long ago, when the thump of every sod jolted his heart", but then refused by a characteristic modulation:

I have left out the wattle—because it wasn't there. I have also neglected to mention the heart-broken old mate, with his grizzled head bowed and great pearly drops streaming down his rugged cheeks. He was absent—he was probably "out back". For similar reasons I have omitted reference to the suspicious moisture in the eyes of a bearded bush ruffian named Bill. Bill failed to turn up, and the only moisture was that which was induced by the heat. I have left out the "sad Australian sunset", because the sun was not going down at the time. The burial took place exactly at midday.

The mourners do not discover the dead man's name until they see it on the plate on his coffin, and this proves to be only "the name he went by", in the rather forced conclusion:

We did hear, later on, what his real name was; but if we ever chance to read it in the "Missing Friends Column", we shall not be able to give any information to heart-broken mother or sister or wife, nor to anyone who could let him hear something to advantage—for we have already forgotten the name.

"The Union Buries its Dead" marks the median of Lawson's creative range. On one side of it lie the more severely documentary studies like "Hungerford", with the dramatic and semi-dramatic sketches like "On the Edge of a Plain"; on the other side are the more searching, more moving and more extended stories like "Joe Wilson's Courtship". Lawson's more enduring work belongs to the period 1888–1902. After *Joe Wilson and His Mates* (1901), which reflects something of his stay in New Zealand in 1897–98, and *Children of the Bush* (1902), the inequality of his writing became more marked, and the stories that appeared between his return from England in 1902 and his death in 1922 lack the vitality of his earlier work. In one series not collected in book-form in his lifetime, *Elder Man's Lane*, Lawson turns his attention to the slum and the larrikin, giving a picture of the city that is more comprehensive than that of his earlier boarding-house stories, but also less vivid.

Uneven as Lawson's work in prose may be, it gains coherence from the vision of life informing it. The outlook of the stories is resigned and sardonic, as though the narrator had had to face the worst, and had accepted it, and now looked to the future without particular hope or illusion; at the same time it is the outlook of a perceptive man, with an undiminished capacity to feel and respond—not made insensitive by his sufferings, but more wryly compassionate. This is the attitude of Mitchell, who has assumed the protective cover of a hardbitten philosopher; of Joe Wilson, looking back nostalgically to his courting days; even of Steelman, the most "successful" of Lawson's characters, shown in all his shrewdness as being as fundamentally disenchanted as the rest.[2] It follows that the success of Lawson's stories is uncertain, and constantly threatened. There is a danger that they may become simply defeatist, presenting a series of characters lost in self-pity at the inequality of the struggle. There is the danger of sentimentalizing values that do stand up in this hostile world, such as mateship, or even the devotion of a man to his dog. Lawson's special feeling for the character who is made vulnerable through his awkwardness, like Malachi or Andy Page, can involve him in the same hazards. His work as a whole makes Lawson the spokesman and recorder of the democratic Australian of his day; his place has been made more secure by the insight and compassion with which he has portrayed his unheroic figures.

Joseph Furphy, in his lifetime, had a much smaller reputation than Lawson, and it was not until after his "rediscovery" in the 1940s that *Such is Life* came to be recognized as the major Australian novel of its period.

Born in 1843 at Yarra Glen in Victoria, Furphy spent his teens "dodging out of farm work, and in learning to mismanage various kinds of portable engine plant",[3] and after an unsuccessful venture in prospecting for gold, married and took up a selection near Lake Cooper. The failure of the farm obliged Furphy to become a bullock-driver, and he drove a team in the Riverina for seven or eight years, and then returned to work in his brother's implement foundry at Shepparton. Furphy therefore came to literature quite late in life (or returned to it, if we recall his juvenile experiments in verse), and his work shows the effect of years of desultory reading and reflection. He contributed paragraphs to the *Bulletin* from 1889 onward, first

[2] See Stephen Murray-Smith, *Henry Lawson* (Melbourne: Lansdowne Press, 1962), pp. 39-40.

[3] A statement cited by Miles Franklin and Kate Baker in *Joseph Furphy: The Legend of a Man and his Book* (Sydney: Angus and Robertson, 1944), p. 22.

under the pseudonym "Warrigal Jack", then as "Tom Collins"—an imaginary person who was held the source of idle rumour and unconfirmed reports, and was always eluding pursuit. To the *Bulletin* he wrote on 4th April 1897, "I have just finished writing a full-sized novel, title, *Such is Life*, scenery, Riverina and Northern Vic.; temper, democratic; bias, offensively Australian". A. G. Stephens wrote back asking to see the manuscript, and his verdict on it is one of those that confirm his judgement as a critic:

> It seems to me fitted to become an Australian classic, or semi-classic, since it embalms accurate representations of our character and customs, life and scenery, which, in such skilled and methodical forms, occur in no other book I know.[4]

The novel that Furphy described in his letter of 1897, and of which Stephens made this prediction, never reached print. Both were speaking of the original form of *Such is Life*, before Furphy was persuaded to abridge and revise it, in an operation he described as "like pulling down a house and rebuilding a skillion".[5] Some of the omitted material was reshaped into *Rigby's Romance*, published serially in 1905–06, and not reappearing in full in book-form until 1946; another omitted chapter was refashioned as *The Buln-Buln and the Brolga*, and remained in manuscript until 1948. The original text of *Such is Life* has not survived, and cannot be reconstructed from the elements of it that remain. The only datum for criticism is the revised text, published after delay in 1903.[6]

The narrator of *Such is Life*, Tom Collins, purports to be expanding a series of extracts from a pocket diary of 1883–4, taking a range of seven months, and choosing the events of the ninth day of each month for amplification and comment. In this way he hopes to "afford to the observant reader a fair picture of life, as that engaging problem has presented itself to me" (p. 2), arguing that if the chronicle will prove rambling and inconsequential, it will nevertheless stand as a faithful record of events:

> The thread of narrative being thus purposely broken, no one of these short and simple analyses can have any connection with another—a point on which I congratulate the judicious reader and the no less judicious writer; for the former is thereby tacitly warned against any expectation of plot or dénouement, and so secured against disappointment, while the

[4] The correspondence is cited in Miles Franklin and Kate Baker, *op. cit.*, pp. 50-53.

[5] Letter to Mr H. Baker, 1st May 1901, in the Booth collection, Melbourne Public Library.

[6] All references are to the 1945 edition (Sydney: Angus and Robertson), which was reprinted in the Sirius Books series in 1962, omitting Tom Collins's "Introduction".

latter is relieved with the (to him) impossible task of investing prosaic people with romance, and a generally hap-hazard economy with poetical justice. (pp. 64–65)

Furphy's rejection of "plot", and his scorn for "the flowery pathway of the romancer", mark the liberation of the Australian novel from the English tradition, the repudiation of the conventions and techniques that had governed it up to that time. Lawson had gained a similar independence in the naturalistic method of his short stories, but Furphy's campaign was far more consciously and deliberately pursued. He derides the writers of the Anglo-Australian school, introducing into *Rigby's Romance* a parody of the episode in *Robbery Under Arms* when Jim Marston rescues the squatter's daughter on the bolting horse, lifting her from the saddle on the edge of the cliff, as her horse goes toppling over,[7] and introducing into *Such is Life* a descendant of Sam Buckley, the hero of *Geoffry Hamlyn*. Buckley's subsequent history—as Collins prolongs it—was to lose Baroona through foreclosure, owing to incompetent management, so that his son became something indefinite in a bank, before being reduced to blacksmith's work, and his daughter went through three husbands before becoming the decayed gentlewoman housekeeper at Runnymede—the Maud Beaudesart of *Such is Life*. In the ineffectual Willoughby, and the insufferable Folkestone with his monocle, the English gentleman who comes to conquer the outback is held up to ridicule, and the narrative is full of asides on the artificialities of the Romantic novel, with its entanglements and improbabilities.

Consciously rejecting the conventions of the Anglo-Australian school, Furphy has capitalized on the looseness of form of *Such is Life* to produce a novel that is unique. The casual, episodic method allows him to catch the pace and texture of nomadic life in the Riverina of the day, recording the Australian idiom with a fidelity no earlier novelist can appoach, and commanding an emotional range extending from the hilarious story of the the lost pants to the controlled pathos of the story of the lost child. The unity of the narrative comes from the presence of the same narrator through the various episodes—Tom Collins, "a solitary wayfarer, wisely lapt in philosophical torpor", seen travelling across the black soil plains in chapter one, heading the cavalcade of his horse, his pack-horse, and his kangaroo-dog, Pup.

The "rediscovery" of Furphy in the 1940s was essentially the full recognition of the subtlety of the design of *Such is Life*. Although Collins claims to be simply amplifying entries from a pocket-diary, a

[7] See H. J. Oliver, "Tom Collins, Lyre-Bird", *Southerly*, XV (1954), 216-17.

closer reading reveals hidden connections between the events so casually described, one incident illuminating another many pages distant, the apparent inconsequence of the narrative masking an intricate pattern of cause and effect. The rôle of Collins himself as narrator is a particular refinement of the technique. The story comes to us as unwittingly distorted by his reflections and theorizings: Collins reveals through his narrative the hidden significance of the events he describes, without ever perceiving it himself. Furphy has dispensed with the artificialities and restrictions of "plot" to deal with life in a more realistic way. He shows how fragmentary is our knowledge of any train of events in which we find ourselves, how the most innocent actions have far-reaching consequences, how chance and accident constantly intervene in human affairs: the book enacts its title, showing that such *is* life.

To classify *Such is Life* as a novel in "temper, democratic; bias, offensively Australian" is not to distil its essence. Yet to regard it as written to demonstate some specific view of life is also hazardous. A. D. Hope, in an influential review-article in *Meanjin* in 1945, began the process of deducing the philosophy of *Such is Life* from Collins' digressions, taking them as an essential part of the fabric of the book. Critical attention since has fixed on the theory of determinism that Collins himself described as consisting in "the unfettered alternative, followed by rigorous destiny" (p. 133). The key reflective passage occurs in Chapter Two, as on approaching Rory O'Halloran's hut, Collins sees a swagman settling into a more comfortable position under a wilga tree. He is about to hail him, when he remembers that it is still a couple of hours before sunset, and if the swagman approached the homestead now, for the traditional hand-out of tea and flour, he would be expected to do some work at the woodheap beforehand. Collins therefore leaves the sundowner under the shade of the wilga, and goes on alone to the hut.

This decision involved a choice between two alternatives—a choice trivial enough in itself, but with grave consequences. On asking Rory O'Halloran next morning whether many swagmen call at his hut, Collins learns that a swagman has been reported in the district nearly blind with sandy blight, his swag discovered on a fence four days ago, but the man himself still missing. Making for the wilga tree in some alarm, Collins finds the man already dead, as a consequence of his choice of the previous afternoon. There are further consequences three chapters later, when after the passage of three months, Collins learns from Thompson of the death of Mary O'Halloran, Rory's daughter. The death of the swagman had worked upon her mind, so that when her father was away from home for a few days, she set out to look for him, and was lost in the bush.

Collins was allowed the initial choice of hailing the swagman or not hailing him, but that decision once made, the consequences followed independently of his volition. In "the unfettered alternative, followed by rigorous destiny" Collins sees his answer to the age-old question whether man controls his own fate, or whether the universe is ruled by the operation of chance. Man has the responsibility of choice between one action and another, but after that initial exercise of will, he submits to destiny and becomes its plaything, powerless to affect the course of events any further:

> Or put it in allegorical form. The misty expanse of Futurity is radiated with divergent lines of rigid steel; and along one of these lines, with diminishing carbon and sighing exhaust, you travel at schedule speed. At each junction, you switch right or left, and on you go still, up or down the way of your own choosing. But there is no stopping or turning back; and until you have passed the current section there is no divergence, except by voluntary catastrophe. Another junction flashes into sight, and again your choice is made; negligently enough, perhaps, but still with a view to what you consider the greatest good, present or prospective. One line may lead through the Slough of Despond, and the other across the Delectable Mountains, but you don't know whether the section will prove rough or smooth, or whether it ends in a junction or a terminus, till the cloven mists of the Future melt into a manifest Present. We know what we are, but we know not what we shall be. (p. 87)

It is almost the "standard" interpretation of *Such is Life* to take this theory of determinism as the philosophy that the book enacts. Yet this is a theory that comes patently not from the mind of Joseph Furphy, but from the mind of Tom Collins, a mind stored with hypotheses that are continually being disproved by events, or else that are so fanciful as to arouse an indulgent amusement. Collins does demonstrate his theory of "the unfettered alternative, followed by rigorous destiny" from the story of the lost child; but the other major demonstration of it, one must emphasize, is the story of the lost trousers. Before crossing the river, Collins is faced by the momentous alternatives of filling his pipe beforehand and smoking it while crossing in the canoe, or waiting to smoke until he has reached the other side. By choosing the second course, the three or four minutes that he does *not* devote to filling the pipe mean that he is punctual in colliding with the log midstream—and so rigorous destiny takes charge, and all the misfortunes of the lost clothes, the mosquitoes and nettles follow.

The philosophy of "the unfettered alternative, followed by rigorous destiny" is clearly another of the theories in the mind of Collins that ridicules itself as the action unfolds. It is part of his character, with no more status than the theory of Stewart of Kooltopa that the world is under "the legislation of an unsleeping Providence" (p. 217), or the belief of Steve Thompson and Warrigal Alf that the misfortunes sent them are a retribution for base actions in their past. What emerges from these divergent hypotheses, and what is dramatized in the action of the book, is surely this: that there is no one system that can account for the baffling quality of experience, no single theory that can comprehend all the facts. This is what Furphy is saying, irrespective of what Collins may be saying, and this is the last ironical exposure of the book: such, Furphy implies, *is* life.

The distinction between the narrator Collins and the novelist Furphy has further consequences for the interpretation of the novel. Furphy's personal adherence to the doctrines of State Socialism is well documented, even though in *Rigby's Romance*, where these doctrines are elaborated, they are attributed to Jefferson Rigby rather than to Collins. Though Furphy's nationalistic views are also well attested, the evidence of *Such is Life* indicates that they are less naïve than is generally assumed. It is easy to see the English aristocrat being lampooned in Willoughby or Folkestone, but which character in the book would an Australian reader choose as his national representative? Would it be Mosey Price, whose code is to take down the other fellow, and boast of his shrewdness in having done so; or another bullock-driver, Priestley, with the mentality of a sullen Neanderthal man, leaning on his whip with a sinister glitter in his eye as Folkestone makes ready to "thump this fellow"? The institution of "mateship" is presented in a curious light in Chapter One, when, as each of the bullock-drivers leaves the group about the campfire to get a pannikin of water, the others take his exit as a cue to join in a mild form of character assassination. Collins gives his views of "the coming Australian" in Chapter Four, in praising Roddy Sollicker to his father ("I tell you we're going to have a race of people in these provinces such as the world has never seen before"—p. 179) —but this representative of the Australia of the future is in fact the illegitimate son of Hungry McIntyre, the boundary-rider's boss. The conception of the Australian national character that emerges from *Such is Life* is of course a composite of all the characters presented in it, but so far as it includes the figures mentioned, it is less naïve and uncritical than has usually been supposed. The kind of subtlety that has been found in the design of the book is to be sought also in the stereotypes and attitudes with which it deals.

The writing of both Furphy and Lawson was nourished by oral tradition, in that both acknowledged the influence of the "bush yarn" on their work—a genre preserved in the many short stories of Lawson that are put in the mouth of an independent narrator, and in the inset narratives of the *Such is Life* trilogy. The distinctive verse of the nineties had a similar "folk" background. The bush ballad, the dominant form of the period, has an ancestry reaching back to the anonymous ballads of the early nineteenth century, some brought by the convicts, others celebrating the exploits of the bushrangers and the stockmen, or the hardships of the digger, the shearer and the overlander. Such a ballad as "The Wild Colonial Boy", recalling the deeds of the bushranger Jack Donahue, has an Irish archetype, and was once sung to the tune of "The Wearing of the Green":

'Tis of a wild Colonial boy, Jack Doolan was his name,
Of poor but honest parents he was born in Castlemaine.
He was his father's only hope, his mother's only joy,
And dearly did his parents love the wild Colonial boy.

CHORUS:
Come, all my hearties, we'll roam the mountains high,
Together we will plunder, together we will die.
We'll wander over valleys, and gallop over plains,
And we'll scorn to live in slavery, bound down with iron chains.

He was scarcely sixteen years of age when he left his father's home,
And through Australia's sunny clime a bushranger did roam.
He robbed those wealthy squatters, their stock he did destroy,
And a terror to Australia was the wild Colonial boy . . . .

It is commonplace for the early ballads to be sung to traditional tunes, as the stockmen's song, "Farewell and Adieu to you, Brisbane Ladies", parodies the old sea-chanty "Ladies of Spain":

Farewell and adieu to you, Brisbane ladies,
Farewell and adieu to the girls of Toowong:
We have sold all our cattle and cannot now linger,
But hope we shall see you again before long—

and as "The Dying Stockman" is sung to the tune of "The Old Stable Jacket":

A strapping young stockman lay dying,
His saddle supporting his head;
His two mates around him were crying,
As he rose on his elbow and said:

CHORUS:
"Wrap me up with my stockwhip and blanket,
And bury me deep down below,
Where the dingoes and crows can't molest me,
In the shade where the coolibahs grow."

Most of the ballads exist in a number of variant forms, modified to reflect different circumstances, and some versions are found in

Ireland, England and the United States as well. Russel Ward has discussed the ancestry of the ballads in *The Australian Legend* (1958), Hugh Anderson has collected the music as well as the words in *Colonial Ballads* (1962), and John Meredith has made a particular study of one set of ballads in *The Wild Colonial Boy* (1960).

However much the early ballads depended on overseas patterns—the only extant texts of some of them are broadsides printed in London—they tended to reflect an Australia that was left unrepresented by the writers of the Anglo-Australian school, a society that was proletarian, hostile to authority, irreverent and independent. These are the qualities that the writers of the nineties came to develop and glorify. Adam Lindsay Gordon had already shown the way, for "The Sick Stockrider" has the anonymous ballad, "The Dying Stockman", behind it. There is nevertheless some distance between the Englishman Gordon and the nineties school—as is suggested by the parody of "How We Beat the Favourite" in the *Bulletin Reciter*—and the man next to Lawson who set the vogue of the bush ballad was A. B. Paterson ("The Banjo"). Paterson made a collection of the anonymous ballads, which he published in 1905 as *Old Bush Songs*: newly edited in 1957 with a more adequate commentary and many more poems, by Nancy Keesing and Douglas Stewart, this still stands as the most comprehensive text of the traditional ballads. (All the quotations given above are from this source.) Paterson was collecting what would have seemed at the time the nearest approach to an Australian folklore—songs of uncertain authorship, acquiring variants in transmission, many surviving only in the memories of those who could recall the words they had heard years ago. The verses which Paterson himself wrote were in imitation of the old bush songs, a translation of them into a deliberate literary mode. This was what the bush ballad of the nineties was, reflecting Kipling as well as the anonymous songster, and established as a current literary fashion.

Andrew Barton Paterson (1864–1941) had more formal education and more literary training than any of the writers of his day whom we have encountered so far. Although he was born in the country, and owned a station on the Murrumbidgee for some years before the First World War, Paterson was educated in Sydney and trained for the law, and spent most of his professional life in newspaper work. He began contributing to the *Bulletin* in 1886, the year before Lawson, and published "Clancy of the Overflow" in 1889, the year the first contribution by Furphy appeared. In 1895 Paterson's *The Man from Snowy River and Other Verses* won an instant popularity, with sales exceeding ten thousand within a year. Banjo Paterson has probably reached a wider public than any other Australian author. His

"Waltzing Matilda" has become an unofficial national song, while generations of schoolboys have been introduced to Australian poetry through the famous ride of the man from Snowy River, or the opening lines of "Clancy of the Overflow":

I had written him a letter which I had, for want of better
  Knowledge, sent to where I met him down the Lachlan years ago;
He was shearing when I knew him, so I sent the letter to him,
  Just on spec, addressed as follows, "Clancy of The Overflow".

And an answer came directed in a writing unexpected
  (And I think the same was written with a thumb-nail dipped in tar);
'Twas his shearing mate who wrote it, and *verbatim* I will quote it:
  "Clancy's gone to Queensland droving, and we don't know where he are."

Paterson's verse is obviously not so much to be studied as to be read, preferably aloud. The secret of its durability is that it succeeded in dramatizing the heroic conception of Australia and the Australian that in the nineties became a living myth. Two generations or more of overseas visitors had by this time recorded their impression of the "typical" Australian as lean and muscular, consciously indolent in the face of authority, living an independent outdoors life. A score or so of observers had also reported their feeling that the "genuine Australia" lay in the vast plains beyond the coastal fringe—the outback which presented a new mode of existence, which made youths into men. This is the Australia which Paterson projects in his verse again and again:

I'm travelling down the Castlereagh, and I'm a station-hand,
I'm handy with the ropin' pole, I'm handy with the brand,
And I can ride a rowdy colt, or swing the axe all day,
But there's no demand for a station-hand along the Castlereagh.

So it's shift, boys, shift, for there isn't the slightest doubt
That we've got to make a shift to the stations further out,
With the pack-horse runnin' after, for he follows like a dog,
We must strike across the country at the old jig-jog . . . .
("A Bushman's Song")

The typical character of a Paterson ballad is a herculean figure like The Man from Ironbark, or the shrewd stranger who rides into Walgett Town, or the scapegrace like Saltbush Bill, and he may hail from Myall Lake or Eaglehawk or the outer Barcoo:

On the outer Barcoo where the churches are few,
  And men of religion are scanty,
On a road never cross'd 'cept by folk that are lost
  One Michael Magee had a shanty . . .

or even from Booligal, reputed worse than Hay or Hell:

> "No doubt it suits 'em very well
> To say it's worse than Hay or Hell,
>   But don't you heed their talk at all;
> Of course, there's heat—no one denies—
> And sand and dust and stacks of flies,
>   And rabbits, too, at Booligal. . . .
>
> "The big mosquitoes frighten some—
> You'll lie awake to hear 'em hum—
>   And snakes about the township crawl;
> But shearers, when they get their cheque,
> They never come along and wreck
>   The blessed town of Booligal. . . ."

Yet Paterson deliberately resisted the grim view of outback Australia that Lawson had given in his work, engaging in a verse debate with him in the *Bulletin* about it. To Clancy gone a-droving belongs "the vision splendid of the sunlit plains extended", and the townsman in his "dingy little office" frets at life that hems him in:

> And in place of lowing cattle, I can hear the fiendish rattle
>   Of the tramways and the buses making hurry down the street;
> And the language uninviting of the gutter children fighting
>   Comes fitfully and faintly through the ceaseless tramp of feet. . . .
>
> And I somehow rather fancy that I'd like to change with Clancy,
>   Like to take a turn at droving where the seasons come and go,
> While he faced the round eternal of the cash-book and the journal—
>   But I doubt he'd suit the office, Clancy, of The Overflow.

Paterson's work provides the nearest equivalent in Australian culture to the values in the United States associated with "the frontier" and "the West". No other poet of the nineties was so skilful in representing Australia in a version the public found appealing, or in producing a poetry to which the average man could so readily respond. This flair of Paterson's was to be seen fully developed once again in C. J. Dennis, whose *Songs of a Sentimental Bloke* became a popular classic in the 1920s.

Diversifying the Pattern

Lawson, Furphy and Paterson represent the main literary tradition of the nineties, in their absorption in the Australian scene and in their chauvinistic attitude to it. Yet a great deal of the writing done in the nineties fails to conform to this image. This is apparent from the series of *Bulletin Booklets* issued from 1889 to 1903, and edited by A. G. Stephens himself. The titles include James Hebblethwaite's *A Rose of Regret*, Roderic Quinn's *The Hidden Tide*, Louise Mack's *Dreams in Flower*, Hubert Church's *The West Wind*—volumes that in varying degrees reflect the "pretty" fashions of late nineteenth-century verse, the modes of Dowson and William Watson. Victor Daley, whose *At Dawn and Dusk* was published by the Bulletin Company in a second edition in 1902, is the main exemplar of this tradition in Australian verse in the nineties. His poem "In Memory of Henry Kendall" dwells on the Romantic strain in Kendall's work —the "dreamer of dreams", not the Australian nature poet—and a typical lyric by Daley could as easily have been written in England as in Australia:

I have been dreaming all a summer day
Of rare and dainty poems I would write;
Love-lyrics delicate as lilac-scent,
Soft idylls woven of wind, and flower, and stream,
And songs and sonnets carven in fine gold.

The day is fading and the dusk is cold;
Out of the skies has gone the opal gleam,
Out of my heart has passed the high intent
Into the shadow of the falling night—
Must all my dreams in darkness pass away?
("Dreams")

The rhyming scheme sustained through the poem as a whole may reflect the cult of such forms as the rondel, the villanelle and the chant royal in contemporary English verse. A. G. Stephens in *The Bookfellow* was in 1899 offering prizes for the best *ballade* submitted, and for translations of poems of Baudelaire and Verlaine. Despite their occasional poems on an Australian scene, the conception of "the poetic" entertained by Daley and other members of the Dawn and Dusk Club in the nineties was very similar to that of the Rhymers' Club in England. Daley departed from it only in the satirical verse he wrote under the pseudonym "Creeve Roe", which remained uncollected until the edition of Muir Holburn and Marjorie Pizer in 1947.

The publication of *At Dawn and Dusk* by the Bulletin Company in 1902 was followed the next year by *Dawnward?*, the first collection of verse by Bernard O'Dowd. Dedicated "To Young Democracy", and with a proem hailing Australia as the possible "Delos of a coming Sun-God's race", *Dawnward?* represents the sentiments of Utopianism and "social protest" characteristic of the *Bulletin* of the day, in which most of the poems included in the book had first appeared. In his manifesto, *Poetry Militant* (1909), O'Dowd was to make a plea for an Australian "poetry of purpose", for the role of the poet as "an Answerer, as Whitman calls him, of the real questions of his age".

In *Dawnward?* he is obsessed with the forces that threaten the Utopian future: poems like "Proletaria", "The City", and "Young Democracy" insist that the injustice and poverty that have crippled other civilizations must not be reproduced in the south. This early verse shows that O'Dowd's method of personification is already habitual, his declaratory manner already established:

> The Babylonian Venus sways
> In every city park;
> Her idiot niece, Abortion, plays
> Beside her in the dark.
>
> Here, Office fawns fidelity
> When stroked by gilded hands;
> In bramble of chicanery
> Belated Justice stands.
> ("The City")

In *The Silent Land* (1906) and *Dominions of the Boundary* (1907) O'Dowd leaves verse of social commentary in order to forge a personal metaphysic, independent of orthodox religion and yet designed to subsume it. The main principle that emerges is his conception of life as a continuum, with the individual mind capable of reaching back into the consciousness of the race:

> Is there behind all men that live
> One all-containing Soul,
> Whose symbols, apt for each one, give
> A transcript of the Whole?

and with the gods representing the aspirations of the human spirit, and in their survival or interplay tracing its evolutionary progress. The later poem *Alma Venus!* (1921) celebrates and elucidates the role of love in this scheme.

O'Dowd's doctrines of the primordial past finding its fulfilment in the present are fused with his idealistic nationalism in *The Bush* (1912). His declaration here is that "Australia is the whole world's legatee", the heir to the myths and gods of the north—

> Who fenced the nymphs in European vales
> Of Pan tabooed from all but Oxford dreams?

—and in the "Great Australia" to come the world will be moulded to shapes of "Freedom, Truth and Joy". If O'Dowd's first volume,

Dawnward?, had in its interrogative title expressed a doubt of Australia's future, in *The Bush* the doubt is resolved.

Critical opinion of O'Dowd is divided, with adverse criticism taking too little account of the coherence of his system, and the favourable critic averting his gaze from the rhetoric in which it is expressed. O'Dowd's work serves at least to show that the poetry of the nineties is more varied than the stereotypes of the period would suggest. He holds to the concepton of the poet as prophet and seer, acknowledging the particular influence of Blake and Nietzsche, and sharing his interest in the occult with Yeats. His poetry has a range of literary allusion not matched by any other of the time, most effective when absorbed into his "conceited" manner:

> Celibate piety with thumb uncouth
> Plastered a fig-leaf over Plato's truth:
> Aquinas thinned, to make a draught divine,
> With holy water, Aristotle's wine. . . .
> ("Alma Venus")

It is instructive that some of the features of O'Dowd's work that seem most insular and parochial—particularly his democratic ideas—are found on enquiry to belong to a larger context. In his early twenties he had fallen under the influence of Walt Whitman, and conducted a correspondence with him during the nineties: O'Dowd read a paper on "The gospel of Democracy as promulgated by Walt Whitman" to the Australian Church Literary Society in September 1890, and named his son Eric Whitman O'Dowd. Whitman sent him reports of the lectures of R. G. Ingersoll, which O'Dowd tried to "place" in the Melbourne press.[8] The extent to which radical sentiment in Australia in the nineties was affected by developments overseas has still to be explored. Joseph Furphy's socialist views were shaped by reading such tracts as Donnelly's *Cæsar's Column*; Henry George visited Australia in 1889, on a lecture tour promulgating the doctrines of *Progress and Poverty*; Edward Bellamy's *Looking Backward* was published serially by William Lane in *The Worker*—the William Lane who in 1893 sailed to found the Utopian New Australia in Paraguay. Australia in the nineties had Bellamy Clubs, Single Tax Leagues, reading circles and debating societies given to the study of "advanced" opinion overseas. This was the intellectual climate in which A. G. Stephens, Lawson, Furphy, O'Dowd and Mary Gilmore all wrote: as representatives of the literary nationalism of the day, they were in contact with ideas of a wider provenance.

[8] See the correspondence of Whitman and O'Dowd in *Overland 23* (April 1962), 8-18, and *Walt Whitman in Australia and New Zealand*, ed. A. L. McLeod (Sydney: Wentworth Press, 1964).

Other writers of the time remind us that literature at any period may escape parochialism through the artist with the vitality and perception to create his own imaginative world. Shaw Neilson was gifted with this perception, and Hugh McCrae certainly possessed the vitality. One of a number of writers whose talent A. G. Stephens encouraged, John Shaw Neilson (1872–1942), was a poet of very little education, who earned his livelihood in such occupations as fencing and road work, and suffered for most of his adult life from defective eyesight. His habit was to compose his poems in the outdoors, and hold them in his head until an amanuensis could be found to write them down. Shaw Neilson had his first poem published in the *Bulletin* in 1895; his diffidence about his work led him to send everything he wrote (from 1905 onward) to A. G. Stephens to "place" for him, sometimes with editorial improvements by Stephens himself.

The special quality of Neilson's work is that it recaptures the untrammelled vision of the child, in the spirit of Wordsworth's ode —"heaven lies about us in our infancy". Shaw Neilson has an instinctive affinity with the unspoilt world of nature, and his poetry records a traffic with it in which the self of the poet is so attenuated that his perceptions are almost unimpaired. As he explained in a comment on "The Orange Tree": "I brought in the young girl because children have a sort of freshness about these things. It's a sort of imagination we all lose later on."[9] He himself never lost it, and in "The Orange Tree" (suggested by "the very beautiful light on the trees in the afternoon" in Merbein) he juxtaposed the two worlds, the one that we have reduced to the familiar and the conventional, the other that is enchanting to the child:

> The young girl stood beside me. I
> Saw not what her young eyes could see:
> — A light, she said, not of the sky
> Lives somewhere in the Orange Tree. . . .
>
> — Listen! the young girl said. There calls
> No voice, no music beats on me;
> But it is almost sound: it falls
> This evening on the Orange Tree. . . .
>
> — Silence! the young girl said. Oh, why,
> Why will you talk to weary me?
> Plague me no longer now, for I
> Am listening like the Orange Tree.

[9] Cited in James Devaney, *Shaw Neilson* (Sydney: Angus and Robertson, 1944), p. 200.

The best of Shaw Neilson's poetry consists in the revelation of the world that remains inaccessible to the girl's insistent interlocutor in "The Orange Tree". Again and again his apparently harmless imagery ("gentle as sunlight on the rain") admits us to a new range of perception, to Neilson's intuitive world of gentleness and delicacy. He could also write poems as painful as "He Sold Himself to the Daisies", on the lot of the man in a rough world who spends his individuality on "things that don't matter—birds, flowers and so on";[10] and in "In the Dim Counties" he contemplates the time "when we all go to bed—underground":

> In the dim counties
>   we take the long calm
> Lilting no laziness,
>   sequel or psalm.
>
> The little street wenches,
>   the holy and clean,
> Live as good neighbours live
>   under the green . . .
>
> Love cannot sabre us,
>   blood cannot flow,
> In the dim counties
>   that wait us below.

Shaw Neilson had never read Blake: it is not easy to trace the influence of any poet upon him, except for Hood. The weaknesses that threaten his particular mode in verse are banality, and the kind of ecstatic exclamation that is so embarrassing in Traherne. The temptation Neilson's critics must avoid, as Judith Wright points out, is of thinking "we are too grown-up to listen . . . [when] perhaps we have not yet grown far enough".[11]

Hugh McCrae (1876–1958) resembles Shaw Neilson in standing outside literary patterns and refusing to be contained in any formula —simply through his insistence on his identity as a poet. McCrae was a man whose vitality overflowed into all that he did, into his friendships, into the playful pen-drawings that illustrated his letters, into the literary talent that spilled into so many forms, from lyric to prose fantasy to poetic drama. He seemed almost to conform to the storybook conception of the poet, quite incapable of understanding such things as "stock exchanges and arbitration courts, booms and depressions", and instead finding his delight in "things of no

[10] *Ibid.* p. 202.

[11] *Preoccupations in Australian Poetry* (Melbourne: Oxford University Press, 1965), p. 130.

importance whatever—the curl of a leaf, the call of a bird, the play of sunlight on the water . . . the music and meaning of poetry, the biting satire of Dean Swift, Chaucer's sly wit, Rabelais' lusty fun".[12]

McCrae became a contributor to the *Bulletin* in 1896 and was represented in *The Bulletin Reciter*, but his first collection, *Satyrs and Sunlight* (1909), was an extraordinary volume to appear in the same decade as *Such is Life*. Here McCrae is already projecting his magical world—a world that is partly classical in its inspiration, as an attempt to recapture the golden age; partly medieval, in its chivalric romance; fanciful, with its nymphs and unicorns, but always rendered with a sensuous excitement. At this distance in time the eroticism may seem artificial, as in "The End of Desire"—

> A flooded fold of sarcenet
> Against her slender body sank,
> Death-black, and beaded with jet
> Across the pleasures of her flank

but the poetry still survives for its meticulous art:

> King Paladin plunged, on his moon-coloured mare
> Athwart the deep shadows of Avalon wood,
> And a heron, afloat on the indolent air,
> Down dropped him a plume in his galloping-hood.

The talent McCrae displays in *Satyrs and Sunlight*—one that he never lost—is for vivid imaginative recreation from myth, literature, or painting, picking up a theme from classical fable or developing a situation from a ballad, and bringing it into his rich and sunlit world. Though this talent is spread over so many forms, in *Satyrs and Sunlight* the best poems are the songs—"Fantasy", "I Blow My Pipes", "Song of the Witless Boy"—for in their carefree spirit we feel the essential McCrae.

The sunlight become clearer in the volumes that follow, as the fantasy becomes more delicate. Nothing in *Satyrs and Sunlight* has quite the exquisite control of "Colombine", or the fantastic wit of "The Mimshi Maiden"; but the effortless lyric that McCrae now has at command is best seen in "Song for Pierrot":

> Dragon-fly and bee are sailing
> Flitter-flutter
> Bright as butter
> Over grass and garden paling.
>
> Rolls the sun a merry eye-lid;
> Who could think it
> Shall he wink it
> Not a flower but is beguiléd . . .

[12] Norman Cowper, "McCrae the Man", *Southerly*, XIX (1958), 67-75.

Water-brooks dance through the meadows,
Little fishes
Have their wishes,
Shadows kiss their fellow-shadows.

Ponies shake and leap for pleasure,
Turning over
In the clover,
Fat, and full of summer treasure.

This song is typical also in the wistfulness of its closing lines:

All can lend of smiles, or borrow —
None so lonely,
I, the only
Pale, impatient child of sorrow.

Through *The Ship of Heaven* (1933), the dramatic fantasy of which this song is part, we are made to share from time to time McCrae's awareness that beauty and vitality must pass, that the sunlight cannot warm us for ever. This realization brings a new tenderness to his final collection, *Voice of the Forest* (1945), when the Camden Town series also shows the conversational relaxation of his later style—a mellow but still exhilarating poet, who could choose as the motto for his last poems *Bibamus!*

Brennan and H. H. Richardson

The literary historian who chose to derive the identity of the period from 1880 to the First World War from Victor Daley's *At Dawn and Dusk*, the bardic utterance of O'Dowd, and the singular achievement of a Shaw Neilson or a Hugh McCrae, would arrive at an image rather different from the more customary one, which reflects the bush balladists and short-story writers of the *Bulletin* school. The necessity to challenge this conventional view of the 1890s is made more urgent by the work of C. J. Brennan and Henry Handel Richardson. Although Paterson, Lawson and Furphy do make this an heroic age in Australian literature—a sometimes inverted heroism, which is nevertheless heroic still—this remains but one aspect of the literary output of the time.

The poetry of Christopher John Brennan (1870–1932) can be understood only in an European perspective. As an undergraduate at the University of Sydney, Brennan was converted to agnosticism in 1890, from reading Herbert Spencer's *First Principles*. His first serious poem, "Farewell, the pleasant harbourage of faith", is a personal response to the theory of the Absolute propounded in the philosophy of the day, written in the style of Swinburne, with one reminiscence of Aeschylus: it also marks the beginning of the metaphysical search that governs all Brennan's later work. Studying in Germany on a travelling scholarship in 1892–4, he made contact with French poetry of the later nineteenth century, especially with the work of Baudelaire, Regnier and Mallarmé. Brennan became convinced that the single impulse behind all the writers of the "symbolist" and "decadent" schools was the aspiration to some pitch of experience, some ideal of beauty that ordinary life denied—and from Mallarmé he learned to formulate this ideal as Eden, the symbol of the lost paradise itself. He found the same impulse expressed in myth, in fables of the Golden Age and the Land of Heart's Desire, and attested in everyday life in the sensation most men have of the imperfection of this life, and in their sense of some fuller life transcending it. All Brennan's poetry—and his metaphysic also, from "Fact and Idea" onward[13]—came to be governed by the sense of a primal harmony lost, and of a further synthesis that mankind is journeying towards. As he wrote later:

> We use poetry to express not the perfect Beauty, but our want of it, our aspiration towards it. Setting it far off in some imagined empyrean, the poet may even, by a paradox, treat with fierce irony of life devoid of all shadow of it or desire for it. More often his theme will be the tragedy of such beauty as this world affords, or the fate that dogs the soul intoxicated with perfection. (*Prose*, p. 19)

The lyrics written in Germany, and on Brennan's reurn to Australia, reflect an effort to realize the Edenic vision in human love. In 1893 Brennan had become engaged to Anna Elizabeth Werth, who was to follow him to Sydney four years later: from the interval of separation came his first volume, *XVIII Poems,* issued in an edition of eight copies in March 1897. This was superseded in July by the enlarged sequence, *XXI Poems: Towards the Source.* Brennan sent a copy to Mallarmé, who replied praising his work, and remarking *"il y a entre vous et moi une parentée de songe".*

Published in the same year in which Furphy sent *Such is Life* to the *Bulletin,* Brennan's *XXI Poems: Towards the Source* falls in the tradition of French symbolist verse. In his articles on "Newer French Poetry" in 1899, Brennan described the emergence in French poetry of the later nineteenth century of the *livre composé,* "the book of verse conceived and executed as a whole, a single concerted poem"

[13] The intellectual search reflected in Brennan's poetry may be traced through its various stages in his prose writings, as assembled in *The Prose of Christopher Brennan,* ed. A. R. Chisholm and J. J. Quinn (Sydney: Angus and Robertson, 1962). This is a companion volume to the *Verse* (1960).

(*Prose*, p. 289). *XXI Poems: Towards the Source* is his own attempt to acclimatize the form. It is not (as *XVIII Poems* had been) a simple collection of poems, but a studiously patterned sequence, with the lyrics grouped in three movements (with an envoi) to allow for the modulation of the theme from one phase to the next.

In the course of the next five years this preliminary sequence was to be extended, and then merged into a more ambitious cycle—still obedient to the symbolist principle of "the unity of the book". From the initial plan of adding a fourth section to *XXI Poems* arose the new series "The Twilight of Disquietude", which led in turn to "The Book of Lilith". This focal section—later renamed "The Forest of Night"—is almost a *livre composé* in itself, the metre ranging from the majestic couplet to *vers libre* in the lyrical passages, the theme deployed through changing situations and rendered at the climax in terms of a mythical drama. In 1900 Brennan turned aside to write *The Burden of Tyre*, a sub-cycle occasioned by the Boer War; but in 1902 the composition of "The Wanderer" brought the main scheme almost to completion. The two smaller units subsequently added, "Pauca Mea" and "Epilogues", absorb a few later poems and provide a retrospect on the whole action traversed.

In the *Poems* eventually published in 1914 Brennan is seen sharing Baudelaire's resolve to "desert the separate *genres* and to condense all his poetry into one book which shall have its unity and its secret architecture" (*Prose*, p. 238). Although most readers have made their first acquaintance with Brennan through isolated poems in anthologies, this is not the way his work is intended to be read. *Poems* (1914) is a single poem in five movements, separately titled, with the text printed in two kinds of type—ordinary type for the text proper, and bold face (rendered as italic in the edition of Chisholm and Quinn) for the epigraphs and interludes that mark the transitions, providing in sum a synopsis of the whole development. The pursuit of the Edenic vision, in its various guises, gives the book its essential coherence, approaching Brennan's ideal formulation of the *livre composé* as "the sublimation of a whole imaginative life and experience into a subtly ordered series of poems, where each piece has, of course, its individual value, and yet cannot be interpreted save in its relation to the whole" (*Prose*, p. 329).

The initial movement, *Towards the Source* (1894–97), preserves seventeen poems from the 1897 sequence (one re-written) and adds thirteen others. Their immediate appeal is as a series of love lyrics, belonging mostly to the "four springtimes lost" between Brennan's leaving Berlin in 1894 and Elizabeth's arrival in Australia in 1897. In the title, "source" is used in the sense of a well or fountain, perhaps recalling the "La Source" motif (a nude figure beside a spring) of

Ingres and Courbet, but made more significant by Brennan's view of the Fountain of Youth as one of the equivalents, in myth, for the lost paradise. It is not merely the prospect of fulfilment in love that dominates the series, but the prospect of a fulfilment beyond it.

Towards the Source comes to chronicle the disappointment of these hopes. It begins with the presentation of the *persona*, pledged to the quest of the lost paradise, as an exile from the happiness of men—and yet possessed of a "desire of the infinite" that is felt in "Dies Dominica! the sunshine burns" (No. 6). The poem's original title, "Sicut Incensum", is from the passage in the Mass which occurs when the priest is incensing the altar: *Dirigatur, Domine, oratio mea sicut incensum in conspectu tuo: elevatio manuum mearum sacrificium vespertinum.* The correspondence of the ascending prayer and the incense rising from the altar finds its equivalent in the breaths of vapour sent up by the morning sun from the dew-soaked fields—a metaphor sustained through three stanzas as a correlative to the poet's aspiration, to dissolve in the fourth in an image of blinding light:

> Dies Dominica! the sunshine burns
> strong incense on the breathing fields of morn:
> lucid, intense, all colour towards it yearns
> that souls of flowers on the air are born.
>
> What claustral joy to-day is on the air
> — expanding now and one with the celebrant sun
> and fills with pointed flame all things aware,
> all flowers and souls that sing—and I am one!
>
> Dies Dominica! the passion yearns,
> and the whole world and singer is but one flower
> from out whose luminous chalice odour burns
> intenser toward the blue thro' this keen hour:
>
> — this hour is my eternity! the soul
> rises, expanding ever, with the sight,
> thro' flowers and colours, and the visible whole
> of beauty mingled in one dream of light.

These conflicting impulses of yearning and disenchantment produce, in the second movement of *Towards the Source*, the stalemate of *ennui*. Brennan follows Baudelaire and Verhaeren in fixing on the city (in "The yellow gas fired from street to street") as the place where the vision is most cruelly thwarted, and "our paradisal instinct" starves. This mood is thrown off in turn, in the third movement, by memories of "the clear enchantments of our single year". With the prospect of the lovers being reunited, the later poems are dominated by the idea of nuptial fulfilment, with its attendant imagery:

> thou common dayspring cease;
> and be there only night, the only night,
> more than all other lone:
> be the sole secret world
> one rose unfurl'd,
> and nought disturb its blossom'd peace intense. . . .

Yet in the two poems (Nos. 28 and 29) written from the standpoint of desire fulfilled, the sense of disenchantment is felt again. There has been a movement from innocence to experience, the *persona* now reflecting on the romantic ardours that had earlier possessed him. In "Four springtimes lost: and in the fifth we stand" he is no longer merely undergoing experiences, but coming to evaluate them also. A passage which Brennan marked in his copy of Arthur Symons' *The Symbolist Movement in Literature* (1899) best sums up the history traced:

> All love is an attempt to break through the loneliness or individuality, to fuse oneself with something not oneself. . . . It is a desire of the infinite in humanity, and, as humanity has its limits, it can but return sadly upon itself when that limit is reached.

With the passage from *Towards the Source* to *The Forest of Night*, Brennan attempts a dramatic projection of the theme through myth —the myth of Lilith. This rabbinical legend he saw as embodying the eternal relationship of mankind to Eden. As the first bride whom Adam renounced for a human mate, Lilith represents the transcendent life that man has forfeited, becoming a memory that he cannot obliterate, and a vision that he cannot regain. As this vision destroys all other satisfactions, Lilith may appear to fallen man in malevolent guises (siren, lamia, vampire), but in her loneliness still has a desire that answers his, so that their reunion would be the recovery of the paradise lost.

But the drama of *The Forest of Night* ends in an impasse. No way of obtaining the vision has been found, nor yet any way of escaping its compulsion. The resolution comes in *The Wanderer* (1902–), produced by the coalescence in Brennan's thinking of the Pragmatist metaphysic of F. C. S. Schiller with the theory of the subconscious mind (cf. *Prose*, pp. 39–48). It is a semi-narrative sequence, the Wanderer setting out in the dusk of an autumn evening, and as he glimpses the firelit windows along the way, longing to share the security of other men, as a refuge from the winds that drive him on his lonely road. In the eighth poem of the series, a counter-movement begins. The warmth and comfort of the fireside come to seem the haven of the "souls that serve", withholding their hands from life: the Wanderer feels a surge of confidence that he is not as they. Then as the chill blast that in the *Koran* presages the end of the world blows out of the west, and as in another dimension the rival powers join in the *Götterdämmerung* and the armies clash at Roncesvaux, the drama is brought to an issue:

> O desolate eves along the way, how oft,
> despite your bitterness, was I warm at heart!
> not with the glow of remember'd hearths, but warm
> with the solitary unquenchable fire that burns
> a flameless heat deep in his heart who has come
> where the formless winds plunge and exult for aye
> among the naked spaces of the world,
> far past the circle of the ruddy hearths
> and all their memories. Desperate eves,
> when the wind-bitten hills turn'd violet
> along their rims, and the earth huddled her heat
> within her niggard bosom, and the dead stones
> lay battle-strewn before the iron wind
> that, blowing from the chill west, made all its way
> a loneliness to yield its triumph room;
> yet in that wind a clamour of trumpets rang,
> old trumpets, resolute, stark, undauntable,
> singing to battle against the eternal foe,
> the wronger of this world, and all his powers
> in some last fight, foredoom'd disastrous,
> upon the final ridges of the world:
> a war-worn note, stern fire in the stricken eve,
> and fire thro' all my ancient heart, that sprang
> towards that last hope of a glory won in defeat,
> whence, knowing not sure if such high grace befall
> at the end, yet I draw courage to front the way.

Brennan made another annotation in *The Symbolist Movement in Literature*, again a comment of Symons on Gérard de Nerval: "He speaks vaguely of the Kabbala; the Kabbala would have been a safety to him, as the Catholic church would have been, or any other reasoned scheme of things". Underlining "safety", Brennan wrote in the margin: *Vivere non necesse est: navigare est necesse.*

Brennan remains by far the most impressive poet of the nineties. For though his cycle was not published until 1914, it had been completed in outline in 1894–1902, and Brennan had contributed more poems to the *Bulletin* during the editorship of A. G. Stephens than to any other magazine. His poetry has a *fin de siècle* quality, influenced as it is by Swinburne and Patmore, and reflecting such period fashions as the rondel and the prose-poem, the cult of the

Fatal Woman (as analysed by Mario Praz), and the convention of the *persona* who draws the experiences of other men and other ages into the compass of his own. In this historical perspective, however, Brennan's work shows how poetry in Australia was widening its horizons even before the turn of the century, acclimatizing the symbolist *livre composé* and looking forward to the "mythical method" of twentieth-century English verse.

During the same period the frontiers of the Australian novel were being extended by Henry Handel Richardson. Ethel Florence Lindesay Richardson (1870–1946) left Australia in 1888 to study music at Leipzig, and lived for most of the time on the continent until 1903. At Leipzig and at Strasbourg she studied the masters of the European novel, particularly Flaubert, Tolstoy, Dostoievsky, and the Danish novelist J. P. Jacobsen (whose *Niels Lyhne* "stirred me as few books have ever done, before or since"[14]). Henry Handel Richardson came to authorship through making translations from Danish and Norwegian: her renderings of *Niels Lyhne* (under the title *Siren Voices*) and of Björnson's *Fiskerjenten* (*The Fisher Lass*) were published in 1896. In the next year she was at work on her own first novel, *Maurice Guest.*

Maurice Guest, set in Leipzig in the 1890s, is a study of the tragic love affair of a young provincial Englishman and an Australian girl there, Louise Dufrayer. Leipzig is presented as an artistic community free from the social restraint common elsewhere at the time, where the *avant garde* read Ibsen and Nietzsche and Schopenhauer: we have the same sense of the *fin de siècle* as in Brennan's early verse. The literary tradition to which the author's allegiance is most obvious is European naturalism. It is felt in the insistent documentation of the early chapters—the recording of circumstantial detail, the specification of time and place, the meticulous description of milieu. But *Maurice Guest* conforms to a more fundamental principle of the naturalistic movement in seeking to present things as they really are, without romantic distortion or sentimental illusion. One of the more startling features of the novel, for the first reviewers of it, was that it presented a-moral behaviour quite dispassionately, without disapproving comment. The author is never concerned to judge the liaison of Maurice and Louise, or the relationship of Krafft and Schilsky: her role is to exhibit and to analyse. From Flaubert (as she explained) she had learned "how a theme was to be handled objectively, without intrusion of the author's personality,"[15] and this moral detachment persists through her later works.

[14] *Myself When Young* (London: Heinemann, 1948), p. 125.
[15] See the autobiographical note in *Twentieth Century Authors,* ed. Kunitz and Haycraft (New York: H. W. Wilson, 1942), p. 1170.

Henry Handel Richardson was to remark to a correspondent in her later years, "I read Freud and his works so early in life—before his *name* was even known in England—that his theories have become commonplace to me."[16] This may help to explain the special quality of her first novel. As Henry Handel Richardson follows the practice of Jacobsen and Dostoievsky in telling the story in terms of the central characters' feelings and motives, she is led into a psychological range still uncharted at the time in English fiction itself. The relationship of Maurice and Louise is a treatment of love in every aspect from its most idealistic to its most sensual, with outbreaks of jealousy, surrenders to desire, moments of bitterness and self-abasement. In Louise the author explores those curious moods in which rational conduct is momentarily suspended, leaving the character in a state of complete numbness or of semi-hysteria; in Maurice she shows an idealistic longing which can turn to violence and fetishism. Heinrich Krafft is a study of a homosexual, the special quality of whose attachment for Maurice foreshadows the disclosure of his relationship to Schilsky. A mere recital of the "plot" of *Maurice Guest* would make it resemble a romantic novelette: the book itself is most carefully wrought—witness the rose motif associated with Louise—and shows a firm psychological grasp.

This grasp does weaken at certain stages of the narrative, usually when Henry Handel Richardson is relying on the mystique of "the artist". *Maurice Guest* had begun as "a novel of a musician who failed to make good", and the theme of the artist already had a long ancestry in German literature by the time Richardson began to write, besides being prominent in each of the two novels she had translated. The weakness of *Maurice Guest* is that it demands assent to a romantic stereotype of the artist, most typically in the portraiture of Schilsky, the Polish violinist and composer with red hair. His inspiration comes and drives Schilsky to the exclusion of everything else, so that he is prepared to live on money provided by women, to seduce Ephie Cayhill—or when the ordeal of composition is over, to seek relaxation in coarse pleasures. Despite the efforts made to interpret Schilsky—and indeed the novel as a whole—in Nietzschean terms, this pattern was established in literature before Nietzsche was born, and the view of the artist as set apart from other mortals was one which Henry Handel Richardson personally found congenial.

Maurice Guest himself conforms to the type described by Goethe as "problematical natures"—Spielhagen's *Problematische Naturen* is one of the books lent to him by Johanna Cayhill.[17] Guest is a young

[16] Letter to Oliver Stonor, 18th May 1939, in the Australian National Library, Canberra.

[17] See Elizabeth Loder, "*Maurice Guest*: Some Nineteenth-Century Progenitors", *Southerly*, XXVI (1966), 94-105.

man of provincial background and bourgeois moral ideas who is brought out of that milieu by the stirring of his musical talent: he has a nature that thirsts for experience, dreams of an heroic life, and yet his indecisiveness renders him inadequate, and his sense of decorum keeps a glass pane between himself and reality. When Maurice's bourgeois principles are cast aside in his passion for Louise, they return to torture him again as he tries to accommodate her to his notions of ideal womanhood. Unable to accept the thought that Louise has ever given herself to others as she now gives herself to him, he eventually destroys their love through his jealousies and persecutions. Maurice is the architect of his own hell, as his moral preconceptions compel him to recreate Louise according to a bourgeois ideal with which she has nothing to do: for both the principals this is a story of suffering in love, which ends in tragedy.

Maurice Guest (1908) was followed by *The Getting of Wisdom* (1910), a gentle and ironic study of the author's schooldays at the Presbyterian Ladies' College, Melbourne, and she then embarked on what proved to be the first novel of a trilogy, eventually assembled as *The Fortunes of Richard Mahony.* Although it was not to be completed for almost twenty years, this massive chronicle is governed by a method that Henry Handel Richardson had arrived at from her study of Flaubert and the naturalistic movement of the nineties, and by the vision she had then come to share with Jacobsen. Her comment on *Niels Lyhne* in an article of 1897 could be applied to *Maurice Guest* and *Richard Mahony* alike:

> *Niels Lyhne* might be called a book of unrealized ideals. Hardly one of the many people that cross its pages attains his heart's desire. All these men and women aim too high; they are none of them satisfied with the lot that has fallen to them, they will have no tree but the sky, all have a touch of divine discontent. And they beat their wings and break them against the unyielding barriers of life, which hem them in as the idea of Fate hemmed in ancient tragedy. Too late Niels learns that the only thing to do is "to bear life as it is, and let it take shape according to the laws that govern life". For most of them the lesson is too hard, and their hearts break in learning it. . . .[18]

Henry Handel Richardson's objectives in the trilogy show her continuing fealty to the naturalistic creed. She saw Australian fiction of the nineteenth century with something of the dissatisfaction felt by Furphy when he came to write *Such is Life*: "tales of adventure", "monster finds and fortunes made in the gold-fields", "the hair-raising

[18] "A Danish Poet", *Cosmopolis*, November 1897. This and other uncollected prose writings by Henry Handel Richardson are assembled in *Southerly*, XXIII, i (1963).

exploits of bushrangers". She chose to turn away from this, to dwell on "another and very different side of the picture":

> What of the failures, to whose lot neither fortunes nor stirring adventures fell? The misfits, who were physically and mentally incapable of adapting themselves to this strange hard new world? I knew of many such; and my plan was to tell the life story of one of them, with the changing face of the country for background . . .[19]

Richard Mahony is an Irish aristocrat who comes to Australia—as Ethel Richardson's father had done— in the gold rush of the 1850s, and becomes a storekeeper on the Victorian diggings. The trilogy records the stages of his career: his resumption of medical practice and his prosperity as a leading physician at Ballarat; his impulsive flight from the rawness of colonial life to England again, where he frets at the dismal climate and caste feeling of an English provincial town; the freedom from professional routine through a lucky investment, that makes Mahony a distinguished figure in Melbourne society of the 1870s; then the financial collapse that means an enforced return to medical practice, and a painfully traced decline into insanity, paralysis, and death.

The first volume, *Australia Felix*, shows a major expansion in Henry Handel Richardson's creative range, with a host of minor characters—Tilly Beamish and John Turnham, Henry Ocock and Purdy—called into existence with surprising ease and sureness, while Mahony's own fortunes describe an ascending arc. The title of the second volume, *The Way Home*, proves to be ironical. It shows the fulfilment of all the wishes cherished by Mahony in *Australia Felix*, and the continued frustration of the man himself. He escapes the vulgarity of colonial society, only to find that the obsequiousness and prejudice of the English class system have now become intolerable; he is freed from the nagging financial worries that had fettered his spirit, but his new leisure makes him more susceptible to trifling irritations and more prone to withdraw from the world. Having thrice crossed the world without assuaging his discontent, Mahony is then compelled in *Ultima Thule* to start earning his living again, and his movement from one failing practice to another is accompanied by a physical and mental decline in which all his nobler qualities disappear, and his sanity is gradually frayed out of existence. This history is the more poignant because Mahony's decline is measured through the fear and hatred that creeps into his relationship with his wife, and because phase after phase of it is reflected

[19] "Some Notes on My Books", *Virginia Quarterly Review*, XVI (1940), 334-47; reprinted with a hitherto unpublished addendum in *Southerly*, XXIII (1963), 8-20.

through the consciousness of his small son, Cuffy. The naturalistic method is remorseless in recording every detail of Mahony's physical ageing—his rounded back, his thin wrists, his stiffening joints, his lean neck—as the blows continue to fall.

It is part of the power of the trilogy that the Flaubertian objectivity is maintained. Henry Handel Richardson confessed that no other book gave her the same pleasure to write as *Australia Felix*: "I was at home in it from the first page, back in a land where the air was crisp and clear, and the sun knew how to shine. . . ."[20] Yet in the novel itself this enthusiasm is suppressed, and Australia is presented as it appeared to the generation with which the story deals—as brash and vulgar, with a pitiless sun and dusty roads to act as an abrasive on the sensibilities of the disappointed migrant. The method goes beyond this again, as even the thinking of the characters is made to observe the bounds and reticences of the Victorian period, and the trilogy re-creates the mental climate of the nineteenth century. Richard Mahony is consistently portrayed as a Victorian intellectual, groping into the unknown through spiritualism, making annotations on the Book of Genesis, and, in the crisis in which he contemplates suicide, questioning the purpose of the universe and its creator. Mahony's intellectual limitations are used to make his fate more moving: he is another who will have no tree but the sky, who will beat his wings and break them against the unyielding barriers of life. It is only the unimaginative characters in the book—Tilly Beamish, or Mary Mahony—who are able to find any content. John Turnham does not become humanly happy despite his success, and expects every new wife to satisfy him in human love; the wasted lives of minor figures like Bolliver and Tangye represent to Mahony, even in his success and prosperity, what his own life is to become. "The history of men on this earth since the beginning of ages", Conrad observed in the preface to *Chance*, "may be resumed in one phrase of infinite poignancy: They were born, they suffered, they died." *The Fortunes of Richard Mahony* shows how one man's experience may exemplify this tragic vision.

The two trends in the general development of Australian writing that were noted at the outset—the extension of European civilization to the south, and the growth of an indigenous culture on our own shores—may plainly be followed through the "nationalist" period just as through the period before. The awareness of overseas movements in someone like Brennan might seem unusual, but it was shared to a large degree by A. G. Stephens, and in another sense by Bernard

[20] "Some Notes on My Books", *Southerly*, XXIII (1963), 15.

O'Dowd. Lawson and the *Bulletin* short-story writers represent a local school of naturalism; Henry Handel Richardson represents the European one. Any monistic approach to the writing of the time must continually break down in the face of the facts. Accommodating Louis Stone's *Jonah* (1911), the minor classic of the larrikin and the "push", it must at the same time prove inadequate to William Hay's *The Escape of . . . Sir William Heans* (1919), the work of a disciple of Meredith and a student of Pater. If the popular tradition in verse is extended by C. J. Dennis, what a distance still separates *The Songs of a Sentimental Bloke* from the poems of 1909–13 that William Baylebridge was to assemble as *This Vital Flesh*! Australian literature from the 1880s to the end of the First World War has a greater range and complexity than literary historians have yet recognized, and by implication a higher value.

3

THE MODERN PERIOD (FROM 1920)

Australian Literature Between the Wars

THERE was of course no decisive break in the continuity of Australian writing in the year 1920. Although the war of 1914–18 produced such poetry as Leon Gellert's *Songs of a Campaign* (1917) and such novels as Frederic Manning's *Her Privates We* (1930) and Leonard Mann's *Flesh in Armour* (1932), these were comparatively isolated works, and the war certainly did not mark the end of one age and the beginning of the next. Banjo Paterson was still publishing in the 1930s; Henry Handel Richardson, who had completed the first volume of *The Fortunes of Richard Mahony* in 1912, was to publish the last one in 1929; the work of Hugh McCrae spans the period from *Satyrs and Sunlight* (1909) to *Voice of the Forest* (1945). Mary Gilmore, who in the 1890s had gone to Paraguay to join the Utopian colony of William Lane, leader of the "New Australia" movement, continued to serve the nationalist ideal through the 1930s, and published her last collection, *Fourteen Men*, in 1954.

Nevertheless there were indications in the 1920s that Australian writing was about to enter a new phase. Katharine Prichard and Vance Palmer had returned from England, and Palmer joined with Louis Esson to form the Pioneer Players, who performed some seventeen Australian plays in 1922–3. In 1923 appeared the magazine *Vision*, with a new programme for Australian poetry and contributors including Norman Lindsay and Kenneth Slessor. R. D. FitzGerald's first collection, *The Greater Apollo: Seven Metaphysical Songs*, was privately published in 1927. The "stream of consciousness" trickled into Australian fiction in Chester Cobb's *Mr Moffat* (1925) and *Days of Disillusion* (1926), and the "chronicle" novel found a new level of sophistication in Martin Boyd's *The Montforts* (1928).

Yet is was in the novel that the continuity with the 1890s was to prove strongest, for over two decades after the war. In 1928 the *Bulletin* insituted the S. H. Prior Memorial Prize for the best novel of each year, and the successive awards show the continuing vitality of the naturalistic tradition. It was extended into the historical field in M. Barnard Eldershaw's *A House is Built* (1929), applied to the life of the small country town in Kylie Tennant's *Tiburon* (1935), wedded to the pioneering saga in Miles Franklin's *All That Swagger* (1936), and developed with a new zest in Eve Langley's narrative of itinerant farm-workers, *The Pea-Pickers* (1942). Over the same period, but more especially in the 1930s and 1940s, the realistic short story was again seen to be one of the more positive achievements in Australian prose, with the appearance of writers like Gavin Casey, Frank Dalby Davison, Brian James, John Morrison, and Peter Cowan.

The two most representative writers of this time, who practised in the novel and short story alike, were Katharine Susannah Prichard (1883–) and Vance Palmer (1885–1959). In Palmer's first collection of stories, *The World of Men* (1915), written with the encouragement of A. R. Orage of the *New Age*, it was already clear that the "documentary" tradition of the 1890s was now passing into more sensitive hands, though in the novels that followed—*Cronulla* (1924) and *The Man Hamilton* (1928) were two of the better ones—Palmer seemed slow to discover where his real ability lay. He was apt to succeed with the minor characters in his novels, and fail with the major ones; his treatment of romantic relationships was usually unconvincing, while the tensions between members of a family could be handled with unusual discernment. With the publication of *The Passage*, which won the *Bulletin* prize in 1930, his particular gifts found their effective scope.

Palmer's talent for bringing out the true quality of the outwardly undramatic life is the main strength of *The Passage*, set in a fishing town on the northern coast. Lew Callaway is contentedly absorbed into the rhythm of existence there, finding in his occupation the satisfaction of all his needs:

> "Time to go in!" thought Lew, watching the dropping sun.
>
> But though the fish had ceased biting he remained with the slack line between his fingers, steeped in reflection. He didn't want to go in; out there on the slowly-heaving water, where there was no craft but his own little boat, he had a sense of harmony he was unwilling to lose. An assurance flowed into him there, had always done so. Life, his own life, was good enough. . . .

Although his mother resists the spell of the Passage, channelling her ambitions through her younger son Hughie, Lew remains the character in the novel with the greatest stability and capacity for fulfilment. There is hidden in him the temperament of a poet, and when the day's work is over he can lie in a "sensuous fatigue", experiencing more keenly "the white wedge on the underside of the black swans' wings as they flew over, the silky swish of the making tide on the shelly inner beach". Palmer works best in the ripples of human experience, rather than in the waves, and he suggests in Lew that simplicity of character that is always so difficult to convey in literary terms.

Although in so many ways *The Passage* calls on Palmer's special powers as a novelist—his skill in suggesting the rhythm of existence in the fishing village, his insight into the vulnerable nature of little Peter Callaway—it also exposes certain of his limitations. The process by which Lew comes to marry Lena Christensen is never convincingly shown: Palmer typically holds back from the treatment that is demanded, and is not on safe ground again until he is dealing with the frictions of the Callaways' domestic life, their silent resentments and oblique tauntings. The same evasiveness is felt in Lena's relationship to Craig, and in Lew's feeling for Clem McNair.

This restricted emotional range finally limits Palmer's achievement. His best work after *The Passage* is probably found in the short story, in the collections *Sea and Spinifex* (1934) and *Let the Birds Fly* (1955). It is true that *The Swayne Family* (1934) allowed Palmer to deal again with the tensions between one generation and another, but to one reviewer it seemed like an experiment "to see how much he can write without a plot". The major enterprise of Palmer's later years was the Macy Donovan trilogy, *Golconda* (1948), *Seedtime* (1957), and *The Big Fellow* (1959), following the career of a union leader who rises to be Premier of Queensland. Although it is a work of some distinction, Palmer's approach is still too sedate and restrained to elicit the full force of his theme, and again the exceptional character proves to lie beyond his range—Donovan leaves an impression of commonplaceness that his achievements belie. Palmer's work will continue to command respect for its patience and sympathy, and the integrity of its craftsmanship: yet too close a scrutiny of it might raise misgivings about the mediocrity of Australian fiction between the wars.

The talent of Katharine Prichard is more striking, but also more uneven. *The Pioneers*, which won the Australian section of the Hodder and Stoughton Dominions Competition in 1915, is a sad commentary on the standard of the other entries, and *Windlestraws* (1916) is almost negligible. Katharine Prichard began to find her feet in *Black Opal* (1921), the first of a series of novels which drew their strength from the environment against which the story is set. Towards the end of the book the heroine, Sophie, comes close to formulating the author's artistic creed:

> "One thing he said has always stayed in my mind: 'Keep close to the earth!' It was not good, he said, to walk on asphalted paths too long . . ."

"Keep close to the earth?" Potch mused.

"In tune with the fundamentals, all the great things of loving and working—our eyes on the stars."

The two novels that follow, *Working Bullocks* (1926) and *Coonardoo* (1929), mark the first peak of Katharine Prichard's achievement, and they both "keep close to the earth", in tune with the fundamentals of loving and working. In *Working Bullocks,* set in the giant karri forests of Western Australia, the relationship of Red Burke and Deb Colburn is traced in terms of the submerged workings of impulse and instinct, and against a natural background that enriches the prose with images of fecundity, vigour and burgeoning growth. The special quality of the novel depends on the exact descriptions of activities like yarding and breaking brumbies, of the splendid exertion of Neil Hansen at the wood-chop, or of the way Red Burke's arm, gripping his whip, "sleeve torn from it, bare to the arm-pits, red and brown with sunburn, glint of fire in the hair on it, muscles and sinews strung out, flung its challenge".

Although Katharine Prichard read and admired D. H. Lawrence, the "cult of the primitive" in her earlier novels is something personal to herself, part of a faith distilled in *The Earth Lover and other Verses* (1932). For all the starkness of her writing, she is by temperament a Romantic, with a keener response to the beauty of the Australian scene than is common in the realistic school. When she began to write, she has explained, "everybody seemed to me to be living in the shadow of Lawson", with a vision of Australia as "a grey and distressing country". Her vision was different: "I wanted to bring a realization of the beauty and vigour of our life to Australian literature. I think I did use colour when most people were writing in neutral tints."[1] Though the world of *Working Bullocks* may be a brutal one, it is also made beautiful by the majesty of the karri forest or the scenery beside the road along which Red drives his team:

> Everywhere the saplings were budding, sunshine making luminous the green of young leaves, ruddy and amber sap in their budding tips. Wild flowers were out, the scarlet spider bush and wild peach showering pink blossoms; low-growing blue, yellow, white and purple flowers strayed across the wheel ruts and into the wilderness of the trees.

There is more of the gauntness and austerity of the outback in *Coonardoo,* set on a cattle station in the north-west, and occupied with the tragedy of a native girl caught between the incompatible demands of black and white society. The effort to "keep close to the earth" continues, in the account of drought-stricken plains and

[1] A letter cited by Henrietta Drake-Brockman, "Katharine Susannah Prichard: The Colour in her Work", *Southerly,* XIV (1953), 214.

withered trees, the strenuous work of mustering and branding, the aboriginal ceremonies that weave Coonardoo to her race by her senses, appetites and instincts. Again the novel explores the blind, elemental level of human behaviour, in a way that is constantly challenging the novelist's range and control: the episode in which Hugh "takes" Coonardoo ("deep inexplicable currents of his being flowed towards her . . . she came to kneel beside him, her eyes the fathomless shining of a well in the shadows") is typical of the hazards to be encountered. *Working Bullocks* and *Coonardoo* are both flawed novels, but in them the naturalistic tradition acquires a new depth and insight.

Their quality is made more emphatic by the tameness of *Haxby's Circus* (1930), which followed. Katharine Prichard's visit to Soviet Russia led to a series of socialist pamphlets in the 1930s, and these came to provide a determining philosophy in her works. It is already influential in her one venture in the introspective novel, *Intimate Strangers* (1937), and becomes much stronger in the goldfields trilogy that followed. This is an attempt to trace the whole history of mining in Western Australia, from prospecting days in *The Roaring Nineties* (1946) to the era of company management in *Golden Miles* (1948), with the third volume, *Winged Seeds* (1950), carrying the chronicle from the depression to the end of the Second World War.

The goldfields trilogy is much more "the story of an industry" (the phrase of the author's preface) than an effective work of fiction. The characters are for too much of the time simply passed from one situation to another, their feelings and responses notified through simple declarations by the author. When Morris kisses Sally, we are told "it was a delirious moment"; when Sally receives news of Lal's death, "her mind whirled crazily in her rage and grief". The dialogue is strained to accommodate the necessary discussions of capitalism and alluvial rights, and in *Winged Seeds* the disquisitions on the Spanish Civil War and the Russo-German Pact show Katharine Prichard's ineptitude with the *roman à thèse*—which cannot be said to have diminished in the more recent novel, *Subtle Flame* (1967). The impressive scope of the goldfields trilogy ensures its place in the work of a writer whose novels traverse the continent from Gippsland to Broome, but her reputation will probably rest more securely on *Working Bullocks, Coonardoo* and *Intimate Strangers,* with the short-story collection *Happiness* as a coda.

Coonardoo shared the *Bulletin* prize in 1928 with M. Barnard Eldershaw's *A House is Built,* which helped to set the vogue of the historical novel in the 1930s. This was the period of Miles Franklin's *All That Swagger* (1936), with the series of novels by her *alter ego,* "Brent of Bin Bin", and of Brian Penton's *Landtakers* (1934) and

Inheritors (1936), aggresively unromantic in their treatment of the pioneering theme. The naturalistic method was at the same time coming to grips with city life, as in Kylie Tennant's *Foveaux* (1939), set in a Sydney slum during the depression. The novel which followed it, *The Battlers* (1941), a boisterous chronicle of the drifting unemployed in the country, set the fashion of "reportage" that was to become standard in the Australian realistic novel—to be pursued by Kylie Tennant herself in *Ride on Stranger* (1943) and *The Joyful Condemned* (1953), and to be taken up later by Ruth Park and D'Arcy Niland. Apart from *The Battlers,* the work of this time which has lasted best is Xavier Herbert's exuberant and indignant novel of life in northern Australia, *Capricornia* (1938).

In all these ways the "documentary" strain of the 1890s, the effort to interpret the Australian environment and character, continued with a new vigour and strength. Yet for a short time in the decade or so after the war, there seemed a possibility that the Australian novel might take another course. Symptoms of this were Chester Cobb's *Mr Moffatt* (1925) and *Days of Disillusion* (1926), already mentioned as marking the entry of "stream of consciousness" into Australian fiction; the introspective, carefully wrought work of Leslie Meller in *Quartette* (1932) and *A Leaf of Laurel* (1937); the strange world illuminated in Christina Stead's *Seven Poor Men of Sydney* (1934); the poise and elegance of Martin Boyd in *The Montforts* (1928); and the technical skill of Eleanor Dark in *Prelude to Christopher* (1933). To look back now on this set of novels is to see the possibility of a renaissance in Australian fiction at that time, or at least of a marked variation in the established pattern.

As it happened, however, neither Chester Cobb nor Leslie Meller published again; Christina Stead and Martin Boyd went overseas, to write a series of "expatriate" novels (*Seven Poor Men of Sydney* had in fact been written abroad); Eleanor Dark moved from the accomplishment of *Return to Coolami* (1935) to a couple of less distinguished contemporary novels, and then embarked on the historical saga, *The Timeless Land* (1941), *Storm of Time* (1948) and *No Barrier* (1953). The one novelist to emerge in these years and hold to his chosen path—if we except Patrick White, whose *Happy Valley* appeared in 1939—was Kenneth ("Seaforth") Mackenzie (1913–55). His first novel, *The Young Desire It* (1937) was a delicate study of adolescence, exploring subtly the innocent and yet sensuous attachment of Charles Fox and the girl he meets on a school vacation and his more perplexing relationship with Penworth, the master who is drawn to him by a quasi-homosexual feeling. A more complex pattern of relationships is analysed in *Chosen People* (1938), where the entanglement of a young man with an older married woman anticipates the situation of *The Refuge* (1954). In between these two novels Mackenzie published *Dead Men Rising* (1951), set in the Japanese prisoner-of-war camp at Cowra where an outbreak had occurred in 1944, but occupied much more with the love of John Sargent and Cathie, the tensions between the various camp personnel, and the personality of the half-Japanese interpreter Orloff. Mackenzie's four published books show him to be one of the most accomplished and perceptive novelists of his time, sensitive to the devious paths of motive and able to catch at the most reticent of feelings. In *Chosen People* the effect may be too claustrophobic, as in *The Refuge* it is finally unconvincing, but *The Young Desire It* is a delicate and eloquent book, and *Dead Men Rising* shows Mackenzie's powers being fully extended.

Novelists so diverse as Katharine Prichard, Vance Palmer and Kenneth Mackenzie can suggest only part of the variety of Australian prose since the 1920s. There were so many other writers whose best work was not in the novel, but the short story. The absence of a single commanding figure, such as Lawson had been at the turn of the century, has prevented the short story of the 1930s and 1940s from receiving the recognition it deserves. Yet so many of those working in this mode proved themselves capable of producing at least one or two stories of first quality: an anthology of the best work of the period would leave *The Bulletin Story-Book* far behind.

During the 1930s and 1940s, the typical Australian short story continued to have an outwardly casual form, with a tight inner control. This was the method followed in F. D. Davison's *Bulletin* stories—since collected, with others, as *The Road to Yesterday* (1964)— and perfected in Gavin Casey's *It's Harder for Girls*, awarded the S. H. Prior Memorial Prize for 1941–2. Casey's stories, the best of them on the disillusionment of married life, looked back to Lawson in their stoic resignation and wry understatement, at the some time catching some of the mannerisms of Hemingway. The more humorous, anecdotal style that Lawson also had at command was extended by Brian James in *First Furrow* (1944) and *Cookabundy Bridge* (1946), and developed in a sparer and more elliptical way in Cecil Mann's *The River* (1945). Dal Stivens had begun to experiment with the "tall" story in *The Courtship of Uncle Henry* (1946), while in yet another direction Margaret Trist was recording domestic and suburban life—with a method of compassionate "reportage"—in *In the Sun* (1943) and *What Else is There?* (1946).

As over these years the Australian short story preserved its "documentary" character, it also acquired a new sensitivity and indirection. This is the singularity of the work of Peter Cowan, Don Edwards or Ken Levis—of Cowan's "Holiday", for example, or

Levis's "The Kid", where the seeming inconsequence and studied obliquity of the narrative are the secret of its effect. If the "proletarian" story was more deliberately naturalistic, in the hands of John Morrison it proved capable of the same imaginative reach. The successive issues of *Coast to Coast*, the anthology first published in 1941, helped to show how flexible and modern the Australian short story had become, while somehow remaining more "Australian" than any other current literary form. Professor A. J. A. Waldock, commenting on Gavin Casey's "Short-Shift Saturday" in a review of the first issue of *Coast to Coast*, asked "Do people still muse on 'the great Australian novel' for which we wait? Casey, I believe, has it in him to write it."[2] Casey was never to write it, but the prediction stands as a testimony to the talent felt to be at large in the Australian short story of that time.

Australian verse, in the first decade after the 1914–18 war, showed more positive signs of a fresh beginning than Australian prose. In 1923 appeared the magazine *Vision*, which, though it survived for only four issues, has since become almost legendary. *Vision* sprang from the discontent of a group of enthusiasts with the state of contemporary writing, and expressed their protest against the lassitude and disillusion that had followed the war. The "Forewords" to each issue resisted this malaise:

> We would vindicate the youthfulness of Australia, not by being modern, but by being alive. Physical tiredness, jaded nerves and a complex superficiality are the stigmata of modernism. We prefer to find Youth by responding to the image of beauty, to vitality of emotion. . . .
>
> We stand for the younger generation: those who had experience in the war and yet had sufficient courage to survive its mental effect. . . . On the shoulders of these lies the burden of the world to-day. Unless they turn to the expression of frankness and laughter, the world is doomed. . . . It must turn to Life with spontaneity of gladness and desire.

Youth, vitality, beauty—these were the leading ideas of the crusade. It was almost as though the Hugh McCrae of *Satyrs and Sunlight* (1909) had found a group of latter-day disciples, and indeed McCrae was a contributor to the magazine—but the vitalist philosophy of Norman Lindsay's *Creative Effort* (1920) was more immediately influential. In its glorification of vigour and impulse, the *Vision* movement attached no special importance to Australianity. It looked to kindred spirits of any age or country—Marlowe, Rubens, Catullus—who cherished "the image of beauty" or "vitality of emotion", rejecting the literal realism of the nationalist in favour of

[2] *Southerly*, II (1941), 34.

writing that "liberates the imagination by gaiety or fantasy". Amid all this exuberance—reflected in the pages of *Vision* in the prancing satyrs and bare-bosomed nymphs of Norman Lindsay's illustrations—was the firm assumption that poetry is above all an art, with virtues of elegance and accomplishment.

Apart from Hugh McCrae, the poet in whose work the artistic ideals of *Vision* were most nearly realized was Kenneth Slessor (1901–). He was one of the editors of the magazine, an editor besides of the *Vision* anthology, *Poetry in Australia* (1923), and after the quarterly had ceased publication in Australia and entered on a brief second life as *The London Aphrodite* (1928), Slessor was a contributor still.[3] His work in this period is represented in *Thief of the Moon* (1924), published in a revised edition in England as *Earth-Visitors* (Fanfrolico Press, 1926). Slessor here revels in a world of vivid fantasy, peopled by Greek goddesses, fauns and buccaneers, trying to capture its excitement in the music and colour of his verse. To a reader accustomed to the beaten track of Australian verse, poems with the flamboyance of "Thieves' Kitchen" and "Earth-Visitors", or with the eroticism of "Adventure Bay" and "A Surrender" would have seemed an exotic innovation:

> When to those Venusbergs, thy breasts,
> By wars of love and moonlight batteries,
> My lips have stormed—O pout thy mouth above,
> Lean down those culverins twain, and bid me spike
> Their bells with kissing, and their powder steal,
> And by night-marches take their garrisons—
> No blood shall stain those battlefields of lace
> But all their snows run dappled with deep roses,
> And thou, I trow, sweet enemy of love,
> Shalt find a conquest in capitulation!
> ("A Surrender")

The sophistication of Slessor's style tends to conceal the relative vacuity of his writing at this stage. Occasionally his romanticism has a more sardonic twist—as in the poem describing Platonic love as "mere rubbing of dim, spiritual flanks"—and at times the excited celebration of passion is tinged with an awareness of its transience

[3] For a discussion of Slessor's involvement in *Vision*, see Jack Lindsay, "Vision of the Twenties", *Southerly*, XIII (1952), 62-71; Kenneth Slessor, "Spectacles for the Fifties", *Southerly*, XIII (1952), 215-19; Jack Lindsay, "Aids to Vision", *Southerly*, XIV (1953), 204-05; and Norman Lindsay, "Reflections on Vision", *Southerly*, XIV (1953), 267-9. An independent account of the *Vision* movement was given by Philip Lindsay in *I'd Live the Same Life Over* (London: Hutchinson, 1941), and the whole period is recalled in Jack Lindsay's autobiographical volumes *The Roaring Twenties* and *Fanfrolico and After* (London: The Bodley Head, 1960 and 1962).

(e.g., "Heine in Paris", "Stars"). But in the more typical poems Slessor bestows all the resources of his art on attitudes that are basically simple, feelings that are unperplexed. This disparity lends a strident effect to his verse, making him appear the exponent of a fabricated romanticism.

Though the whole *Vision* crusade must wear this aspect now, it was important in the 1920s in seeking to provide Australian poetry with new standards and values—in particular, with new standards of craftsmanship. Slessor was soon to leave his *Vision* phase behind, but the sense of poetry as an art remained paramount with him, and no one else in the thirties was so alert to experiments overseas. In his lecture on "Modern English Poetry" in 1931, he discussed the work of the Imagists, Ezra Pound, T. S. Eliot, the Sitwells and E. E. Cummings, with comments on Owen's experiments in rhyme and on the possibilities of free verse. Making clear the direction in which his own verse was moving, Slessor declared that the whole structure of English poetry "rests on the use of the image, the choice of the concrete where the abstract would be less racking to the creator".[4]

In *Trio* (1931) and *Cuckooz Contrey* (1932) there was a change of mood in Slessor's verse, as certain romantic themes from his earlier poems were treated over again in a spirit of cynicism and bitterness; and a change of poetic milieu, as he drew away from the past of myth and fable to the more sober past of history. "Five Visions of Captain Cook", the major poem of this period, has been taken as inaugurating the cult of historical narrative in subsequent Australian verse. The Lindsayan metaphysic persists here, as the successive "visions" show the power of Cook's personality, whether at the moment of decision that commits his ship to the discovery of the east coast of Australia (I), or in the spell he casts over the officers serenely pointing their sextants at the sun amid the perils of the Barrier Reef (II), or as he figures in the reminiscences of midshipman Trevenen, as a god in human form, mapping the coast with one eye cocked for game (IV). This heroic conception is however "distanced" in part III ("Two chronometers the captain had"), which sets the whole enterprise in the perspective of Time:

> One ticked fast and one ticked slow,
> And Time went over them a hundred years ago—

and is questioned in the final vision, where Cook's career is recalled by Captain Home, retired on a pension of half-a-crown a day, blind, and talking to empty chairs. Although Home is derided by his termagant wife Elizabeth, the experiences he shared with Cook then

[4] The lecture, given to the English Association, was reported in the *Union Recorder* (Sydney University), 1st October 1931.

lifted him out of mere existence into life, in a way that Elizabeth can never understand:

> Elizabeth, a noble wife but brisk,
> Who lived in a present full of kitchen-fumes
> And had no past—

just as Cook's own decision in the Coral Sea made its dent in the indifference of Time, with consequences still to be felt now:

> So, too, Cook made choice
> Over the brink, into the devil's mouth,
> With four months' food, and sailors wild with dreams
> Of English beer, the smoking barns of home.
> So Cook made choice, so Cook sailed westabout,
> So men write poems in Australia.

If "Five Visions of Captain Cook" still upholds the doctrines of *Creative Effort*, they are nevertheless being treated in a more realistic way. In other poems in *Trio* and *Cuckooz Contrey*, Slessor forsakes the past of history and the past of fable alike, to observe and comment on the world about him. The romantic blur of the *Vision* poems gives way to the sardonic picture of "Country Towns":

> Country towns, with your willows and squares,
> And farmers bouncing on barrel mares
> To public-houses of yellow wood
> With "1860" over their doors . . .

or the more incisive imagery of "Crow Country":

> Gutted of station, noise alone,
> The crow's voice trembles down the sky
> As if this nitrous flange of stone
> Wept suddenly with such a cry;
> As if the rock found lips to sigh,
> The riven earth a mouth to moan;
> But we that hear them, stumbling by,
> Confuse their torments with our own. . . .

In *Five Bells* (1939) the pattern of Slessor's development is completed. All the resources of verse are here mastered and at command, as equal to the hynotic effect of a poem like "Sleep" as to the ironic portraiture of "Vesper-Song of the Reverend Samuel Marsden", while the magic world lost with *Vision* is now recovered in another guise—in the city environment, seen most often after nightfall. Poems like "Last Trams" and "William Street" mark the "discovery" of the modern city in Australian verse, with a degree of accomplishment lacking in Furnley Maurice's *Melbourne Odes*:

The red globes of light, liquor-green,
The pulsing arrows and the running fire
Spilt on the stones, go deeper than a stream;
You find this ugly, I find it lovely.

Ghosts' trousers, like the dangle of hung men,
In pawnshop-windows, bumping knee by knee,
But none inside to suffer or condemn;
You find this ugly, I find it lovely. . . .

When the contents of *Five Bells* fell into place as the final section of Slessor's collected volume, *One Hundred Poems* (1944), they also confirmed his stature as a reflective poet. Though for thirty years he had used verse to conjure up magic worlds, evoke the historical past, explore his own perceptions and sensations, at no stage had his work been altogether free of misgiving. The exotic world of *Earth-Visitors* had been touched by regret for the ephemerality of beauty and joy; a spirit of disillusion was felt in *Cuckooz Contrey*, where an anti-romantic piece like "The Old Play" is full of overtones of bitterness and mockery. In *Five Bells*, the reflections that had earlier attached themselves to beauty and passion come to focus on the concept of Time, envisaged as a merciless, unceasing, impersonal flow. In "Out of Time", the poet yearns for a moment of freedom from this blind current, a moment he likens to the miniature world imaged in the sheen of a bubble, as its surface reflects the scene around it. As the scene itself is in time, while its radiant reflection is not, so for an instant he is "fixed in a sweet meniscus, out of Time";

Out of the torrent, like the fainter land
Lensed in a bubble's ghostly camera,
The lighted beach, the sharp and china sand,
Glitters and waters and peninsula—

The moment's world, it was; and I was part,
Fleshless and ageless, changeless and made free.
"Fool, would you leave this country?" cried my heart,
But I was taken by the suck of sea.

Only for a moment is personality or identity possible; then the impersonality of Time resumes, as remorselessly as the bubble world vanishes in air.

In "Five Bells" (title-poem of the 1939 volume) the soundings are deeper. It is a reverie by the Harbour one evening, on a friend who has died by drowning—the tide has flowed over him (as over Cook, a hundred years ago); he is now lost in time. The poem operates through a dual conception of time: first the "time that is moved by little fidget wheels", chronometer time, measured by the sound of five bells. Then there is the other time, the time between the strokes, as it were; and the dead man lives again in this time, he "lives between five bells".

Time that is moved by little fidget wheels
Is not my Time, the flood that does not flow.
Between the double and the single bell
Of a ship's hour, between a round of bells
From the dark warship riding there below,
I have lived many lives, and this one life
Of Joe, long dead, who lives between five bells.

Deep and dissolving verticals of light
Ferry the falls of moonshine down. Five bells
Coldly rung out in a machine's voice . . .
Why do I think of you, dead man, why thieve
These profitless lodgings from the flukes of thought
Anchored in Time? You have gone from earth,
Gone even from the meaning of a name;
Yet something's there, yet something forms its lips
And hits and cries against the ports of space,
Beating their sides to make its fury heard.

The poet, in one dimension, is trying to communicate with the dead man in another, trying to catch his voice in the silence between the bells. As the poem relives the different phases of their relationship, recorded in "the bumpkin calculus of Time"—arguments in Sydney by the flare of "penny gaslight on pink wallpaper", the five-mile tramp in the dark on a country track—the dead man is seen to have some of the attributes of the Lindsayan rebel, talking of "Milton, melons and the Rights of Man", and arguing about blowing up the world. As the elegiac mood is now crossed with truculence, now heightened in bewilderment, the poem comes to test the validity of human aspiration, as "Five Visions" had, and the dead man symbolizes the whole riddle of time and death:

Where have you gone? The tide is over you,
The turn of midnight water's over you,
As Time is over you, and mystery,
And memory, the flood that does not flow . . .
If I could find an answer, could only find
Your meaning, or could say why you were here
Who now are gone, what purpose gave you breath
Or seized it back, might I not hear your voice?

The poet goes on gazing over the Harbour, with an alertness that is assuaged to calm lucidity, and then subsides in resignation:

I looked out of my window in the dark
At waves with diamond quills and combs of light
That arched their mackerel-backs and smacked the sand
In the moon's drench, that straight enormous glaze,
And ships far off asleep, and Harbour-buoys
Tossing their fireballs wearily each to each,
And tried to hear your voice, but all I heard
Was a boat's whistle, and the scraping squeal
Of seabirds' voices far away, and bells,
Five bells. Five bells coldly ringing out.
Five bells.

In the late 1930s, when *Vision* was forgotten, another movement arose which might earlier have been regarded as a counter-offensive —the Jindyworobak school. Its founder was Rex Ingamells (1913–55), whose pamphlet *Conditional Culture* (1938) insisted on the importance of "environmental values" in Australian poetry, with the further claim that a truly Australian literature could be founded in the culture of the aborigines. In the work of Ingamells and others in the Jindyworobak anthologies published annually from 1938 onward, attempts were made to incorporate aboriginal terms and to develop a distinctly "Australian" imagery in verse. The Jindyworobak movement was not simply a reversion to the literary nationalism of the nineties. It was closer to the ideas of P. R. Stephensen, whose essay on "The Foundations of Culture in Australia" Ingamells had read in *The Australian Mercury* for July 1935. Stephensen—who was critical of the *Bulletin* for having "presented a larrikin view of Australian life"—held that only an Australian literature that was first truly national could prove itself truly universal, and that no progress was possible towards this goal until local writers ceased merely to imitate European patterns.

Although the Jindyworobak movement aroused so much controversy at the time, it simply failed to produce an impressive body of verse. The plan to find inspiration in aboriginal culture, despite occasionally effective poems by Ingamells or Ian Mudie, proved impossible to sustain, and as the successive anthologies became broader in scope, the movement lost its special identity. Contributors to the 1943 issues, for example, included James McAuley, A. D. Hope and R. G. Howarth. Any reader looking back on this period now must wonder why the Jindyworobaks continued to attract so much attention, while the work of poets like Kenneth Mackenzie and Ernest G. Moll was attracting so little.

Kenneth Mackenzie, whose *Our Earth* (1937) was illustrated by Norman Lindsay, asks to be grouped with McCrae and Slessor for the sensuousness and artistry of his verse, though his posthumously published work has shown him to be a poet of greater range and depth than acquaintance with *The Moonlit Doorway* (1944) might suggest. Ernest G. Moll (1900–) has also gained steadily in reputation since *Native Moments* (1931) disclosed his curiously astringent lyrical gift. Yet the poet who contributed to *Vision* in the twenties, and who continued to dominate Australian verse into the 1950s, is R. D. FitzGerald (1902–), who has sometimes been seen as the heir to Brennan in modern Australian poetry.

FitzGerald is a poet who from the first has been intent to establish a point of view on the universe, and the main feature of his work over the years has been its consistent intellectual challenge. The predicament from which it arises is already defined in the youthful volume, *The Greater Apollo: Seven Metaphysical Songs* (1927), where in the poem that gives the sequence its title, the *persona* is drawn on the one hand to the thought of a transcendent reality, a "greater Apollo" exceeding "the man-made gods of earlier days", and on the other hand to the conviction that the material world is the only reality:

> The valley path is calm and cool
> As I walk here between green walls—
> And those are diamond waterfalls;
> This is a bird; and that's a pool:
> I heard their loud insistent calls,
> And gladly have returned to these.
> What is revealed to me and known
> Beyond material things alone?
> It is enough that trees are trees,
> That earth is earth and stone is stone.

This confidence in the reality of the world where "this is a bird; and that's a pool" is to uphold FitzGerald's work over the years, contending with rival possibilities as time goes on, but keeping his poetry fixed in the "tangibles and actualities" that he sees as its proper subject.[5] Whatever the difficulties FitzGerald encounters in holding to his metaphysic, there is no resort to the security offered by a supra-natural order: if indeed there are greater realities lying beyond the world of things, then the only access to them—setting aside the way of the mystic—must be through what is offered to us as matter, space, time and consciousness.

The attitude of *The Greater Apollo* is nevertheless a Romantic one. The poet's stance is that of a man confronted by an inscrutable universe, and responding to it in a spirit of affirmation. This persists

[5] See R. D. FitzGerald, *The Elements of Poetry* (St Lucia: University of Queensland Press, 1963), especially the chapter "Poetry's Approach to Reality".

in *To Meet the Sun* (1929), a collection absorbing the earlier sequence and supplementing it with other poems, lyrical, descriptive and aphoristic. Although the volume is a medley, its title and one or two key poems (e.g., "Consecration", "Sindbad") place an emphasis on intellectual adventure—"I go to meet the sun with singing lips".

Confidence in the reality of the material things of the world must eventually be troubled by the thought that they do not endure, and this prospect FitzGerald faces in *Moonlight Acre* (1938), in the two long poems, "The Hidden Bole" and "Essay on Memory". The immediate occasion of "The Hidden Bole" is the death of the dancer, Pavlova, seen as part of the material world which in its beauty is vulnerable to the processes of time. The poem becomes an exploration of the nature of beauty, offering one possibility after another to be contemplated and discarded, and coming to the conclusion that beauty eludes death, paradoxically, because it is a transient thing, finding one incarnation after another, surviving through its impermanence. "The Hidden Bole" is one of the most fascinating of FitzGerald's poems because its affirmation is so precariously achieved: it is beset by possibilities he might prefer to exclude (is beauty after all some Platonic form, do its successive incarnations depend on the human mind recognizing them?), the tremors in the structure becoming expressive of the complexity of the problem.

"Essay on Memory" is a poem of greater assurance. Here FitzGerald delivers himself of the conception of life as an eternal energy stretching back an immeasurable distance into the past, carried on from one generation to the next in an unbroken chain. Memory is the primordial past still existing in the present, symbolized in the rain and the wind that are the most primitive forces we know in nature. In this continuum the individual life has value and purpose only if we *act*, so carrying the development onward:

> This hour, a gulp in the long throat of the past,
> swallows what once was future, but soon spent;
> this hour is a touch of hands, an accident
> of instants meeting in unechoing vast . . .
>
> Then knot this hour's activity as a rope
> in strength of climbing hands; for still our hope
> best clings to shoulders swarming—from the mouth,
> black-gaping, of loss and failure; all we know
> is this jerked ladder of change whereby men go
> with gasping struggle, vigour of movement—up!
> Wherefore all good is effort, and all truth
> encounter and overcoming . . . .

FitzGerald has now grasped securely the concept of renewal for which he was reaching in such poems as "The scored sea cliff . . ." in *The Greater Apollo.* Although individual men may die, life itself is endless: when we ourselves have been consumed in the past, our future may be fulfilled in the present of those who succeed us, in an inexhaustible series. Although the confidence and assertiveness of the "Essay" have won due notice, the darker features of FitzGerald's conception need remarking too. Memory is seen in terms of primeval darkness and rain, presented to the conscious mind in images ("wind's voice in the crevice", rifler of "bleak tombs") that are threatening or malign, so that the origins of the endless chain of living seem themselves to lie in the darkness and menace in which Memory is rooted. In the later poem, "The Face of the Waters", FitzGerald seems to try to read these origins, to probe consciousness until it yields to the unknown. Although (the poem seems to argue) the mind may strain back to where matter becomes nothing, life itself becomes non-being, this state is unrecognizable except at the point where matter becomes actuality again, non-being becomes being: what ultimately exists is energy—motiveless perhaps, but as far as we can tell, inexhaustible. Life is a supply that has not yet run out, and there is no evidence that it ever need do so. Representing perhaps the utmost stretch of FitzGerald's thinking, "The Face of the Waters" accounts for the facts that demand to be accounted for, but without abandoning the world of "tangibles and actualities" for some transcendent order.

The shorter poems in *To Meet the Sun* and *Moonlight Acre* represent FitzGerald's earlier effort as a lyrical poet. Although the effort occasionally succeeded (as in "Long since I heard the muttered anger of the reef", one of the poems set in Fiji), FitzGerald has acknowledged ruefully "I don't think anybody would say of a poem of mine 'That's lovely, I want to learn it'."[6] His more characteristic manner is seen in "Essay on Memory", where an impatient intellectual energy is expressed in a style that is sometimes congested and discordant, and in imagery appealing typically to the muscular sense—climbing a jerked ladder of change, hammering links in a chain, stretching canvas in the wind.

After the appearance of *Moonlight Acre* (1938), FitzGerald published no further collection for fourteen years. The work that appeared in the interim, in journals and anthologies—"Heemskerck Shoals" (1943), "Said the Don" (1946), "Fifth Day" (1947)—in some ways suggested that he was making a new beginning. He was experimenting with the long poem, and more especially with the

[6] See the interview reported in the *Sydney Morning Herald,* 7th August 1965.

historical narrative—the form that has since become known as the "voyager poem", exemplified also in Rosemary Dobson's *The Ship of Ice* (1948) or Francis Webb's *A Drum for Ben Boyd* (1948). It is a poem re-creating an historical situation, where the narrative is given not for the interest of "what happens next", but as the vehicle of some other enquiry—not for the action itself, but for what the poet can express through the action. This was the mode FitzGerald adopted in *Between Two Tides*, the long poem that occupied him during the 1940s, though not published until 1952. "Heemskerck Shoals" and the other poems that represented approaches to it were then collected in *This Night's Orbit* (1953).

There proves to be no discontinuity between these two volumes and the three that preceded them. FitzGerald is dealing with the same issues as before, but projecting them now in the careers of men. In "Heemskerck Shoals" the expedition of Tasman, narrowly escaping disaster on the Nanuku Reef, frustrated by the "councils and committees" that have made its instructions too rigid, is shown to retain its worth in terms of heroic endeavour:

> that
> was what the thought in his mind was biting at:
> the necessity in men, deep down, close cramped,
> not seen in their own hearts, for some attempt
> at being more than ordinary men,
> rising above themselves.

In "Fifth Day", an episode from the trial of Warren Hastings is held under the microscope to insist again on the enduring value that an isolated moment in the past may possess, as an embodiment of the human spirit:

> Attitude matters: bearing. Action in the end
> goes down the stream as motion, merges as such
> with the whole of life and time; but islands stand:
> dignity and distinctness that attach
> to the inmost being of us each.

Between Two Tides, with its shifting points of view and oscillating movements in time, shows this fragmentary, allusive technique fully developed. The characters appearing momentarily in the narrative become significant for the decisions they have made: Captain Duck, who chose "the defiance, the challenge of living, personal pride"; the governor of Tola, looking back to the enterprise of Pizzaro, to whom life now is "the good coat I wear and the clean linen". All become part of the experience of Will Mariner, the survivor of the massacre on the *Port au Prince*, who is adopted by the Tongan chief

Finau. The centre of *Between Two Tides* is in Finau and the choices that confront him: he works to unite Tonga for its own good, yet using the feuds and treacheries the past has presented; he has a mind of greater guile and duplicity than any observer could fathom, and yet an imagination that condemns the acts to which necessity and ambition drive him. Finau is a type of the leader, seen in the same perspective as Napoleon or Alexander, with the poem insisting that

> Wars, dates and histories
> are footprints on the shores of each discovery
> that men make of their world,

and that in the flux of history

> Only by acts
> of resolution does any man mould himself
> to something he'd know to-morrow.

As Finau's "acts of resolution" are pondered in the reflecting mind of Will Mariner, the assertiveness of "Essay on Memory" is tempered and subdued. *Between Two Tides* is still exploring and assessing human enterprise, but seeing it now as part of a hunger for the unattainable that cannot be assuaged:

> All aims, all effort
> seek to fill somehow emptiness of hands reaching
> to what the heart would have which still desires
> (beyond man's little capacity) something not known—
> except as mirrored in symbols. . . .
> And under longings
> man was eternal unrest that no place satisfies,
> content never overtakes and no year ends.

The action is "distanced" as it is probed and evaluated: it is seen as a retrospect on Mariner, now "the sound stockbroker, the reliable agent", and again as recorded by Dr Martin, the scholar and recluse, at another remove. As the enthusiasm and rhetoric of the earlier poems give way to a more mature and temperate wisdom, *Between Two Tides* completes a second phase of FitzGerald's development, as "Essay on Memory" had completed the first. His work since will be noticed in a later section.

The Contemporary Scene

Australian literature of the last fifteen or twenty years has yet to fall into historical perspective. It is possible to single out individual writers who have risen to prominence since the war—Judith Wright and A. D. Hope in poetry, Patrick White in the novel—and to remark certain trends—like the renaissance of Australian drama in the 1950s—that have stood out from the pattern of events. The main general development is that Australian writing in these years has acquired a breadth and diversity that it did not possess before. Fiction now ranges from the allegorical experiments of Randolph Stow to the cosmopolitan, best-selling novels of Morris West and the colloquial humour of Nino Culotta's *They're a Weird Mob*. Whereas at the end of the war there were but two literary magazines, *Southerly* (1939–   ) and *Meanjin Papers* (1940–   ), there are now about a dozen to provide an outlet for both creative and critical work. Some areas of literature uncultivated before have suddenly become productive: autobiography is a conspicuous example. Some of the most distinguished prose writing in recent years is to be found in Hal Porter's acutely sensuous reliving of the past in *The Watcher on the Cast-Iron Balcony* (1963), in Alan Marshall's autobiographical sequence, *I Can Jump Puddles* (1955), *This is the Grass* (1962) and *In Mine Own Heart* (1963), or in the mellow reminiscences of A. R. Chisholm in *Men Were My Milestones* (1958) and *The Familiar Presence* (1966). There has been a flow of European migrants to Australia since the war, an accelerated pace of industrial development, a growing affluence, an increase in urban population: all these changes have their reflection in Australian writing.

Of the new novelists to emerge after the war, some naturally found their first subjects in the war itself. T. A. G. Hungerford's tautly written novel of the New Guinea campaign, *The Ridge and the River* (1952), was followed by *Sowers of the Wind* (1954), dealing with the occupation of Japan. Likewise Jon Cleary first won notice with his stories of war service, *These Small Glories* (1946), as did Eric Lambert with *Twenty Thousand Thieves* (1951) and David Forrest with *The Last Blue Sea* (1959). Although Dymphna Cusack had been publishing in the 1930s, her particular talents found their best expression in *Come In Spinner* (1951), treating civilian life in Sydney during the war (written in collaboration with Florence James). It is doubtful if the work of any of these writers since has advanced significantly on the novels that first brought them attention. It may be that the major consequence of the war for Australian fiction was that it contributed to the return of two expatriate novelists, Martin Boyd and Patrick White.

Martin Boyd (1893–   ) has been a neglected figure, possibly because his best novels look back to a past age, and deal with a leisured and cultivated society that is now disappearing. *Lucinda Brayford* (1946), in which Boyd turned his attention again to the Australian scene, was in some degree a re-writing of *The Montforts*, which had been awarded the Gold Medal of the Australian Literature Society in 1928. *The Montforts* Boyd has described as "a pseudo-

Galsworthian account of my mother's family over five generations, full of thinly disguised portraits"[7]—a family which in the seventeenth and eighteenth centuries had had its seat in England, one branch migrating to Australia before the gold rush, and becoming established as part of the colonial aristocracy there. Boyd shows the divided loyalty that the Montforts come to feel, with their physical roots in Australia and their cultural roots in England, with the family estate as a magnet drawing them periodically over the seas. He has already in this early novel discovered the theme, the social class and the historical period with which his most distinctive work is to deal—the work he resumed, after an interval of eighteen years, in *Lucinda Brayford.*

Lucinda Brayford follows the history of the Vane family over four generations: from William Vane, who migrated to Australia in the mid-nineteenth century, on being sent down from Cambridge for cheating at cards; his son Fred, who made a fortune on the land and became a leader of Melbourne society in the 1890s; Fred's daughter Lucinda, who married Hugo Brayford, the A.D.C. to the Governor, and returned to his family's estate at Crittenden; to her son Stephen, whose unsuccessful marriage is followed by the violence of the Second World War and the sufferings of a conscientious objector, which result in his death and the extinction of the earldom to which he is heir. A. D. Hope has pronounced *Lucinda Brayord* "perhaps the best novel since Henry Handel Richardson's *The Fortunes of Richard Mahony*".[8] It is a poised and moving book, with a penetrating awareness of the interaction of Australian and English cultures, brilliant in its evocation of the manners of its period, and written in a prose that is lucid and firmly controlled. The wit and suavity of *The Montforts* is felt again in *Lucinda Brayford,* but now joined with a deeper insight and compassion. Boyd is the elegist of the social class whose history he records, from the William Vane who flung his fellow-student from Clare Bridge into the river, as the first of the misdemeanours that led to his emigration to Australia, to Stephen Brayford his descendant, whose ashes are dispersed over the water from the same bridge as the story closes.

Boyd himself returned to Australia in 1948 and settled there for some years. In 1952 he published *The Cardboard Crown,* the first novel of the Langton series, continued with *A Difficult Young Man* (1955) and *Outbreak of Love* (1957), and completed with *When Blackbirds Sing* (1962). This tetralogy, written by Boyd in his sixties, shows him now in full command of his powers, using the structure

[7] See his autobiography *A Single Flame* (London: Dent, 1939), p. 204.

[8] A. D. Hope, *Australian Literature 1950-1962* (Melbourne University Press, 1963), p. 12.

that can best deploy them, and working in the period and with the social class that he has made his own. The period is Melbourne from the 1890s to the First World War, recalled in its glitter and assurance in *Outbreak of Love,* with Government House as the centre, and the eligible young men the English officers in the Governor's entourage. The class is that colonial aristocracy for whom the means of subsistence is automatically provided, whose living is predominantly social and intellectual, who look back on a long ancestry and whose assumption is that life is to be enjoyed. *The Cardboard Crown* exposes some of the scandals behind the decorum of these lives; the series as a whole defines most piquantly the ideals that sustained them. Assured of their position in the social order, the Langtons never consciously think of it, and lack the anxieties about proper dress and behaviour that afflict the socially ambitious. The notion that eminence might be conferred by the school one had attended is strange to them, as it is to Dominic's parents in *A Difficult Young Man*:

> To them a school was simply something you made use of like a shop, and the idea that grew up with the nineteenth-century middle class, that one derived social standing from a school, had not reached them. They would have thought it as absurd to derive social importance from their dentist. (p. 63)

While Boyd's discrimination and alertness to social nuance make the Langton tetralogy the consummation of his achievement as a novelist of manners, it also makes plainer a further dimension in his work, common to his English and Australian novels alike. A recurrent figure in Martin Boyd is the young man who regards the world as full of innocence and beauty, and has his vision cruelly denied by the circumstances he meets. Such had been Michael Kaye in *The Lemon Farm* (1935), and Stephen in *Lucinda Brayford*, and the two most moving novels of the tetralogy, *A Difficult Young Man* and *When Blackbirds Sing*, are devoted to such another, Dominic Langton. The disappointment they experience is shared in different ways by Lucinda Vane, by Alice in *The Cardboard Crown*, by Diana von Flugel in *Outbreak of Love*. Either the world fails to deliver the promise it offered them in youth, or fulfils it when the circumstances have so changed as to make the fulfilment ironical. Through all Boyd's work there runs this motif of opportunity lost, hope dulled into disillusion, aspiration cherished but finally denied. The lonely integrity of a Stephen or a Dominic may for a time stand out, but it is then tragically submerged in a current of indifference. Boyd has described his own outlook on the world and defined his personal scale of values in the autobiographical books *A Single Flame* (1939),

Much Else in Italy (1958) and *Day of My Delight* (1965). He was wise to have made these personal statements independently of his novels: in his creative work his special vision is more compelling when it is felt not as a thesis, but in terms of the wistfulness and irony of the lives of the romantics and idealists (as a bourgeois mentality would classify them) that are traced with such detachment and compassion. From *The Montforts* onward Boyd's career has been occupied with successive attempts to write one novel, the novel he began to succeed in writing with *Lucinda Brayford*, the novel he wrote at last in the Langton series of 1952–62.

If Martin Boyd has remained an unobtrusive presence in contemporary Australian fiction, perhaps more highly esteemed abroad that at home, the international reputation won by Patrick White (1912–) has had a more decided impact on the local scene. This reputation dates from the appearance of *The Tree of Man* (1955), and White has since won recognition as a playwright and short-story writer as well. His early novels attracted little notice. Yet the first of them, *Happy Valley* (1939), set in the snow country of New South Wales, shows already White's preoccupation with the solitariness of human beings, the impossibility of building a bridge from one life to another: the epigraph declares that "the law of suffering" is the one indispensable condition of human existence, that "progress is to be measured by the amount of suffering undergone". The two characters in the book with most capacity for experience, Oliver Halliday and Alys Browne, who come to think that they may find fulfilment in their relationship to each other, have this hope taken from them at the end—and it is then made to seem just a further illusion, of a piece with Oliver's early ambition to be a nature poet, and with Alys's desire to be "distinguished", reading Tolstoy and playing Schumann in the late afternoon. The happiness won by the second pair of lovers, Clem Hagan and Sidney Furlow, is almost worthless. The only ones to escape defeat are the "intuitive" characters like Margaret Quong, who helps her uncle and aunt in the general store:

> They never spoke very much, the Quongs. They sat there at tea, eating a tin of herrings, sitting in the room behind the store, Amy and Arthur and Margaret, and they were very complete, they ate stolidly, they passed each other the things, their hands touched and sundered, and it was enough to be there, the three of them, that was quite enough.[9]

While *Happy Valley* has, at one level, the competence of a novel

[9] *Happy Valley* (London: Harrap, 1939), p. 96. Page-references to White's novels are to the first English editions, except that quotations from *The Living and the Dead* are from the second edition (Eyre & Spottiswoode, 1962).

of the circulating-library type, it is more significant for the preoccupations that may be seen emerging. The chief of these is a concern for unfulfilled lives, which becomes central in *The Living and the Dead* (1941). Its setting is Bloomsbury in the 1930s, where in a house in Ebury Street, Elyot Standish looks back on his life, and is brought to realize that his existence has been no more than an extension of the more positive lives of others—that he has tried to "build a cocoon of experience away from the noises in the street" (p. 19). His sister Eden has tried to escape this sterility by compulsively "giving" herself, forming an attachment to a carpenter who goes to fight in the Spanish Civil War; his mother, Catherine Standish, has sought fulfilment in a number of roles—the emancipated girl who has read Shaw and Ibsen, the hostess of a smart set in pre-war London—maintaining a life of brittle elegance, with her fear of stagnation driving her from one liaison to another. Hers is the most positive life in the book—leaving aside her servant Julia Fallon, another intuitive character—though this may not have been the impression White intended. The novel ends with Elyot leaving the house and catching one of the London buses, as though turning from the dead to the living.

The Living and the Dead is a study of characters seeking their identity, painfully coming to conceive of "an intenser form of living" (p. 331). The theme of the novel is re-enacted in White's play *The Ham Funeral* (prompted by his return to his lodgings in Ebury Street in 1947, though not performed until some years later). The character corresponding to Elyot Standish is the Young Man, the introverted spectator; the role of Mrs Standish is developed by Mrs Lusty, the landlady in the basement, who stands for the life of the flesh. Mrs Lusty is one of a series of characters in Patrick White who represent that acceptance of life, at any level, from which the Young Man shrinks—Pearl Brawne in *The Aunt's Story*, Nola Boyle in *The Season at Sarsaparilla*, Daise Morrow in the short story "Down at the Dump". Although it is Mrs Lusty who forces the Young Man into the experience of living, in spite of himself, yet at the end of the play she is as lost and confused as he had been in the course of it. It is not she who has the secret the Young Man has tried to discover, but her husband Will Lusty, the landlord who is now dead. He has a serenity and insight of which all the other characters are aware, though they are unable to share it. Nor can he communicate it to them, except in such a remark as "This table is love . . . if you can get to know it." The issues that fascinate the early White are heightened in *The Ham Funeral*, but not resolved there: they find their first resolution in *The Aunt's Story*, the most moving and accomplished of his early books.

The Aunt's Story (1948) is separated from the two novels before it by the experience of the war, which left White at demobilization with the alternatives of remaining in England, "in what I then felt to be an actual and spiritual graveyard", or of "returning home, to the stimulus of time remembered".[10] The stimulus of time remembered is felt especially in Part I of *The Aunt's Story,* in the passages recalling Theodora's girlhood at Meroë, the station property that to her comes almost to represent the earth in its golden age. Theodora Goodman is a dark, thin sallow child, whose life is summed up in the unspoken thoughts of her headmistress:

> Theodora, I shall tell you the truth. Probably you will never marry. We are not the kind. You will not say the things they want to hear, flattering their vanity and their strength, because you will not know how, instinctively, and because it would not flatter *you.* But there is much that you will experience. You will see clearly, beyond the bone. You will grow up probably ugly, and walk through life in sensible shoes. Because you are honest, and because you are barren, you will be both honoured and despised. You will never make a statue, nor write a poem. Although you will be torn by all the agonies of music, you are not creative. You have not the artist's vanity, which is moved finally to express itself in objects. But there will be moments of passing affection, through which the opaque world will become transparent, and of such a moment you will be able to say: My dear child. (pp. 67–68)

Theodora experiences the isolation, the failure of human contact, that had tormented White's earlier characters, but she is capable also of the visionary awareness that the landlord possessed, of moments through which the opaque world may become transparent. She shares moments of insight with her father, and with others she encounters quite casually in her life— the Man who was Given his Dinner, the 'cellist Moraïtis—and she can also find a liberation from the self in music. Theodora most resembles the landlord in her capacity to shed her identity in phenomena of the created world, as she does in contemplating the little hawk:

> After this, Theodora sometimes walked in the paddocks alone. Once the hawk flew down, straight and sure, out of the skeleton forest. He was a little hawk, with a reddish-golden eye, that looked at her as he stood on the sheep's carcase, and coldly tore through the dead wool. The little hawk tore and paused, tore and paused. Soon he would tear through the wool and the maggots, and reach the offal in the belly of the sheep. Theodora looked at the hawk. She could not judge his act, because her eye had contracted, it was reddish-gold, and her curved face cut the wind. Death, said Father, lasts for a long time. Like the bones of the sheep that would

[10] See his autobiographical statement, "The Prodigal Son", *Australian Letters,* I, iii (1958), 37-40.

> lie, and dry, and whiten, and clatter under horses. But the act of the hawk, that she watched, hawk-like, was a moment of shrill beauty that rose above the endlessness of bones. The red eye spoke of worlds that were brief and fierce. (p. 31)

As Theodora loses her consciousness in the activity of the hawk ("her eye had contracted, it was reddish-gold, and her curved face cut the wind") she experiences an eclipse of the self, and isolation is momentarily overcome.

Part I of *The Aunt's Story* traces the process by which Theodora resists the conformity that other lives would impose upon her, avoiding marriage with Frank Parrott and Huntly Clarkson because it would be an impairment of her integrity. Her mother's death frees her of all human relationships but the one with her niece Lou, which she reluctantly resigns also. Her goal is the extinction of the self, the achievement of "that desirable state . . . which resembles, one would imagine, nothing more than air or water" (p. 151). Part II, set in the Hôtel du Midi in the south of France, continues the process of purgation, re-enacting episodes of the past by a surrealist method, and teaching Theodora to reconcile opposing aspects of her experience as she participates in other lives. Part III is occupied with her journey across America, and her decision to get off the train and cast aside her identity altogether. Her true homecoming, as the Odyssean references make clear, is to a deserted farmhouse where she meets the hallucinatory figure Holstius, a composite of all the men who had been sympathetic to her in her life. Holstius explains what is left to happen:

> "They will come for you soon, with every sign of the greatest kindness," Holstius said. "They will give you warm drinks, simple, nourishing food, and encourage you to relax in a white room and tell your life. Of course you will not be taken in by any of this, do you hear? But you will submit. It is part of the deference one pays to those who prescribe the reasonable life. They are admirable people really, though limited."
>
> Theodora nodded her head to each point she must remember.
>
> "If we know better," Holstius said, "we must keep it under our hats." (p. 341)

The novel ends with Theodora having gone what we should call mad.

The Aunt's Story, the third of White's earlier novels, is the most sensitive and compassionate, imaginatively realized and beautifully written. It is also central in his development, shedding the perplexity and uncertainty of *The Living and the Dead* and *The Ham Funeral*, and yet raising problems of another kind. *The Living and the Dead* had ended with Elyot's gesture of renouncing his introverted existence to assert kinship with the noises in the street; in *The Ham Funeral* the Young Man had been forcibly confronted with Mrs Lusty as the life he should accept. Yet *The Aunt's Story* seems to demonstrate the rejection of life as it is normally lived: although Theodora, having achieved the extinction of the self, will (according to the assurances of Holstius) live more abundantly, she will live—like the landlord in *The Ham Funeral*—cut off from common mortals, and offering no help to them. White's later work is troubled by a nervous insistence on the values of the workaday world, which conflicts with a steadily increasing emphasis on characters who find fulfilment not in that world, but beyond it.

In *The Tree of Man* (1955), the novel that established White's international reputation, the resolution to fix some essential values in the activities of ordinary living is most conspicuous. The book traces the lives of one man and one woman, who establish a holding in the wilderness, see their shack become part of a settlement, then of a wider community, until near the end suburbia is encroaching. Stan and Amy Parker feel a bond with the earth as they hoe the cabbages or milk the cows, and the stages in their relationship are measured by a flood, a bushfire, a drought, until their existence seems a paradigm of Life itself. White's prose is masterly in the early chapters in showing the Parkers as inseparable from the activities in which they are engaged, bringing out the simplicity of their life, and at the same time making it seem timeless and universal.

Inarticulate as they are, Stan and Amy both strain after some illumination that escapes them, the state of lucidity that Theodora Goodman had finally achieved in the extinction of reason. Amy Parker is the more bewildered and exposed, her plight imaged in Gage's painting of a laborious naked woman reaching up with ponderous hands to a savagely dazzling sun. She becomes resentful and possessive, while Stan finds release in the moments when he feels his consciousness deflected on to objects in the natural world ("This table is love . . . if you can get to know it"). This is how his sense of personal identity slips away from him in the storm:

> The rain buffeted and ran off the limbs of the man seated on the edge of the veranda. In his new humility weakness and acceptance had become virtues. He retreated now, into the shelter of the veranda, humbly holding with his hand the wooden post that he had put there himself years before, and at this hour of the night he was quite grateful for the presence of the simple wood. As the rain sluiced his lands, and the fork of the lightning entered the crests of his trees. The darkness was full of wonder. Standing there somewhat meekly, the man could have loved something, someone, if he could have penetrated beyond the wood, beyond the moving darkness. But he could not, and in his confusion he prayed to God, not in specific petition, wordlessly almost, for the sake of company. Till he began to know

every corner of the darkness, as if it were daylight and he were in love with the heaving world, down to the last blade of wet grass. (p. 152)

Stan's illumination is meant to imply not only a loss of identity in the created world, but a selfless love for it—of every blade of grass, of the veins of a leaf, the stubble of a field. At the end of the book he explains to the young evangelist that God for him can be found in a gob of spittle.

Yet the strength of *The Tree of Man* comes not from Stan's achievement of illumination (which is hard to render in terms that make it seem other than vacuous), so much as from his blunderings towards it, his bewilderment and uncertainty, his painful effort to interpret such knowledge as he is given. Despite the emphasis on Stan's absorption in the workaday world, our strongest sense is finally of his isolation. His relationships are characterized by fumbling and awkwardness: he lives all his life with Amy, but cannot share his deepest experiences with her; in trying to make contact with Ray, he causes the boy apprehension and embarrassment; he struggles to communicate with his fellows, but even at the moment of his death he is powerless to share his vision. For all the insistence in *The Tree of Man* on immersing oneself in the ordinariness of living, the novel itself shows that fulfilment lies in liberation from that condition—lies in transcendence.

The way of transcendence is examined in *Voss* (1957). Voss leads an expedition across the Australian continent in order to mortify and exalt himself by suffering, as though in rivalry with Christ, to prove that man may become God. He seeks his selfhood in disdaining the ordinary values—disdaining the conventions and usages of the society in which he is placed, rejecting the natural beauty of the world for a private world of "desert and dreams", and condemning the values that the mass of men revere. The conception owes something to White's study of the explorers Eyre and Leichhardt, and to his war experiences "trapesing backwards and forwards across the Egyptian and Cyrenaican deserts, influenced by the arch-megalomaniac of the day".[11]

Voss seeks transcendence through a supreme egotism. What makes him so compelling a figure, however, is rather his vulnerability in this attempt. He must try to extinguish all human feeling in himself, not only by welcoming the privations of the journey, but also by repelling all emotions of fellowship—the suspicion that he may be thought to love his dog, Gyp, compels him to execute her forthwith. He seeks to establish an ascendancy over each of the members of his party, exposing their values as illusions, lest they should undermine

[11] "The Prodigal Son", *Australian Letters,* I, iii (1958), 37-40.

his own—and so must fear the stability of Judd, the Christian humility of Palfreyman, and above all the love of Laura Trevelyan, as a threat to his self-sufficiency. Voss is tormented also by "a sense of almost intolerable beauty" (p. 17) in the created world—the world where Stan Parker found God in a gob of spittle—and his struggle to resist this force becomes another index of his predicament. The evening when the expedition descends the valley at Rhine Towers is an occasion where natural beauty is so intolerable that Voss succumbs to it:

It was the valley itself which drew Voss. Its mineral splendours were increased in that light. As bronze retreated, veins of silver loomed in the gullies, knobs of amethyst and sapphire glowed on the hills, until the horseman rounded that bastion which fortified from sight the ultimate stronghold of beauty.

"*Achhh!*" cried Voss, upon seeing.

Sanderson laughed almost sheepishly.

"Those rocks, on that bit of a hill up there, are the 'Towers' from which the place takes its name."

"It is quite correct," said the German. "It is a castle."

This was for the moment pure gold. The purple stream of evening flowing at its base almost drowned Voss. Snatches of memory racing through him made it seem the more intolerable that he might not finally sink, but would rise as from other drownings on the same calamitous raft. (p. 137)

For this moment of surrender he must scourge himself, remaining seated on his horse "with his mouth folded in" as the Sandersons offer their hospitality to the party:

Everyone was expecting something.

"I did not think to impose upon you to this extent, Mr Sanderson," the German released his lip and replied. "It would embarrass me to think such a large party should inconvenience you by intruding under your roof-tree. I would prefer to camp down somewhere in the neighbourhood with my men, with our own blankets, beside a bivouac fire."

Mrs Sanderson looked at her husband, who had turned rather pale.

"It would not enter my head," said the latter.

Since it had entered the German's, his eyes shone with bitter pleasure. Now the beauty of their approach to Rhine Towers appeared to have been a tragic one, of which the last fragments were crumbling in the dusk. He had been wrong to surrender to sensuous delights, and must now suffer accordingly. (p. 138)

The eclipse of the self in the natural world has been seen already in the experience of Theodora (as a state that seemed morally neutral) and in the experience of Stan Parker (with a moral value being affixed, in terms of unfocused love). In *Voss* this state—glimpsed in the episode at Rhine Towers, and resisted throughout by

Voss as an assault on his selfhood—is seen in terms on one hand of surrender and humility, and on the other of exaltation. This difficult theme is celebrated in Le Mesurier's prose-poems, extended in the aboriginal myths about the migration of spirits, and pursued through Voss's final experiences in the desert and their aftermath. To achieve a state of oneness with the created world is at once a process of humbling (in the dissolution of the ego), and a process of transcendence (in the dispersal of the spirit through nature after death). "Voss did not die," Laura Trevelyan claims. "His legend will be written down, eventually, by those who have been troubled by it" (p. 477). This claim is itself viewed realistically in the concluding chapters, where with the unveiling of the bronze statue in the Domain, those who have been "troubled" by the legend—Laura, Judd, Colonel Hebden—are a little company indeed. But for them, as for Mrs Poulter in *The Solid Mandala*, the whole *Zeitgeist* has been changed by the experience.

The third of White's later novels, *Riders in the Chariot* (1961), has this same uncertain magnificence. Here the "acceptance of life" that had become mandatory in *The Ham Funeral* is felt in the choice of the four illuminates who have a vision of the chariot—Miss Hare, the grotesque spinster living in Xanadu, a decaying mansion on the outskirts of Sydney; Mordecai Himmelfarb, an ugly Jewish refugee from the gas-chambers of Germany; Mrs Godbold, the washerwoman living in the shack below the post-office at Sarsaparilla, with a drunken husband and a brood of children; and Alf Dubbo, the half-caste aboriginal with tuberculosis. All are figures whom genteel bourgeois society would find worthless or distasteful, and they seem to have been selected for exactly that reason. Miss Hare occupies the now familiar role of the mystic who loses her identity in the natural world, peering at the veins of a leaf or sucking a smooth pebble instead of sweets. Himmelfarb is a scholar who has sought through study and contemplation what Miss Hare knows by intuition, and comes to the conclusion that "the intellect has failed us". The job he finds in the Brighta Bicycle Lamps factory, boring a hole in a sheet of metal, becomes "a discipline without which my mind might take its own authority for granted". Dubbo the half-caste has a mind stocked with Biblical imagery by the parson who brought him up, and is haunted by a picture he once saw of Apollo driving a chariot with four figures in it: he comes finally to realize his vision through art. Mrs Godbold, the only one of the visionaries to survive at the end, is sustained by a naïve religious faith which leads her to accept her lot uncomplainingly and express herself in acts of charity towards others, in a sometimes stifling way.

The organization of the novel around these four characters makes

Riders in the Chariot White's major study of the alienated, tortured consciousness, a study that is pursued even further in the desiccated and sometimes grotesque personalities of his short-story collection, *The Burnt Ones* (1964). Although the chariot is again a symbol of transcendence, there is more emphasis in this novel on the visionaries in relation to those about them, and especially on Mrs Godbold as an exemplar of "lovingkindness"—the ethic further defined in the play *The Season at Sarsaparilla* (1962). In showing the rejection of the illuminates by the society in which they are placed, however, White seems to present the inhabitants of Sarsaparilla as preternaturally malevolent, and the inhabitants of Paradise East as caricatures: as a result the book gives a sense of aversion to life as it is commonly lived, and to those who commonly live it. Although White's comic skill and sharp powers of observation may be seen at their best in these scenes, there is finally a great gulf fixed between the four visionaries and almost everyone else in the book—those most in need of "lovingkindness" are the least compassionately treated. This vision of things may be fully worked out in White's fourth play, *Night on Bald Mountain* (1964), where Miss Quodling forsakes the human race to live on a mountain with the goats.

In *The Solid Mandala* (1966) the perspective has altered. "Who and where were the gods?" Arthur Brown asks himself, taken as a child to a performance of *Götterdämmerung*. "He could not have told, but knew, in his flooded depths" (p. 217). Arthur Brown is brought up in Terminus Road, Sarsaparilla, by a mother who has married out of her class, and whose gods are her memories of a vanished gentility, and by a father who is a rationalist, but reads the Greek myths and adds a classical pediment to his house (which, like Xanadu for Norbert Hare, might be George Brown's contribution to the truth). Regarded as "a dill", Arthur is an intuitive who does come painfully to articulate his vision. As a child he is fascinated by glass marbles for their completeness, the fathomless unity that seems to lie in their depths; later he comes upon a passage in an encyclopaedia explaining the mandala as "a symbol of totality", but cannot understand what it means—except to realize that his father's explanation (" 'Totality is the quality of being total' . . . it means 'that which is a whole' ") is futile. Arthur learns to give a psychological reality to his vision in trying to read *The Brothers Karamazov*: his discovery is essentially of the need in humans to "find somebody to worship" (p. 200), which is frustrated because they are afraid to love.

Those who are afraid to love are represented in Waldo, Arthur's twin. Waldo is the intellectual, accepted by "the tight world, of tidiness and quick answers, of punctuality and unbreakable rules"

(p. 229); but he is arid, nervous, introverted, sterile in his aristocratic and literary pretensions. He is one of White's most compassionate studies, and the book creates a poignant sense of what it is like to *be* Waldo—a sense lacking in the portraiture of Mrs Jolley and Mrs Flack. Although Arthur is able to establish bonds with so many others—Mrs Musto, Dulcie Feinstein and her father, Mr Allwright—who are not deterred by his need to touch, or push his face up close, Waldo proves finally to be beyond his protectiveness. The existence of Arthur, as a cause of humiliation, breeds hatred in Waldo until he dies of it—Arthur's effect on the lost soul he most wanted to save proves in the end to be lethal.

"Who and where were the gods?" Although the mandala, like the chariot, may be regarded as a symbol of perfection, the idea of transcendence is now diminished further. In the *Götterdämmerung* of the twentieth century (to formulate one reader's view of the impression left by the book) most value is to be found in the liberation that may come from overcoming the fear to love, or from sensing the plight of others and helping them (as Arthur helps the Saportas) and then becoming unnecessary to their lives. Achievements may be minor, and failures (as with Waldo) may be disastrous. The final section of the book shows the consequences of Arthur's life for a Sarsaparilla housewife, Mrs Poulter. The process by which she rejects suburban Christianity, and comes to accept Arthur as her saint, is open to dispute: but to have chosen her as the inheritor of Arthur's "legend" (in the sense the word has at the end of *Voss*), and to have shown her possession of the vision as completely compatible with getting Bill Poulter's tea, is White's most daring stroke so far.

White is unquestionably the major novelist writing in Australia at present, his books drawing their extraordinary power from his exploration of territories uncharted before, and from his insight into minds that remain closed to nine novelists out of ten. His achievement in fiction and drama prompts the same reply to "malignant criticism" as Dr Johnson made in his preface to his *Dictionary*: that if flaws may be found in his work, "let it not be forgotten that much is likewise performed", and that if the enterprise as a whole is less than triumphant, then he has "only failed in an attempt which no human powers have hitherto completed".

A rough measure of the attainment of Australian fiction between the wars was found (in an earlier section) in the novels awarded the *Bulletin* prize, which gave recognition to such writers as Katharine Prichard, Vance Palmer and Gavin Casey. Since the 1950s, another index has been offered by the Miles Franklin Award. Patrick White won it in 1957 with *Voss*, and in 1961 with *Riders in the Chariot*.

While this helps confirm his exceptional place in contemporary fiction, a glance at the prize-winning novels of other years suggests, at the same time, that White's work is part of a trend. It is not so isolated as might at first appear. In 1958, for example, the Miles Franklin Award went to the young novelist Randolph Stow for his third novel, *To The Islands.* In 1966 it was awarded to Peter Mathers for *Trap,* and in 1967 to Thomas Keneally for *Bring Larks and Heroes.* Collectively such writers represent a movement away from the naturalistic tradition, a movement towards the baroque, the impressionistic, the allegorical, the symbolic.

Randolph Stow (1935–), an admirer of Patrick White, may illustrate these tendencies most clearly. In *A Haunted Land* (1956), Stow had already begun to establish a special relationship with the Australian environment, using the bare landscape relieved by a pool beside the trees, or the decaying station homestead with the scent of oleanders in a darkened room, as a means of mediating his vision. *A Haunted Land* and its sequel *The Bystander* (1957) demonstrated Stow's special feeling for the unbalanced or diseased mind, as portrayed through the perplexity and compassion aroused in others. This was developed further in *To The Islands,* in the embittered missionary Heriot whose loss of faith drives him on a pilgrimage of self-discovery to the aboriginal islands of the dead. *Tourmaline* (1963) is set in a drought-stricken ghost township, to which a water-diviner comes mysteriously from the desert, as a messiah seeming to offer salvation. Though all look to him for guidance, he is proved finally to be deluded and spiritually corrupt, and Tourmaline is left to its thirst.

Randolph Stow's novels are made memorable by their symbolic landscapes and the tortured beings inhabiting them, and at their best have the imaginative force that is also found in his two volumes of poetry, *Act One* (1957) and *Outrider* (1962). There is nevertheless a feeling of evasiveness in Stow's work, a sense of a vacuum at its centre. This may be encouraged by the elusiveness of the characters in the earlier novels: a leading figure like Maguire is exhibited mainly through his effect on others; someone vital to the evolution of the theme, like Diana Ravirs, is allowed to remain almost unknown. *To The Islands* and *Tourmaline* are each made perplexing by the irresolution at the end. Whatever the values Heriot seeks by repudiating Christianity and journeying to the islands sacred in aboriginal belief, the state to which he is finally brought seems a state characterized by the absence of all values; the rejection of the corrupt gospel of Random at the end of *Tourmaline* is followed by the return of Kestrel—another dictator, but an invulnerable one, equally repugnant to the ideals of Tom Spring—and the significance to be given to Deborah's child is left equivocal.

Stow broke away from the growing schematism of these novels in *The Merry-go-Round in the Sea* (1965), exploring a rich lode of boyhood reminiscence. Although Rick Maplestead, in his loneliness and suffering, is allied to the maimed protagonists of the earlier books, he is "placed" in the fresher and uncomplicated vision of young Rob Coram. Although Rob's own development cannot be fully traced in the book, the perspective it supplies is transforming—later chapters of this history will be awaited with interest.

Hal Porter (1911–) had begun writing much earlier than Stow, issuing his first collection, *Short Stories*, in 1942, but he was little known until his work began to appear in the *Bulletin* in the mid-1950s. The appearance of *A Bachelor's Children* (1962) established Porter as one of the most original of Australian short-story writers, and this was followed quickly by the success of *The Watcher on the Cast-Iron Balcony* (1963), his first volume of autobiography. *The Watcher* is still the most striking single manifestation of Porter's talent, and a centre to which his other work—in verse, in drama, in the short story and the novel—may in some way be referred. It shows the fund of experience on which his writing draws and his extraordinary powers of recall, exercised most often through sensuous detail; it reveals his distinctive sensibility, in the fastidious recording of the bizarre and the repellent: it shows also (as an autobiography) his artistic control of his own presence in his writing, through the clinical detachment with which the self-revelation is made.

Although these qualities are not so striking in the second autobiographical volume, *The Paper Chase* (1966), they do sustain the short stories in *A Bachelor's Children* (1962) and *The Cats of Venice* (1965). The world of Porter's stories is the familiar world seen as slightly askew, the personalities sometimes neurotic, the events sometimes macabre. Porter has praised in Katherine Mansfield the ability to catch "the breathtaking surface texture and, simultaneously, what the X-ray showed".[12] The surface texture is caught in his nervous, impressionistic prose; he has also an uncanny feeling for the sinister that lies beneath a polished or genteel surface—a recurring theme in his stories is the betrayal of illusion, the rude awakening from innocence. The narrator himself typically adopts the standpoint of a fascinated observer: to him human beings are enigmatic and astonishing, and he watches for the revealing word or gesture, the mannerism or turn of phrase, that betrays their secret to him.

Porter's first novel, *A Handful of Pennies* (1958), set in Japan during the Occupation, was too flimsy a work for a writer of his

[12] "Beyond Whipped Cream and Blood", *The Bulletin*, 28th April 1962, p. 66.

abilities. In *The Tilted Cross* (1961), however, set in Tasmania in the 1840s, his preoccupations are more deeply involved and his idiosyncratic manner is fully extended. This is another study in betrayal: Porter conveys powerfully the cunning and self-interest lurking beneath the aristocratic life of Cindermead, the vulnerability of Queely Shiell, the ineffectualness of the eccentric denizens of Campbell Street, and in all this succeeds in making the most improbable personality—the cripple Asnetha Sleep, the black boy Teapot—convincing and compelling. There are however signs of strain in the book, in the presentation of Queely as a Christ-figure, and in particular scenes (e.g., the amputation at the hospital) that draw attention to themselves as though existing as entities apart. The arresting but uneven achievement of *The Tilted Cross* is perhaps indicative of Porter's work as a whole. Although his talent has been expressed in so many forms—including the verse collections *The Hexagon* (1956) and *Elijah's Ravens* (1968), the plays *The Tower* (1963) and *The Professor* (1966)—there is no one work in which it is fully realized. Porter seems to have better work in him than he has so far got out.

The movement away from naturalism in White, Stow and Porter is reflected also in the rediscovery in the 1960s of the work of Christina Stead (1902–). The critical acclaim won in the United States with the republication in 1965 of *The Man Who Loved Children* (1940) coincided with the reissue in Australia of *Seven Poor Men of Sydney* (1965), *The Salzburg Tales* (1966) and *For Love Alone* (1966). Christina Stead's work seems to have sprung from as fundamental a questioning of the novelist's role as is found in Virginia Woolf's classic essay of 1919. "Life escapes", Virginia Woolf wrote, "and perhaps without life nothing else is worth while".

> Examine for a moment an ordinary mind on an ordinary day. . . . The mind receives a myriad impressions—trivial, fantastic, evanescent, or engraved with the sharpness of steel. From all sides they come, an incessant shower of innumerable atoms; and as they fall, as they shape themselves into the life of Monday or Tuesday, the accent falls differently from of old . . . if [a writer] could base his work upon his own feeling and not upon convention, there would be no plot, no comedy, no tragedy, no love interest or catastrophe in the accepted style, and perhaps not a single button sewn on as the Bond Street tailors would have it. Life is not a series of gig-lamps symmetrically arranged; life is a luminous halo, a semi-transparent envelope surrounding us from the beginning of consciousness to the end. Is it not the task of the novelist to convey this varying, this unkown and uncircumscribed spirit, whatever aberration or complexity it may display. . .?[13]

[13] "Modern Fiction", in *Collected Essays*, ed. Leonard Woolf (London: Chatto & Windus, 1966), ii, 105-06.

This could almost be an account of Christina Stead's practice. *Seven Poor Men of Sydney* was first published in 1934, and the effect of the novel relies heavily on the physical description of Watson's Bay and the harbour foreshores, Chamberlain's printery in the squalor of Wooloomooloo, of George Street West and the University, as a setting for the iconoclasts, idealists and lost souls whose lives are traced with such strange exuberance. The 'Loo is described on a stifling evening:

> The lamps were lighted. The dwellings on the borders of the hot asphalted pavement were holes in which moved dimly a world of heaving bosoms, gasping mouths, fanning arms. There were visible black-socked feet and bare feet in slippers, bare arms starting upwards from a bush of black hair at the armpit; locks "straight as candles" hung wet and tangled, hairy men's breasts gaped in the vees of open work-shirts. The oil-lamps or gas-jets lighted corsets and stockings carelessly thrown on beds, discoloured with sweat and dirt. The rancid breeze blew in from the wharves with the smell of weeds grown on the piles, beer from the saloons, rotten vegetables from the garbage-tins. There came the clanking of winches at ships' sides, and the fitful songs of men at the waterfront. The last cries of children came from the old streets by the Plunkett Street school or from the other side, where they were dashing up into the rank grass of the Domain to wrestle, smother their giggles, lie on their backs, tell inane tales, sing parodies of songs, and contemplate the high southern constellations through the sensuous summer evening. (p. 139)

Despite the semblance of naturalism, the technique is more that of "collage". The detail is selective and purposeful, catching the garishness of the interiors ("gas-jets lighted corsets and stockings"), the images create motifs (heaving bosoms, armpits, gaping vees of open shirts), and the "sweat and dirt" of the homes is juxtaposed with the children wrestling in the rank grass and with "the high southern constellations" above. The scene is shown in its aberration and complexity, and (as we see only what an outsider might) in its mystery too. The lives of the characters themselves mingle kaleidoscopically—the novel deals typically with seven poor men, a motley group, not a single character—and as we are again shown what an observer would see, even someone like Michael Baguenault remains unfathomable, his suicide enigmatic.

Christina Stead's is a supra-realistic method, seen more fully developed in the description of Malfi's wedding in *For Love Alone*. Exploring the predicament of Teresa Hawkins, the successive chapters of that novel exhibit contrasting aspects of love—the narcissism of Andrew Hawkins, fixed in the opening sentence ("Naked, except for a white towel rolled into a loincloth, he stood in the doorway . . . with powerful chest and thick hair of pale burning gold"), the semi-prurient vulgarity of a suburban wedding-party, the isolation experienced amid family relationships, Teresa's naked fantasies in her room, the theories of the two girls on the ferry. The book is not organized in terms of plot, though it does come to focus increasingly on Teresa's relationship to Jonathan Crow. Teresa is one of Christina Stead's studies of the human being who is starved of affection, living in emotional dependence on others (although she wins freedom at the end); Crow reflects her fascination for the predatory quality of human relationships, for the person who preys continually on others, experimenting with them. Both preoccupations are combined in Nellie Cook in *Cotters' England* (1967), whose desperate, cajoling loquacity demonstrates how Christina Stead's characters work on one another through *talk*, as though in obedience to demons that drive them. However monstrous the corruption of Crow or the egotism of Nellie, they do not forfeit the author's understanding and compassion: Nellie is seen as a member of an "unnamed rebel battalion . . . outcasts, criminals, the misunderstood" (p. 34). The seven poor men had marched in that battalion, joined by so many charlatans and misfits in the books that followed. While the grotesque, carnival world of Christina Stead is so remote from Virginia Woolf's, it is governed by the same need to capture "this varying, this unknown and uncircumscribed spirit, whatever aberration or complexity it may display".

In writing *Voss* (1957), Patrick White had professed himself above all "determined to prove that the Australian novel is not necessarily the dreary, dun-coloured offspring of journalistic realism".[14] Ten years later the proof had become abundant. The superlatives that greeted Thomas Keneally's gifted but confused third novel, *Bring Larks and Heroes* (1967), may even suggest the establishment of a fashion. At the same time the kind of book that had been a rarity in the 1920s and 1930s, when written by Leslie Meller or Seaforth Mackenzie, has become almost a commonplace event. Novelists of the sophistication of Thea Astley and George Turner (who shared the Miles Franklin Award in 1962) have been publishing every year —for example Mungo MacCallum (*A Voyage in Love*, 1956), Christopher Koch (*The Boys in the Island*, 1958), John Iggulden (*The Storms of Summer*, 1960), David Martin (*The Young Wife*, 1962), or Elizabeth Harrower (*The Watch Tower*, 1966), to name only one work of each. To these might be added expatriates like Clive Barry (*Crumb Borne*, 1965) and Shirley Hazzard (*The Evening of the Holiday*, 1966).

Yet it is not possible now, just as it had not been possible in the 1890s, to confine Australian fiction to one dominant mode. The

[14] "The Prodigal Son", *Australian Letters*, I, iii (1958), 37-40.

movement towards the non-naturalistic novel, plus the growing tendency to look inward rather than outward, are but strands in a more varied pattern. The tradition of "reportage" has continued unabated, and is at any moment likely to produce so striking a "documentary" novel as George Johnston's *My Brother Jack* (1964), or—in another key—so perceptive a study as Margaret Trist's *Morning in Queensland* (1958). The controversy aroused by Frank Hardy's *Power Without Glory* (1950) has made it something of a landmark in the social-realist novel, which has more recently become concerned with the plight of the aboriginal—as in F. B. Vickers' *The Mirage* (1955) and Donald Stuart's *Yandy* (1959). Colin Johnson's *Wild Cat Falling* (1965) is the first novel by a writer of aboriginal blood. Two recent novels of factory life, Dorothy Hewett's *Bobbin Up* (1961) and Mena Calthorpe's *The Dyehouse* (1961), combine a realistically described setting with a plot that relies on romantic clichés, in the manner of Dymphna Cusack. These limitations are overcome in the better work of Judah Waten, and notably in John Morrison's short-story collection, *Twenty-Three* (1962).

It has already been remarked that Patrick White and Hal Porter are playwrights as well as novelists. The resurgence of drama in Australia, after a long record of failure, has been one of the features of the 1950s and 1960s. Although the Australian theatre had a lively existence during the nineteenth century, its boards had rarely been occupied with Australian plays—except for dramatizations of *His Natural Life* and *Robbery Under Arms*, and later of Steele Rudd's *On Our Selection*—and the progress in other literary fields that so signalized the 1890s had no counterpart in the indigenous drama.[15] Such groups as the Melbourne Repertory Theatre (1910–17) and the Pioneer Players (1922–3) gave some scope to the slender dramatic talent of Louis Esson and Vance Palmer, and during the 1930s the plays of Sydney Tomholt and Dymphna Cusack were achieving performance or print. Louis Esson's *The Drovers* (1920), Betty Roland's *The Touch of Silk* [1930], and Tomholt's *Bleak Dawn* (1936) remain as plays with a more than historical interest, together with Dymphna Cusack's *Morning Sacrifice* [1942] and Max Afford's thriller, *Lady in Danger* (1944).

The first sign of distinction in modern Australian drama, however,

[15] For the history of the Australian theatre in the nineteenth century, see Leslie Rees, *Towards an Australian Drama* (Sydney: Angus and Robertson, 1953), and Hal Porter, *Stars of Australian Stage and Screen* (Adelaide: Rigby, 1965). In the references to plays in the pages following, dates in square brackets are those of performance, and dates in round brackets are those of publication.

came with the verse plays of Douglas Stewart (1913–). Although it seemed isolated at the time, and has had no perceptible influence on other playwrights since, Stewart's work may be seen now as in some respects anticipating the course of Australian drama in the renaissance of the 1950s. In *Ned Kelly* (1943) he made a reappraisal of a leading Australian folk-hero, and in *Shipwreck* (1947) resorted to Australian history again in treating the disaster that overtook Pelsart's expedition at the Abrolhos. The radio play, *The Fire on the Snow* [1941], had dealt with R. F. Scott's tragic expedition to the South Pole in 1912. Stewart's plays are at once a counterpart in drama of the cult of historical narrative in modern Australian verse, an expression of the concept of the heroic that probably reflects Stewart's admiration for Norman Lindsay, and—in *Ned Kelly* especially—a beginning of that re-examination of the Australian "myth" that was soon to engage playwrights like Lawler and Seymour.

As verse drama, Stewart's radio plays *The Fire on the Snow* and *The Golden Lover* are his most accomplished. *The Golden Lover* (1944) is the more delicate and fanciful, a dramatization of the Maori fable of a woman who lives with her husband by day but spends her nights with a lover from "the people of the mist". Despite the playful treatment of Tawhai's domestic difficulties, *The Golden Lover* has the same preoccupation as Stewart's other plays—the situation of the dreamer, who would live a life of illusion, compelling reality to conform to his vision.[16] The heroism of Scott in *The Fire on the Snow* is shown as having this quality, and this is what most demands the resources of verse for its expression:

> This journey is one man's dream
> As it is one man's burden
> And the man is Scott, the leader.
> The others do what they're bidden
> Bearing their share of the load,
> But cannot tell what it means . . .
>
> The dreamer knows he is master,
> As every dreamer has been
> Who ruled men's minds or bodies
> Who had no will of their own.
> Nothing the future bodes
> Or the past has done can hurt
> The hour when the dreamer walks
> Alive in the dream of his heart.

[16] See further J. F. Burrows, "An Approach to the Plays of Douglas Stewart", *Southerly*, XXIII (1963), 94-108.

At the end Scott is forced to account to himself for the deaths of his followers, and receives his answer from Wilson—that they came to share his dream, and turned its defeat into triumph through their endurance, which remains like a tongue of flame in the snow:

> We dreamed, we so nearly triumphed, we were defeated
> As every man in some great or humble way
> Dreams, and nearly triumphs, and is always defeated,
> And then, as we did, triumphs again in endurance.
> Triumph is nothing; defeat is nothing; life is
> Endurance; and afterwards, death. And whatever death is,
> The endurance remains like a fire, a sculpture, a mountain
> To hearten our children. I tell you,
> Such a struggle as ours is living; it lives after death
> Purely, like flame, a thing burning and perfect.

In *Ned Kelly* and *Shipwreck*, the two plays written for the stage, the visionary is seen as flawed and suspect. In *Shipwreck* he is Cornelius, the usurper who assumes despotic control of the marooned party after Pelsart has gone for help. Cornelius aspires to be a king, possessing the beauty of Lucretia and the wealth of the ship's treasure, using others as his instruments like the Finau of *Between Two Tides*—the bid fails, but in making it Cornelius has expressed something beyond the pettiness and hesitancy of his ordinary nature, has lived momentarily a larger life than the one he knew.

The hero of *Ned Kelly* does not have the same inherent complexity as Cornelius, but the interplay of the forces around him makes his situation more complex. Ned Kelly is the almost legendary Australian bushranger, a symbol of the defiance of constituted authority, seen as representatively "Australian" in his youth and gameness, able to elude the law for so long because of the hostility of the outlying districts to the police. Stewart sees him as at once acting a cavalier rôle, yet dwelling on his wrongs and nervously trying to justify the murder of the three troopers at Stringybark Creek; sensing the enmity of the sedate and respectable that must finally bring him down, and yet intent on the reckless escapade that is to make the "Kelly country" a kingdom of his own. The verse is at its most energetic in suggesting the powers that beset the Kelly gang, and the outlaws' defiance of them:

> You see before you
> As fine a stallion as ever took to the bush
> For a brumby mare called Freedom, to breed from her
> The white-eyed bucking colts the Kellys ride.
> I could have won the ribbon at the Show,
> I could have won my races, then gone to grass
> With the knock-kneed station fillies, too tame to pig-root,
> But I jumped the blooming fence

—but at the same time Ned is shown to be in the grip of a neurotic dream, his delusions carrying his comrades on to disaster. This half-admiring, half-disbelieving attitude to the Australian "myth" becomes characteristic of the drama of the 1950s.

Sumner Locke-Elliott's *Rusty Bugles,* set in an Australian tropical army camp during the war, led the way with its emphatically "realistic" method and its vernacular idiom. The alleged profanity of the soldiers' dialogue caused the censorship of the play in 1948. Then with the performance of Ray Lawler's *The Summer of the Seventeenth Doll* [1955], Australian drama seemed to have found a new footing. *The Doll* was so "Australian" a play that it was to prove a revelation to audiences in London—and was also performed in New York, and even Iceland—while at home it suggested that the self-discovery that had occurred in the other fields in the 1890s had now come about in the native drama. The leading characters, Barney and Roo, are two cane-cutters who toil in the Queensland climate for seven months of the year, then spend the "lay-off" with their unmarried wives in Carlton. Sixteen souvenir dolls decorate the ground-floor front room. Roo is the leader and champion cutter of his gang, Barney has a vitality that makes him a Lothario to women, and Olive's idea of them both embodies the myth of the natural superiority of the broad-shouldered outdoors man:

> They'd walk into the pub as if they owned it—even just in the way they walked you could spot it. All round would be the regulars—soft city blokes having their drinks and their little arguments, and then in would come Roo and Barney. They wouldn't say anything—they didn't have to—there'd just be the two of them walkin' in, then a kind of wait for a second or two, and quiet. After that, without a word, the regulars'd stand aside to let 'em through, just as if they was a—a coupla kings.

The play is writen not to uphold the myth, however, but to scrutinize it. In the seventeenth summer Roo comes home broke, his place in the gang taken by a better man, Johnnie Dowd; the irresistible Barney has found his advances greeted with laughter, and Nancy has left him for the security of marriage. The ideal of mateship is critically tested, as Barney stayed with the gang after Roo left it, and has continued to cultivate Dowd. The course of the action brings self-recognition to Roo, who takes a job in a paint factory, and also to Barney, now "the great has-been": the situation of Olive is more poignant, as she clings to the romantic dream, refusing to accept the reality. *The Doll* makes two sentimental concessions to the myth it examines, in the naïve hopes of Bubba Ryan and the attempt at the end to re-assert the mateship of the two men, but otherwise it escapes the local context to become a study of what one is to do with one's disillusionment in middle age.

Lawler's second play, *The Piccadilly Bushman* [1959], probing into the love-hate relationship to Australia of the returned expatriate, had much less impact than *The Doll.* But already other playwrights had joined in exploring the unpretentious lives of the apparently drab inner suburbs, the rich possibilities of the vernacular, and other accepted features of the Australian myth. In *The Shifting Heart* [1957], set in the backyard of a Collingwood terrace, Richard Beynon looked critically at the egalitarian tradition in Australian life. Although the Australian characteristically sees himself as a democrat in a classless society, his egalitarianism does not always extend to the migrant—the dago, the Balt, the reffo—a somehow inferior being. Beynon, like Lawler, chooses a typically inarticulate Australian as the centre of the play—Clarry Fowler, who by marrying into an Italian family finds that he is still influenced by the Australian antipathy to the foreigner even as he tries honestly to overcome it. Clarry is established expertly through the laconic dialogue (as is Leila Pratt) : the image of his helplessness and confusion after Gino has been beaten up at the dance hall is the scene in which he pounds his fist against the paling fence. Although the image is blurred by the tameness of the conclusion, *The Shifting Heart* painfully makes its point.

The title of Alan Seymour's *The One Day of the Year* [1961] refers to Anzac Day, when Australians of two world wars march to commemorate Gallipoli, and celebrate afterwards at reunions that by tradition are often alcoholic. To Alf Cook, it is the one day when he can escape from the hopelessness of his life and rise above the frustrations of working as a lift-driver; to his son Hughie, a University student, the illusions about the day have become intolerable, and he has accepted the assignment of photographing drunken diggers lying in gutters for the University paper. *The One Day of the Year* turns a searching light on another hallowed Australian institution, besides showing how blunted and thwarted the existence of the ordinary man can be in "the workingman's paradise", and questioning the myth of the classless society. Alf Cook remains the triumph of the play, either in his moments of bitter eloquence, or in his drunken recital of the way he has celebrated his day:

> I've had a bloody lovely day. . . . We went into every pub, every pub we come to, we went in every pub, there was ten of us by then, ten of us so someone says Come on let's get some other bastards 'n' make it a round dozen, so we grabs two ole blokes and turned out they was real old diggers, real Anzacs, 'ear that Wack, Anzacs, they was sittin' 'avin' a quiet yarn to themselves, we soon fixed that—we got 'em and shouted 'em and Ginge 'e made a speech, 'e said these are the blokes wot started the Anzac legend,

> these done the trick, soldiers and bloody gentlemen and we poured bloody beer into the poor old cows till they couldn't stand up, they was rotten, then silly bloody Johnny 'Opkins 'as to go 'n' muck things, 'e turns round too quick and gets dizzy and spews, did 'e spew, brought it all up all over the bloody bar, all over the mob, in their beer, all over the floor, all over 'mself, laugh . . . Jeez, I never laughed so much in all me. . . .

The larger themes of the play—the conflict of the generations, every man's need of an illusion—are left unresolved at the end, but *The One Day of the Year* achieves the same effect of painful "exposure" as *The Doll* and *The Shifting Heart.* Not that these plays should be seen as unduly solemn. There is a robust comedy in them all—as there is in Ray Mathew's *We Find the Bunyip* [1955] and (more temperately) *A Spring Song* [1958]—providing some of the most successful acting parts.

In 1960 Hugh Hunt voiced a concern at the vogue of "backyard realism" in Australian drama,[17] as a too limited mode to be permitted to monopolize the stage. As though to allay his concern, Patrick White's *The Ham Funeral* was produced the following year. Its place in White's development has already been discussed: in the development of Australian drama it marks a conscious swing away from naturalism, as White acknowledged in the programme note:

> It is not a naturalistic play. The chief problem was how to project a highly introspective character on the stage without impeding dramatic progress. I have tried to overcome this, partly through the conflict between the Young Man and those human symbols Mr and Mrs Lusty, the figures in the basement with whom he wrestles in his attempt to come to terms with life, partly through the dialogues between the Young Man and his anima, the Girl in the room opposite. The Relatives become an expression of the conscience, with its multiple forebodings. As for the two scavengers, a lapse of time and a change of scene were necessary, so I gave way to my weakness for music-hall.

In performance *The Ham Funeral* seemed to rely overmuch on a dated expressionism, but it was startling in its alternation of humour and tragedy, of the crude effect and the subtle, finding out poetry in frowsy lives.

In White's second play, *The Season at Sarsaparilla* [1962], the stage was occupied by the kitchens and backyards of three adjoining houses in Mildred Street, Sarsaparilla—the fictitious outer suburb of Sydney which is also the setting of some of White's novels and short stories. The dramatic method, however, is not realistic, but expressionist: the play is subtitled "A Charade of Suburbia"; certain

[17] Hugh Hunt, *The Making of Australian Theatre* (Melbourne: Cheshire, 1960), p. 17.

of the characters from time to time lapse from dialogue into a non-naturalistic, choric utterance; the title itself betrays a crude symbolism, referring to the "season" when the canines of Sarsaparilla are on heat. The play's life from moment to moment on the stage comes from White's witty exposure of the domestic routine and genteel pretensions of Australian suburbia; beneath this surface the action depends on the juxtaposition of the various relationships, all shallowly presented. The exception is Nola Boyle, the woman of generous and responsive sexuality who is more firmly realized than Mrs Lusty, and in whose relationship with her husband White gives actuality to the "lovingkindness" which Judy Pogson expounds to Roy Child. The scene between the two after Nola has yielded to Rowley Masson, in its tact and control, is a step forward in White's development as a playwright.

White's third play, *The Cheery Soul* [1963], was based on a short story of the same title. Despite the brilliant characterization of Miss Docker, it seems something of an interlude. *Night on Bald Mountain* [1964] attempts a larger statement, and is also more violent in its action (although the death of Stella has a precedent in the suicide of Julia in *The Season*), and more intense in its portrayal of the sterility of those who live by intellect or pride. Yet Miss Quodling, who forsakes the world of "the destroyers" to live on Bald Mountain with her goats, finds this refuge violently invaded too. From the wreckage at the end of the play, there is a painful movement towards the idea of renewal, as Sword claims that "Failure is sometimes the beginnings of success", and Miss Quodling in her mourning turns from the nothingness she has envisaged when Bald Mountain itself has been ground to dust: "There is no such thing as nothun! (*Softer*) The silence will breed again . . . in peace . . . a world of goats . . . perhaps even men!"

Another departure from naturalism is registered in the plays of Hal Porter. In his idiosyncratic history, *Stars of Australian Stage and Screen* (1965), deploring the involvement of Oscar Asche in the "bejewelled muck" of *Chu Chin Chow*, Porter asserted that "the silliest farce and the most absurd melodrama are, in intention, nearer to the heart of the matter" (p. 100). His own plays *The Tower* (1963) and *The Professor* (1966) are perhaps attempts to explore the possibilities of civilized and cultivated melodrama, the one set in Tasmania in the 1850s—almost the period of *The Tilted Cross*—and the other dealing with a colony of Australians in post-war Japan. In both plays the life of an aristocratic or genteel group is made to erupt into a "Gothic nightmare" (Miss Medlin's phrase in *The Professor*), revealing the hidden selves of the characters as concupiscent, self-centred, even homicidal. Porter seeks out the barbarism underlying the civilized exterior, exerting such control through his alert sense of stage-effect and his corrosive dialogue that his vision imposes its own terms.

Although Porter's work is in one respect isolated, it does in others represent the experimental tendency of Australian drama in the 1960s. No one play has had the same impact as *The Doll* had in 1955. Lawler's own later work, as represented in *The Unshaven Cheek* [1963] and the television play, *A Breach in the Wall* [1967], has had overseas settings. Other playwrights have shown a continued awareness of Australia in their emphasis on a specific time and place, like David Ireland in *Image in the Clay* [1960] and Anthony Coburn in *The Bastard Country* (1963). Jack McKinney's *The Well* [1960] showed naturalism itself being transformed, while Patricia Hooker's *The Lotus Eaters* [1968] carried it cleverly in the direction of farce. Experiment and improvisation have been the main source of vitality, whether in the linguistic energy of Thomas Keneally's *Halloran's Little Boat* [1966], in Rodney Milgate's skirmishings with Greek myth in *A Refined Look at Existence* [1966], or in the adventurousness of the Jane Street production *Terror Australis* [1968].

Australian poetry has also undergone a rapid development since the war. Of the poets already established in the 1940s, Slessor has since written very little. His collection, *One Hundred Poems* (1944), contained no work later than *Five Bells* (1939), and although the new edition *Poems* (1957) was augmented by the hauntingly beautiful "Beach Burial" and a few other verses, Slessor's work now seems to be complete. R. D. FitzGerald, on the other hand, has pressed on to *The Wind at Your Door* (1959) and *Southmost Twelve* (1962), and in 1965 assembled the collection *Forty Years' Poems*. His later writing has become more stringent as it has become more confessional. In "The Wind at Your Door", the historical narrative is drawn into the tighter form of the soliloquy, the poet himself reflecting on his subject and coming to terms with his experience. Other poems are a new form of lyric: to be read as testimony still, but with the sometimes strident manner of the earlier verse yielding to an eloquent simplicity. All the central preoccupations are found again here, caught in a finer lens. Within the compass of a poem like "Strata" FitzGerald can see present civilization as the latest cooling in the process of geological change, and at the same time find an athletic pleasure in its "tangibles and actualities" still:

> So that I count this gift
> priceless: that I have been
> never so far adrift

from cliff, creek, ravine
and red gravel of the ridge
that from my youth on
I could not find some ledge
neighbourly to the sun.

A third seasoned poet to be grouped with these two is Douglas Stewart. His non-dramatic verse goes back to *Green Lions* (1936), though Stewart established himself more authoritatively with *The Dosser in Springtime* (1946) and *Glencoe* (1947). *Glencoe* was a ballad sequence prompted by an earlier unsuccessful attempt to write a verse drama on the Highland massacre of 1692. The singularity of *The Dosser in Springtime*—which also inclined towards ballad measures—was to have defined the middle range of Australian verse in the 1940s: the typical poetry of the open air, humorous and ironic, apparently relaxed in form but controlled by an easy discipline, and impossible to imagine as having been written anywhere else.

As the poet likely to be nominated as the most "typically Australian", Douglas Stewart has yet acknowledged the early influence of the nature verse of W. H. Davies and Edmund Blunden, a period of fealty to Roy Campbell, and a special debt in his later work to Yeats, whose "natural style" was the main shaping influence on Stewart's Australian ballads.[18] In the same way the poetry of one so at home in the Monaro landscape as David Campbell is informed by the example of Elizabethan lyric, and Geoffrey Dutton playfully accommodates a European fashion in "Venus by the Torrens". Douglas Stewart's *Collected Poems 1936–1967*—which won the Townsville Foundation for Australian Studies Award for 1967—shows him as the most versatile of these poets of the "middle range", with a feeling for the outdoors that is as adequate to the miniature world of *Sun Orchids* as to the desert scenes of *The Birdsville Track*, expressing the inter-relatedness of all created things; with the gift for fantasy seen in "Heaven is a Busy Place" or "The Man from Adaminaby"; and with the intellectual penetration to develop the "voyager" poem from the "Worsley Enchanted" sequence to the world of that modern explorer, the scientist Rutherford. Stewart's more recent poems (headed "The Flowering Place" in the collected volume) are those of a mature writer obeying his own injunction to "be yourself" in poetry,[19] taking his subjects from the world about—like a fence or a parking meter—and writing with an assurance that is at once indulgent, sceptical, and shrewdly perceptive.

There is some logic in grouping Slessor, FitzGerald and Stewart as

[18] See his television interview of 7th January 1965, reported in *Southerly*, XXVII (1967), 188-98.
[19] *Ibid.*

three poets who had all published before the war, and separating them from those who have emerged since, to give contemporary Australian verse a new aspect. Among these Judith Wright, A. D. Hope, and James McAuley stand out, with Rosemary Dobson, Francis Webb, Vincent Buckley, Roland Robinson—or to add some more recent names, Gwen Harwood, Bruce Dawe, Rodney Hall, and Thomas W. Shapcott. This necessarily selective account must begin with Judith Wright (1915-).

Very few Australian poets have made the same impact with their first volume as did Judith Wright with *The Moving Image* (1946). Here was a collection of poems addressed to the persistent task of coming to terms with the Australian environment, that at once broke away from the stock attitudes of the bush balladist and put an end to "nature" poetry in the Wordsworth-Kendall mode. Judith Wright was fully aware of her Australian identity, while at the same time conscious of the older European tradition in which her poetry must also fall. To the nineteenth-century poet, she has observed, Australia presented "the *tabula rasa* on which the European consciousness expected to write",[20] and for the contemporary poet the landscape is still something that will not allow itself to be taken for granted—it calls for attention, demands to be reckoned with first. Judith Wright's own reckoning with it is recorded in *The Moving Image*. It is the New England landscape that she observes and re-creates, with a sense of its past living on into the present, harsh and frostbound and beautiful:

> South of my days' circle, part of my blood's country,
> rises that tableland, high delicate outline
> of bony slopes wincing under the winter,
> low trees blue-leaved and olive, outcropping granite—
> clean, lean, hungry country.

These lines take their authority from a sheer individuality of perception, which is sustained through later passages in the poem:

> The walls draw in to the warmth
> and the old roof cracks its joints; the slung kettle
> hisses a leak on the fire. Hardly to be believed that summer
> will turn up again some day in a wave of rambler roses,
> thrust its hot face in here to tell another yarn . . . .
> ("South of My Days")

The Moving Image is a book in which perceptions are held and explored, the titles of the poems reading like talismans—"Trapped Dingo", "Northern River", "Soldier's Farm", "The Surfer". The

[20] See "The Upside-down Hut", *Australian Letters*, III, iv (1961), 30-34.

poet is as yet unsure of what she wants finally to *do* with what she has perceived, so that the conclusion to "The Surfer" or "Trapped Dingo" may seem overstated. The attempt to read the given experience more deeply is more fruitful when it probes into the past —to the convict shepherds first exiled to the countryside which is now "safe with bitumen and banks", or to the eponymous suicide of "Nigger's Leap: New Fngland". In the well-known poems "Bullocky" and "Remittance Man", figures are drawn from the Australian "myth", but re-interpreted and presented with a fresh insight. The mind of the bullocky is seen as crazed by his privations:

> Beside his heavy-shouldered team,
> thirsty with drought and chilled with rain,
> he weathered all the striding years
> till they ran widdershins in his brain:
>
> Till the long solitary tracks
> etched deeper with each lurching load
> were populous before his eyes,
> and fiends and angels used his road.
>
> All the long straining journey grew
> a mad apocalyptic dream,
> and he old Moses, and the slaves
> his suffering and stubborn team . . . .

—though in this hallucination a deeper truth is glimpsed, through the identification of the pioneers with the prophets leading their people to the promised land:

> Grass is across the wagon-tracks,
> and plough strikes bone across the grass,
> and vineyards cover all the slopes
> where the dead teams were used to pass.
>
> O vine, grow close upon that bone
> and hold it with your rooted hand.
> The prophet Moses feeds the grape,
> and fruitful is the Promised Land.

—the effort to strain beyond the immediate experience, to discover the reality behind it, is to characterize all Judith Wright's poetry. The title, *The Moving Image*, is a reference to Plato ("Time is a moving image of eternity"), and through the sequence is felt a sense of the destructiveness of time, its hostility to permanence—a feeling sharpened in the poems that reflect the menace of the war. In the direct treatment of the theme of time in the title-piece, "The Moving Image", there is some effort to see time also as the means of renewal and continuity, but the poem as a whole is not an artistic success. In the more concrete situation of "The Company of Lovers", love is offered as a precarious refuge as "Death draws his cordons in"; in "Waiting" the individual life is seen as at the mercy of what the unknown future may hold:

> . . . the circling days weave tighter, and the spider
> Time binds us helpless till his sting go in.

The link between *The Moving Image* and *Woman to Man* (1949) is that the second collection asserts an answer to the problem left unsolved in the first, celebrating "the principle of love" (in the words of the epigraph) as "the summary or collective law of nature . . . impressed by God upon the original particles of all things, so as to make them attack each oher and come together". Love is seen as a force of creativeness and regeneration, resisting destructive time:

> All things that glow and move,
> all things that change and pass,
> I gather their delight
> as in a burning-glass . . .
>
> since love, who cancels fear
> with his fixèd will,
> burned my vision clear
> and bid my sense be still.
> ("The Maker")

Although it is love in this wider sense that is celebrated in *Woman to Man*, the special quality of the volume comes from the lyrical poems on human love, love that has been consummated and made fruitful of new life:

> The eyeless labourer in the night,
> the selfless, shapeless seed I hold,
> builds for its resurrection day—
> silent and swift and deep from sight
> foresees the unimagined light.
>
> This no child with a child's face;
> this has no name to name it by;
> yet you and I have known it well.
> This is our hunter and our chase,
> the third who lay in our embrace. . . .
> ("Woman to Man")

The poems in this range of experience have the immediacy and vitality of the best work in *The Moving Image*. In the collection as a whole, however, the situations are not always so concrete and specific:

in poems like "The Cycads" and "Camphor Laurel" the observed subject is more involved in the reverie of the poet, the descriptions are not hard and detailed so much as suggestive. It is a purposeful development, as Judith Wright still has the earlier manner at her command, as in the first stanza of "Flame-tree in a Quarry":

> From the broken bone of the hill
> stripped and left for dead,
> like a wrecked skull,
> leaps out this bush of blood . . .

or in the dramatic portrait of the "Metho Drinker":

> His white and burning girl, his woman of fire,
> creeps to his heart and sets a candle there
> to melt away the flesh that hides the bone
> to eat the nerve that tethers him in Time.

But she is reaching now towards a different kind of poetry, a search that continues in *The Gateway* (1953) and *The Two Fires* (1955).

The immediate impression made by these two collections is that Judith Wright's poetry is losing its grasp on the actual world, retreating into the impersonal and the abstract, becoming vague and uncertain in its effect. To the reader who values *The Moving Image* and *Woman to Man*, *The Gateway* may at first seem like a collection of the poems rejected from those earlier books. The world as perceived, which has hitherto been the main source of Judith Wright's poetic inspiration, no longer dominates her field of vision. Instead it offers now a starting-point for reflection, as in "Phaius Orchid"; or a symbolic situation to be explored, as in "The Pool and the Star"; or it is translated from literal reality into a sphere of imagination and dream, as in "Lion". Although *The Two Fires* was written in response to the threat of the atomic bomb, the later poems in that collection illustrate the same development.

In both these books, the individual poems gain from their relationship to one another, and from the total movement of which they are part. It is significant that the epigraph to *The Gateway* is taken from Blake (while a later poem is addressed to Thomas Traherne) and that of the Australian poets whom Judith Wright has studied, she has written most sensitively of Shaw Neilson. The instinct that she has possessed from the first, to tease out the underlying meaning of a specific experience, is now becoming more insistent and searching. A possible way of access to her later work is through the concept of the "two lives", to which she herself has referred in discussing the poetry of Chris Brennan.[21] He gave his own formulation of it in his lectures on symbolism in 1904:

> There are, as most of us feel, two lives: that lies in the brightness of truth, this stumbles in error; that is radiant with love and beauty, this is vexed with its own littleness and meanness; that is unfettered, lying beyond good and evil, this is caught in the quagmire. . . . Poetry, mediating between the two, necessarily enters into the conflict . . . its part is both to exasperate and reconcile that war. (*Prose*, p. 87)

In *The Gateway* and *The Two Fires*, the contingent world has become both an earnest of the ideal world and a denial of it, at times a prison and at times a means of release.

Thematically the most important of these later poems is "The Gateway" itself, which takes up the idea of the journey that figures in other poems like "The Lost Man" and "The Traveller and the Angel". Through the gateway lies the land where the world falls away and self is the "sole reality"; the way leads on until the path itself vanishes and the self is dissolved in turn—then from nothingness, it is remade:

> To say that I recall that time,
> that country,
> would be a lie; time was not,
> and I am nowhere.
> Yet two things remain—
> one was the last surrender,
> the other the last peace.
> In the depths of nothing
> I found my home.
>
> All ended there,
> yet all began.
> All sank in dissolution
> and rose renewed.

This is the only poem in which the transition from the one world to the other is completed, and then only at the level of descriptive statement. More often the renewal offered is a rebirth into the natural cycle, which makes spring so agonizing in "The Cicadas" and "The Cedars":

> Spring, returner, knocker at the iron gates,
> why should you return? None wish to live again.

The natural world, obedient to its own law, can nevertheless present an enviable harmony and rightness (as in "Birds"), and by contrast prove a torment to the divided self:

[21] In "Australian Poetry to 1920" in *The Literature of Australia*, ed. Geoffrey Dutton (Ringwood, Victoria: Penguin Books, 1964), p. 72.

How to live, I said, as the flame-tree lives?
To know what the flame-tree knows—to be
prodigal of my life as that wild tree
and wear my passion so?

but the folly of holding to the world of time is bitterly exposed in "The Harp and the King":

This is the praise of time, the harp cried out—
that we betray all truths that we possess.
Time strips the soul and leave it comfortless
and sends it thirsty through a bone-white drought.
Time's subtler treacheries teach us to betray.
What else could drive us on our way?
Wounded we cross the desert's emptiness
and must be false to what would make us whole.
For only change and distance shape for us
some new tremendous symbol for the soul.

"The Harp and the King" is the concluding poem of *The Two Fires*, and it restates more painfully the dilemma in which the poet had found herself at the outset. Nevertheless both *The Gateway* and *The Two Fires* are positive in their intention, in the effort to cling to love as a dynamic principle, in the struggle towards the integration of the self ("Eden"), and in the longing for the illumination that will transcend the whole conflict—the state symbolized by silence ("The Cup") and by the perfection of the dance ("Song"). In some of the later poems of *The Two Fires*, like "At Cooloolah", there is a renewal of feeling for the world accessible to the senses—a feeling that becomes more acute in *Birds* (1962). Poems like "Parrots" and "Dotterel" are more exquisite in their perceptions than anything in *The Moving Image,* though "Eggs and Nestlings" shows that the cruel contrast of the "two lives" can make itself felt even here:

The moss-rose and the palings made
a solemn and a waiting shade
where eagerly the mother pressed
a sheltering curve into her nest.

Her tranced eyes, her softened stare,
warned me when I saw her there,
and perfect as the grey nest's round,
three frail and powdered eggs I found.

My mother called me there one day.
Beneath the nest the eggshells lay,
and in it throbbed the triple greed
of one incessant angry need.

Those yellow gapes, those starveling cries,
how they disquieted my eyes!—
the shapeless furies come to be
from shape's most pure serenity.

Birds was followed in 1963 by *Five Senses,* Judith Wright's own choice from all her previously published work, with the addition of a new series, "The Forest". Her verse since *Woman to Man* is seen more clearly in this collection as fulfilling poetry's role of mediating between the two worlds, sometimes exasperating but more often reconciling their conflict. Judith Wright has provided an autobiography of a sort in her successive poems on the task of the poet, from "The Maker" in *Woman to Man* to "For Precision" in *The Two Fires* and "Poem and Audience" at the end of *Five Senses.* Where a reconciliation has been achieved, it has been in answer to the plea of "For Precision"—the plea to make things cohere, to "pin with one irremediable stroke"

what?—the escaping wavering wandering light,
the blur, the brilliance; forming into one chord
what's separate and distracted; making the vague hard—
catching the wraith—speaking with a pure voice,
and that the gull's sole note like a steel nail
that driven through cloud, sky, and irrelevant seas,
joins all, gives all a meaning, makes all whole.

The drive to make all cohere, felt also in the poems on the dance, is an effort to win "shape's most pure serenity" from an incoherent and imperfect world, but not by writing in the depersonalized style of *The Gateway.* It is instructive that the title of the collection should be *Five Senses*—from a piece published some seven years earlier, and perhaps to be seen as defining the motif of Judith Wright's work over that period. The emphasis in "Five Senses" is upon the poet's activity as creative, "forming into one chord what's separate and distracted", so that what is fashioned from the imperfect world has a perfection that transcends it:

Now my five senses
gather into a meaning
all acts, all presences;
and as a lily gathers
the elements together,
in me this dark and shining,
that stillness and that moving,
these shapes that spring from nothing,
become a rhythm that dances,
a pure design

while the poet's activity in turn is guided by something beyond his knowing, so that the poem at once embodies the union of his creative mind and the world outside it, and is the symbol of a reality beyond them both:

> While I'm in my five senses
> they send me spinning
> all sounds and silences,
> all shape and colour
> as thread for that weaver,
> whose web within me growing
> follows beyond my knowing
> some pattern sprung from nothing—
> a rhythm that dances
> and is not mine.

At such moments— and poems as early as "Wonga Vine" are their record—the "two lives" become one.

While the consciousness of dualities which refuse to be resolved into singleness persist in *The Other Half* (1966)—notably in the title-poem and "Naked Girl and Mirror"—the style of oracular profundity that had begun to accompany it is here balanced by the development of a vein tapped earlier in "Request to a Year". Poems like "Eve to her Daughters", "Remembering an Aunt", and "Turning Fifty" are nourished by a humane reminiscence, and an engaging humour. May this cheerfulness continue to break in.

Three years before the publication of *The Moving Image* (1946), there had appeared in Sydney a brochure, now extremely rare, called simply *No. 1*. It was followed in 1944 by *Number Two*, and in 1948 by *Number Three*, then publication ceased. These fugitive pamphlets marked the first appearance in book-form of the poems of A. D. Hope (1907–), joint author with Harry Hooton and Garry Lyle of *No. 1*, and joint author with Hooton and Oliver Somerville of *Number Two*. Though his work became known to a wider audience through the inclusion of some poems in H. M. Green's *Modern Australian Poetry* (1946; revised edition 1952), almost ten years elapsed before Hope issued his own first volume, *The Wandering Islands* (1955).

Recognition was immediate. Perhaps because satire had been relatively undeveloped in Australian verse, except by poets like F. T. Macartney and Ronald McCuaig, Hope was first identified as a satirist and iconoclast. The truculence and pungency of "Observation Car", "The Lingam and the Yoni", "Australia", and "Standardisation" help to explain this reaction to *The Wandering Islands*: these are poems written from the standpoint of a critical observer, intent to expose fake and sham wherever they are found. They had all been first published in the 1940s, along with "Conquistador", "The Return from the Freudian Islands", and "The Damnation of Byron". The fundamental principle of Hope's earlier poetry is the vision of a world lacking any heroic dimension. If this is something common to all social satire, it is also a theme that he deliberately presses. "Conquistador" relates the odyssey of the contemporary hero, Henry Clay:

> Each day he caught the seven-thirty train
> To work, watered his garden after tea,
> Took an umbrella if it looked like rain
> And was remarkably like you or me.
>
> He had his hair cut once a fortnight, tried
> Not to forget the birthday of his wife,
> And might have lived unnoticed till he died
> Had not ambition entered Henry's life.

Henry's adventure comes from an encounter with a huge girl in a hotel lounge, and from her invitation to accompany her home:

> . . . in her quiet room they were alone.
> There, towering over Henry by a head,
> She stood and took her clothes off one by one,
> And then she stretched herself upon the bed.
>
> Her bulk of beauty, her stupendous grace
> Challenged the lion heart in his puny dust.
> Proudly his Moment looked him in the face:
> He rose to meet it as a hero must;
>
> Climbed the white mountain of unravished snow,
> Planted his tiny flag upon the peak.
> The smooth drift, scarcely breathing, lay below.
> She did not take the trouble to smile or speak.
>
> And afterwards, it may have been in play,
> The enormous girl rolled over and squashed him flat;
> And, as she could not send him home that way,
> Used him thereafter as a bedside mat.

The modern hero is a pigmy, who when he stands up to life finds that it rolls over and squashes him flat. Henry's final indignity is to be processed:

> Speaking at large, I will say this of her:
> She did not spare expense to make him nice.
> Tanned on both sides and neatly edged with fur,
> The job would have been cheap at any price.

> And when, in winter, getting out of bed,
> Her large soft feet pressed warmly on the skin,
> The two glass eyes would sparkle in his head,
> The jaws extend their papier-maché grin.

Although the wit and the aggressiveness of Hope's early satires have led critics to see him as "alienated" and nihilistic, he is a poet with a fierce integrity, trying modern society by the heroic standard and finding it wanting. This underlying seriousness in his earlier work is made plainer in the major poem of the time, *Dunciad Minimus* (1950), in the definition of the function and purpose of satire in Book III.[22]

The Wandering Islands, besides collecting poems published more than ten years earlier, made it clear that Hope's work by 1955 had become too versatile to be contained in the category of satire. In the title-poem, as in "Chorale" and the "Death of the Bird", the assertive poetry of observation is seen yielding to a poetry of reflection and enquiry, with a control and sensitivity that had not been encountered before. Equally arresting are the poems on myth, in their calculated reversal of the normal interpretation of the story—the switching of sympathies in "The Return of Persephone", or the determination in "Imperial Adam" to make the reader confront certain brutal facts. Other poems, including "The Muse" and "Pyramis or The House of Ascent", show Hope's attraction to the theme of the poet, which is a preoccupation of his later verse.

"Pyramis" was suggested by one of the theories presented in I. E. S. Edwards' *The Pyramids of Egypt*, that the Pharoahs built the pyramids as a stairway to heaven, challenging the gods:

> This is their image: the desert and the wild,
> A lone man digging, a nation piling stones
> Under the lash in fear, in sweat, in haste;
> Image of those demonic minds who build
> To outlast time, spend life to house old bones—
> This pyramid rising squarely in the waste!

Then attention turns to the builders of the pyramids of art, who spent their energies like slaves toiling in the sun:

> I think of other pyramids, not in stone,
> The great, incredible monuments of art,
> And of their builders, men who put aside
> Consideration, dared, and stood alone,
> Strengthening those powers that fence the failing heart:
> Intemperate will and incorruptible pride.

[22] The *Dunciad Minimus* is still unpublished, though an outline and substantial extracts were given in *Southerly*, XXIV (1964), 104-15.

The man alone digging his bones a hole;
The pyramid in the waste—whose images?
Blake's tower of vision defying the black air;
Milton twice blind groping about his soul
For exit, and Swift raving mad in his—
The builders of the pyramid everywhere!

The first heroic personality to emerge in Hope's verse is the personality of the poet, seen as one of those who "put aside/ Consideration, dared, and stood alone". The poets named are Blake and Swift, both rebels against the values of their age, and Milton, last exemplar in English of the tradition of the heroic poem. Akin to the Pharoahs, who took "like genius, their prerogative/Of blood, mind, treasure", the poet is seen as a godlike figure, and yet also as crazed and demonic—a kind of inspired lunatic. The vehemence of "Pyramis" perhaps comes from Hope's conviction of the antithesis between the poet and the unheroic world about him, which he re-affirms in "William Butler Yeats" and in a poem published a year after *The Wandering Islands*, "Persons from Porlock". Coleridge was fortunate to have suffered but one intrusion, to have lost only the remainder of "Kubla Khan": consider his fate had Porlock controlled his upbringing, drawn him into its social routine, supplied him with

Neighbours from Porlock, culled from Porlock's best,
The sweetest girl in Porlock for his bride,
In due course to surround him with some young
Persons from Porlock, always giving tongue.

Eight hours a day of honest Porlock toil,
And Porlock parties—useless to refuse—
The ritual gardening of Porlock soil,
Would leave him time still for a spare-time Muse—

if then "Kubla Khan" had come to him in a dream, how would he have rendered it?

'In Xanadu . . .'—He know the words by rote,
Had but to set them down.
To his despair
He found a man from Porlock wore his coat,
And thought his thoughts; and, stolid in his chair,
A person fresh from Porlock sat and wrote:
'Amid this tumult Kubla heard from far
Voices of Porlock babbling round the bar.'

The poet, in Hope's view, has fought a losing battle against the values of Porlock since Coleridge's day. In his essay "The Discursive

Mode: Reflections on the Ecology of Poetry" in 1956[23] Hope resumed a theme of his 1952 inaugural lecture at Canberra University College: the decay, in the last two hundred years or so, of such major poetic forms as the epic, verse tragedy, the ode, the great philosophic poem—and with them other traditional forms like the epistle, the elegy, the pastoral, the verse satire. The great narrative poem began to decline in the seventeenth and eighteenth centuries (Hope argues) with the rise of the domestic novel; satire persisted through the eighteenth century, but died with Byron; the ode and the elegy and the verse epistle, scarcely surviving into the nineteenth century, were then extinguished by the doctrine of Poe, that "Poetry in its purest form . . . was to be found in the lyric." With the prevalence of the heresy that narrative, argument, excogitation and description are alien to poetry, the majestic forms of the past have now been superseded by "little poems of reflection, brief comments, interior monologues, sharp critical barks and hisses, songs that never become articulate".

The decay of the great forms is for Hope a token of the decay of civilization itself. When the epic died and the novel replaced it, "something noble in the mind of man died . . . and something more comfortable and amusing took its place". The diagnosis is pursued in "Conversation with Calliope", the longest of Hope's poems next to the *Dunciad Minimus.* In a parable, the Muse explains to her balding protégé how the evolutionary process has advanced from the order of plants to the order of the conscious mind, then to the age of "social man": the next step, the conscious mind moving towards ends as yet unseen, is delayed by the present reign of "the great Unculture", in which over-population and mass production have cheapened and diluted all the arts. The epic is a casualty of an age where the arts are "sterilised and tinned and tested", and when the last tame poet is tethered on the campus, the last vineyard replaced by a coca-cola factory, the evolutionary process will have come to a halt. The future depends on the isolated poet preserving his values through a barren and hostile age, ready

> through his art to bring to birth
> New modes of being here on earth.

Hope's "mystique" of the poet, developed from the chest-beating stance of "Pyramis or The House of Ascent", gives coherence to the work that has followed *The Wandering Islands.* His essay on "The Discursive Mode" was a plea for the revival of the middle form of poetry—the equable style in which Chaucer wrote his tales, Dryden

[23] *Quadrant,* I (1956), 27-33, reprinted in *The Cave and the Spring* (Adelaide: Rigby, 1965).

his *Religio Laici,* Browning his monologues, Robert Frost some of his New England poems. The rehabilitation of the poetry of discourse is seen as the first stage in a programme to reclaim the desert to which the poetic landscape has been reduced by the erosion of the last two centuries. As the flexible style that is adequate for exposition, argument, narrative and meditation, it can begin to restore some of the areas laid waste by the heresy of Poe, with formal satire notable amongst them.

Poems (1960) shows Hope pursuing this design. He revives one form after another in the middle style of poetry—the epistle, the elegy (in the piece sub-titled "Variations on a theme of the Seventeenth Century"), the fable (in "Lambkin")—besides approaching the ceremonial dignity of the ode in "Soledades of the Sun and Moon". Some of the most impressive of the newer work is devoted to defining and celebrating the poet's role and mission. "An Epistle from Holofernes" looks to the myths as a repository of truths that persist down the centuries, transcending the accidentals of time and place to "speak to us the truth of what we are", and stresses the insight of the poet as re-awakening their significance:

> . . . the myths will not fit us ready made.
> It is the meaning of the poet's trade
> To re-create the fables and revive
> In men the energies by which they live.

In "An Epistle: Edward Sackville to Venetia Digby", the poet is likened to the lover whose torments exalt him to "surpass the single reach of man", giving access to "fresh modes of being, unguessed forms of bliss". In "Soledades of the Sun and Moon" the world of myth finds an equivalence in the constellations in the heavens, changeless and immortal, yet isolated one from the other by the very order and harmony of the motion to which they are bound. It is through the poet that they become articulate:

> The mortal hearts of poets first engender
> The parleying of those immortal creatures;
> Then from their interchange create unending
> Orbits of song and colloquies of light;

and the poet is wooed and entreated by the gods of song, their rivalries forgotten, so that the cosmic dance itself seems almost to pay homage to the poets of the world, even as it embodies the "enchanted motion" that they celebrate:

For you the gods of song forgo their quarrel;
Panther and Wolf forget their former anger;
For you this ancient ceremony of greeting
  Becomes a solemn apopemptic hymn.
Muses who twine the ivy with the laurel
In savage measures celebrate you, Stranger;
  For you the Maenads trim
Their torches and, in order due repeating
The stately ode, invoke you. Wanderer, Ranger,
  Beyond the utmost rim
Of waters, hear the voice of these entreating!

It is easy to appreciate why reviewers of *Poems* (1960) should have hailed such poems as Hope's most important work so far. Yet admiration must be tinged with disquiet. Although the doctrines about poetry enunciated in "An Epistle from Holofernes" are obviously important to Hope, they are not made dramatically relevant to the situation with which the poem itself deals. The theorizing that concludes "An Epistle: Edward Sackville to Venetia Digby" is again responsible for a degree of discontinuity in the poem, subtracting from the moving account of separation in love—a treatment of love in which "sex" is incidentally transcended. There is a general tendency for these poems—and for "Conversation with Calliope"—to go on for too long, losing force and impact.

The appearance of Hope's *Collected Poems 1930–1965* declared the range of his output, and justified his conception of poetry as a "celebration of the world", an act of joy.[24] This celebration is found equally in discursive pieces like "A Letter from Rome" (on the girl taking love as a post-graduate course) as in the reaching after "new modes of being" in the beautiful "Ode on the Death of Pius the Twelfth", with which the volume concludes. There is a particular fascination, however, in the new poems on myth. The most delicately modulated of them, "The Double Looking Glass", reinterprets the story of Susannah and the Elders by tracing her reverie as she bathes alone, indulging the fantasy of a lover in her charmed world—so that the irruption of the elders finds her guilty in thought, though not in deed. "Faustus" resumes the fable of the man who sold himself to the devil in exchange for complete knowledge and complete experience: when the moment of reckoning comes, he finds that with the power to fulfil every wish, his will has already decayed; reason has atrophied, with no problems to exercise it; love has withered, untried by passion—the devil has his soul already. The earlier poem "Fafnir" had dealt in the same way with the Siegfried legend,

[24] See the television interview reported in *Southerly*, XXVI (1966), 245-6, and "Poetry and Platitude" in *The Cave and the Spring*, pp. 15-16.

presenting the hero the morning after, foreseeing his death in Gudrun's eyes; "The End of a Journey" had been a study of the returned Ulysses, "an old man sleeping with his housekeeper".

These poems do not rely on quite the same shock tactics as "Imperial Adam". They have a more questioning, a more exploratory quality. Each looks again at some human ideal—the heroism of Siegfried, the fabled chastity of Susannah, the magian knowledge of Faustus—and presents it in a more disturbing light. The poet who had begun by testing the world against an heroic standard may have come to question that standard itself. Does a greater wisdom lie in the visionary prospect of the "Ode on the Death of Pius the Twelfth"? Hope remains the most restless and unpredictable of contemporary Australian poets, his work demanding to be evaluated afresh at every stage.

When J. D. Pringle published *Australian Accent* in 1958, he linked Hope, James McAuley and Harold Stewart as the leaders of a "counter-revolution" in Australian poetry, resisting the nationalism of the Jindyworobaks and returning, like a new Augustan school, to the classical forms. Hope's cultivation of eighteenth-century modes is, as we have seen, part of a different crusade, and Pringle himself confessed two years later that his chapter on poetry "would have been better without the rather 'gimmicky' notion of a counter-revolution which no one in Australia had ever heard of until he invented it" (*Hermes*, 1960). It is nevertheless worth recalling the association of Hope and McAuley in the early 1940s, and the association of McAuley and Stewart that led them one afternoon in 1944 to concoct the apocalyptic poems of Ern Malley, from sources such as an American report on the drainage of breeding grounds for mosquitoes.[25] The three poets have since developed in such different ways that it would be impossible to regard them as a "school"; and McAuley's work in particular needs to be separately considered.

James McAuley (1917–) won early recognition from a relatively small output of verse. *Under Aldebaran* (1946) included work that went back to his undergraduate years, and the studious arrangement of the contents, the careful dating of the poems, and the "Notes" supplied all suggested that McAuley was a writer taking seriously—perhaps too seriously—his own intellectual and poetic development. The singularity of *Under Aldebaran* is the hard and lucid style that McAuley is shaping, still uncertainly sustained in "serious" poems like "The Blue Horses" and "Celebration of Love", but capable of a natural precision in a more sardonic piece like "The True Discovery of Australia". Although this last poem is dedicated to A. D.

[25] For a full account of the Ern Malley affair, see *Ern Malley's Poems*, ed. Max Harris (Melbourne: Lansdowne Press, 1961).

Hope, the main quality which McAuley at this time shares with Hope is an awareness of the whole European tradition accessible to him—whether in Blake or Nietzsche, Rilke or Valéry.

He did not publish another book for ten years. The major event for McAuley in this interval was his conversion to Roman Catholicism, with the hard thinking that preceded and followed it. His steady reappraisal of literature and art is reported in the essays later collected as *The End of Modernity* (1959). Here modern literature is seen as the expression of a culture in disintegration, of a liberalist outlook "opposed both to the *philosophia perennis* and to what one may call *religio perennis*, the natural pieties of the human mind" (p. vi). McAuley's subject is really "the anti-metaphysical modern mentality", and the consequence for the arts of "the idea which is creeping like a deathly chill over the Western world that the *normal* mind is the uncommitted mind, without fixed principles or certainties" (p. 40).

His new standpoint is reflected in *A Vision of Ceremony* (1956). Only one poem, "A Letter to John Dryden", is written as polemic. It is a diagnosis of this "vacant sly/Neurotic modern world", in which order and tradition have been lost:

> You chose for your attempt a kind of verse
> Well-bred and easy, energetic, terse;
> Reason might walk in it, or boldly fence,
> And all was done with spirit and with sense.
> But who cares now for reason?—when we see
> The very guardians of philosophy
> Conceive it as their task to warn the youth
> Against the search for philosophic truth . . .

and to crown the educational process

> that enigmatic pile
> Where ancient wisdom scarce evokes a smile,
> The University, confronts the land,
> Neutral of course, and secular, and bland;
> Where Christ, Augustine, and the Stagirite
> Lie dead and buried, neither wrong nor right,
> Under a sneer of silence cold as arctic night.

Although the indignation of "A Letter to John Dryden" is not typical of McAuley's work in this second volume, it springs from a concern at the falling away from the *philosophia perennis* and *religio perennis* celebrated in the other poems, to a state where

> A formless relativism ends our days,
> And good and evil are but culture-traits.

As the title implies, the intention of *A Vision of Ceremony* is to evoke and celebrate such qualities as harmony, serenity, and order. It begins with the poem headed "Invocation":

> Radiant Muse, my childhood's nurse,
> Who gave my wondering mouth to taste
> The fragrant honeycomb of verse;
> And later smilingly embraced
> My boyhood, ripening its crude
> Harsh vigour in your solitude:
>
> Compose the mingling thoughts that crowd
> Upon me to a lucid line;
> Teach me at last to speak aloud
> In words that are no longer mine;
> For at your touch, discreet, profound,
> Ten thousand years softly resound . . . .

The new authority McAuley's verse has acquired is felt in these lines, as in poems like "Mating Swans" and "To a Dead Bird of Paradise" is felt a new perceptiveness—each somehow suggests a moment of startling clarity born of austerity and self-discipline. The most ambitious poem, "Celebration of Divine Love", does not achieve this lucidity, perhaps because its tone is too declarative. McAuley can yet write most sensitively in an "oracular" style, as in "An Art of Poetry (To Vincent Buckley)":

> Since all our keys are lost or broken,
> Shall it be thought absurd
> If for an art of words I turn
> Discreetly to the Word?
>
> . . . Scorn then to darken and contract
> The landscape of the heart
> By individual, arbitrary
> And self-expressive art.
>
> Let your speech be ordered wholly
> By an intellectual love;
> Elucidate the carnal maze
> With clear light from above.

A Vision of Ceremony was greeted without fervour at the time of its publication, if not with some misgiving at the loss of the warmth and humanity felt in McAuley's earlier work. He has furnished a possible reply to this criticism in the essay "Tradition, Society and the Arts" in *The End of Modernity*, in the distinction there made between "secular" and "liturgical" literature:

What attracts us to secular literature is its immense variety of subjects, its free development of passion and mood, its psychological subtlety, the wealth of imagery that it amasses by laying the whole world under contribution, the enchanting touches of fantasy and even inconsequence it can wear. Compare with this the austere simple strength, the impersonality, the narrow range of subject and imagery, of the Ambrosian hymns, whose precept is:

Laeti bibamus sobriam
ebrietatem spiritus.

But if we shift our point of view from the outer to the inner realm . . . it is the secular work that is narrow, because of its concentration on visible detail, emotional and sensual variety, and worldly concerns; while the liturgical work is limitlessly wide, because of its rigorous concentration on the most universal themes which contain through their simplicity an endless wealth of significance. (pp. 17–18)

Although there is a place for both the "secular" and the "liturgical", McAuley has elected in his later verse to forgo the one for the more austere and demanding practice of the other—to concentrate on "the most universal themes which contain through their simplicity an endless wealth of significance".

He has faced his most exacting task in his third volume, *Captain Quiros* (1964). The historical narrative is a well established form in modern Australian verse, but McAuley's undertaking has different motives from those behind *Leichhardt in Theatre* or *Between Two Tides.* One symptom of the deterioration of modern literature is for him "the dethronement of poetry" by prose fiction, and even the forfeit to the novel of things that are the natural business of poetic narrative and drama: a work like Patrick White's *Voss* challenges the poets with having allowed their art to fall away from the greater tasks. *Captain Quiros* is an attempt at the epic, and it is capable of description in the terms McAuley has applied to *Voss* itself. He sets out to present "a significant action, examined in all its levels of psychological penetration, pathos, irony, moral and metaphysical meaning".[26]

Pedro Fernandez de Quiros was the navigator who committed himself to the search for the Great South Land, and to the dream of winning it for Catholic Christendom. His story is told by his secretary, the poet Belmonte: Part One describes Quiros's role in the expedition of Mendana to the Solomon Islands in 1595; Part Two his own quest for the southern continent, which he believed he had found in the New Hebrides, dedicating it to the Holy Spirit

[26] See James McAuley, "The Gothic Splendours: Patrick White's *Voss*", *Southerly,* XXV (1965), 34-45. He says here "I may as well confess that in my recollection there is a link between my reaction to *Voss* and my decision to write *Captain Quiros.*"

(*Austrialia del Espiritu Santo*); Part Three is concerned with the final expedition seven years later, halted by Quiros's death at Panama. The larger significance of the tale is suggested in the Proem to Part One, where the search for Terra Australis is seen as a search for the new Eden, an enterprise which human imperfection itself must defeat:

> *Terra Australis* you must celebrate,
> Land of the inmost heart, searching for which
> Men roam the earth, and on the way create
> Their kingdoms in the Indies and grow rich,
> With noble arts and cities; only to learn
> They bear the old selves with them that could turn
> The streams of Eden to a standing ditch.

A work on the scale of *Captain Quiros* cannot rely on the special intensity which McAuley achieved in the compass of his shorter "liturgical" poems, and its spare and disciplined style is a severe test of the artistic tenets to which he has pledged himself. The poem is sustained by its dramatic structure: it is a working out of a collision between the "secular" and "liturgical" worlds, the study of a visionary whose dream is nourished and frustrated by circumstance, ennobled even as it is doomed to failure by aiming at more than it is possible for man to achieve. The involvement of Quiros in the brutality and corruption of Mendana's voyage is a "hard apprenticeship" that nevertheless leaves his idealism unimpaired,

> Refining what was wavering or uncouth
> To a clear purpose, tempered and serene—

so that he becomes the leader with a bloodless sword of another company

> bound for a new heaven and earth—
> Our voyage was to be a solemn rite,
> A passing through the waters to rebirth
> In a new world, created in despite
> Of the demonic powers that rule the age.

Although the poem is so articulated that no intensity can be merely "local", the narrative is most luminous and radiant in the voyage southward towards the Isle of Beautiful Folk, and in the claiming of the New Hebrides as "the South Land of the Holy Ghost". The misadventures that then overtake Quiros lead him to ask of the friar

> "Where was the fault, that we have merited
> No more than this from Heaven?"

and to receive this reply—

> "Conformed to Christ in longing, we aspire
> To re-create creation, and restore
> All things in Justice, perfect and entire:
> This is indeed our task and privilege;
> This in our voyage was our sacred pledge,
> Yet under limits we may not ignore.
>
> "For in the midst of time God has not willed
> The end of Time. Not ours to bring to birth
> That final Realm; nor shall our labours build
> Out of the rubble of this fallen earth
> The new Jerusalem, which will never be
> Christ's perfect Bride save in eternity."

There can be no more than "broken efforts" until this dispensation gives way to the next, with present failures themselves an earnest that "all shall be made perfect at the last". A vision of this future perfection is allowed to Quiros on his deathbed in Panama, after he has embarked too late on a second expedition, a victim of the temporizing of statesmen and prelates.

With its austere style and controlled architecture, *Captain Quiros* is a poem that gains from re-reading, and from being seen in relationship to McAuley's whole *oeuvre*, from the poems about Henry the Navigator and Mercator's maps in *Under Aldebaran*. Though he initially won recognition from a small output, McAuley is one of a number of Australian poets writing at present whose recent work has called for the reappraisal of their achievement. In the same way *The Ghost of the Cock* (1964) has forced attention on the talent of Francis Webb, though *Birthday* (1953) and *Socrates and Other Poems* (1961) passed almost unnoticed; and Rosemary Dobson has added so steadily to *In A Convex Mirror* (1944) that she is now the foremost woman poet, next to Judith Wright.

If contemporary Australian poetry remains too fluid and varied to reveal any single pattern, one aspect of it does conform to the larger scheme that this essay has been concerned to trace. To find part of the singularity of McAuley's work in the sense of a wider European tradition informing it is not to deny that his poetry is distinctively Australian, and also completely personal. This holds for A. D. Hope also, and for younger poets in University positions like Vincent Buckley, Evan Jones, Chris Wallace-Crabbe, and Vivian Smith. It is more important to recognize that what may appear a singularity of these writers is in fact a singularity of most modern Australian verse, that any account of Australian literature in the twentieth century would be distorted—as the typical account of the 1890s has been—by the assumption that the only important shaping influences have been local ones.

It would be false history to think of any given Australian poet as explicable simply through his relationship to the Australian poetry preceding him. The work of Eliot and Auden was as accessible to poets of the 1930s and 1940s as the work of any local predecessor, and sometimes more accessible. Slessor was constrained to point out to a reviewer in 1945 that he had "never had the opportunity of reading C. J. Brennan's *The Wanderer*, or any other of his poems, except *The Chant of Doom* and a few pieces which have been printed in anthologies";[27] he has also acknowledged Tennyson as his master in the technique of verse. R. D. FitzGerald is a known student of Brennan, but he has named Matthew Arnold as "a big influence in my own work which none of the critics seem to have spotted", and emphasized that he "read *The Ring and the Book* again and again before I wrote *Between Two Tides*".[28] The influence of T. S. Eliot has been felt, whether in the wittiness of Ronald McCuaig's earlier verse or in the resistance it has encountered from McAuley and Hope,[29] while Judith Wright—the interpreter of the Australian environment—can base her "Typists in the Phoenix Building" on a situation from Yeats, and Rosemary Dobson's recent work reflects her enthusiasm for Robert Lowell. In the same way a novelist like Patrick White writes from a consciousness of the whole European tradition, in painting and music as well as literature, without surrendering any part of his own individuality. Australian literature began as an extension of European civilization to the south, and it is still the richer for having the larger tradition behind it—while that tradition itself may now be fructified in turn by the vitality it encounters.

[27] In a letter to *Meanjin Papers*, IV (1945), 221-2.

[28] See his lecture "Modern Poetry and its Interpretation in the Classroom", in *The Teaching of English* (October, 1963), p. 19, and an interview reported in the *Sydney Morning Herald* on 7th August 1965. His article on "Narrative Poetry" in *Southerly*, XXVI (1966), 11-24, stresses the example of Masefield.

[29] Hope pillories the *Four Quartets* in *Dunciad Minimus*, and McAuley's view of Eliot is hinted in "A Letter to John Dryden":

> Perhaps you'd choose T. Eliot's mighty line,
> To drift, and flutter, hesitate, opine,
> Hint at meaning, murmur that God knows,
> And gently settle in a soup of prose.

NEW ZEALAND LITERATURE

1

INTRODUCTION

THE EUROPEAN history of New Zealand is brief and its literary history even briefer. Abel Tasman, the Dutch navigator who discovered the islands in 1642, Captain James Cook, who rediscovered them in 1796, and the various French explorers such as the brilliant Dumont d'Urville and D'Entrecastaux, who followed, left their records of a land whose physical grandeur and variety excited their admiration as much as its cannibal inhabitants, the Maoris, excited their horror or pity. The whalers, sealers, traders, missionaries, convicts escaped from the Australian penal settlements, and others who filtered into the country in the wake of the discoverers during the period in which it was an Australian colony, also bequeathed their scattered records, reminiscences, and narratives. All of these have their obvious historical value, but very rarely a literary one.

The production of imaginative literature began only with the arrival of planned groups of colonists from Great Britain sponsored by the New Zealand Company early in the nineteenth century, and the formal annexation of New Zealand by the British Government in 1840. On February 5 of that year, a treaty between Queen Victoria and the Maoris was signed, and on May 21, Captain Hobson, the Queen's representative, proclaimed British sovereignty over the whole country. To the new settlements at Christchurch, Wellington, Dunedin, and Auckland there came in the two following decades a mixture of various types of colonists; some people of means and education, others assisted immigrants of humbler station. Attempts to preserve English class distinctions collapsed under the weight of the problems of breaking-in a land that possessed none of the civilized amenities. As one early woman settler from England observed: "The look and bearing of the immigrants appear to alter soon after they reach the colony . . . I like to see the upright gait, the well-fed, healthy look, the decent clothes (even if no one touches his hat to you) instead of the half-starved, depressed appearance, and the too often cringing servility, of the mass of our English population."

Although a tradition has grown up that, in contradistinction to the convict settlement of Australia, New Zealand was founded primarily by groups of selected migrants, largely gentlemen, in fact, after the 1840's, a great haphazard influx of settlers, including Scots at Waipu, Irish at "Fencible Settlements" around Auckland, French at Akaroa, Bohemians at Puhoi, and miscellaneous migrants from Australia made up the majority of the new arrivals. By 1854, there were about 32,500 people in New Zealand, most of them from the lower middle-class English group, and the greater number involved in farming and mining.

The literate arrivals, of whom there was a high proportion, however, brought with them the current books from England—the works of Dickens, the Brontes, Carlyle, Tennyson, Browning, volumes of sermons and essays, and the works of the lesser Victorians—Samuel Smiles, Felicia Hemans, and Martin Tupper among them. A Pickwick Club, dedicated to spreading the fame of the "inimitable Boz," was formed in Port Nicholson just three months after the arrival of the first New Zealand Company settlers there in 1840, and the first quarter's report proudly records the possession of a library of 100 volumes. Nevertheless, the earliest literary efforts in the new colony inevitably took a pragmatic form—journalism, letters and diaries (often later issued as books), pamphlets and leaflets, histories, instruction-manuals. The art of versifying sprouted fairly early, too, in the contribution to the "Poets' Corner" of the newspapers, and in the work of local bards, usually tried out on a receptive audience before seeing print.

On the whole, however, as Arthur S. Thompson, New Zealand's first historian, put it, ditchers were more esteemed than poets. For, in the opening-up period, the practical arts were of prime importance: the early settlers were faced with the tasks of breaking-in land, felling bush, ploughing, building homes and cities, establishing laws, and creating a society. There was scant entertainment, except for sport and occasional balls. Men spent most of their leisure in pubs, dance-halls, and gambling-dens. The heterogeneous community life of gold-rush days tended to accentuate the coarser aspects of social behavior. In such a society, writing was regarded mainly as a practical instrument, and was most highly prized when it was informative.

The first verse arose out of the celebration of special occasions, in the form of topical pieces recited or sung at a "social." As it developed more self-consciously literary manners, it graduated as a branch of minor Victorian verse, with its post-Keatsian worship of "Beauty," its vague generalizations and personifications, its bardic fervors, and its sentimentality. Shopworn in sentiment, uninventive in form, mediocre in content, and weighed down with unassimilated local color, the first New Zealand verse reflects the worst features of its models. So, too, the plays written later in the century belong to the crude tradition of Victorian melodrama, and the novels owe more to Pierce Egan and Theodore Hook than they do to Thackeray and George Eliot.

The lack of any quantity of significant writing in nineteenth-century New Zealand may be explained, simply, by the absence of writers of real talent: while there was a will to make, there were not the necessary skills. Only in flashes, and then almost, it seems, by chance, do the more "literary" poets of the time produce a line or two that looks like poetry. But other factors made it difficult for any real literature to flourish. Apart from the imperative practical demands that hampered them, the early settlers suffered from a divided personality which prevented them from drawing strength and inspiration from their immediate surroundings. They were exiles, men and women whose bodies were in the new land, but whose spirits were still in "The Old Country." This is, of course, an inevitable colonial condition, but, in the case of the New Zealand migrants, it was aggravated by the particular island character of the land and its distance from Europe; those geographical facts bred a sense of physical isolation which led to a compensatory closer clinging to the image of Britain.

In the absence, too, of any local literary tradition, the first New Zealand writers adhered firmly to English ones, which with their class-values and their reflection, both conscious and unconscious, of a special type of society and particular ideals and aims, bore only the faintest relation to the realities of life in the new land, with its comparative lack of privilege, its need for hard work from all, and its strikingly egalitarian atmosphere. For at least three generations, writing in New Zealand reflected this pain of separation and dichotomy of spirit, a clash between the Victorian sensibility and colonial pragmatic realities; and there was no poet able to get sufficiently outside this division to make rewarding poetry from it. It is not surprising, then, that much of the writing of the age shows an uncertainty as to the identity of the writer and indeed of his audience. In the absence of a local market of any size, novels were written for English readers and exploited the exotic appeal of the new land. As for the poets, unless they had aimed at the most elementary responses, they would have had no audience at all.

For the early writers, New Zealand was an outpost of Britain; the homeland they had left behind became idealized as the center of what was most gracious and worthwhile in life and art. The concept of the new country as a community with its own special character and of the New Zealander as a person with specific problems of adaptation was indeed in the minds of several of the first writers, but so long as England remained "Home," with all that that nostalgic name implied by way of dependence, the writer was an exile, and wrote as such, belonging in spirit neither to the older society nor to the new one.

The possibility of building some kind of native tradition seemed to be promised in the South Island, with its great sheep-runs, its gold-fields and its early prosperity. Out of the Scottish settlement of Otago came an interesting variant of Scots vernacular literature, in the work of Barr, Golder, Bathgate, and others. But the changes that shifted the economic center to the North Island (not to mention the attractions of a better climate), so that, in the later twentieth century, one-third of the population lives in the Auckland province, meant that any chance of continuity was shattered. In fact, the influx of a heterogeneous population attracted by gold discoveries in the 1860's broke the Scottish hegemony fairly early.

For a time, it appeared that some kind of native literary tradition might develop from contact with Australia. The vigorous ballad-type poems of Adam Lindsay Gordon and Henry Kendall had local imitators later in the century in David McKee Wright and Arthur H. Adams. But, despite a certain amount of cross-traffic, despite, too, the fact that for many years New Zealand poets were gathered under the Oxford University Press's umbrella of *An Anthology of Australasian Verse,* the contact between the two very different cultures—different in geographical character, in the nature of their society, in their religious composition (for an important cultural factor has been the much higher proportion of Nonconformists in New Zealand) and, indeed, in the extent of their emotional dependence upon Britain—was at bottom artificial. No native tradition of bush-ballads, folk-songs, or work-songs ever grew in New Zealand to match the sturdy Australian crop: those few New Zealand possesses are almost all variants of English or Australian ones. The local attempts to capture the vigor of Gordon, Kendall, or "Banjo" Paterson are literary imitations usually as remote from the originals as the New Zealand contemporary poetasters' lyrics are from those of Tennyson.

Fiction exploiting the exotic landscapes and the savage Maoris and the trials of pioneers for the delectation of a British audience and poetry concerned with "Nature," domestic sentiment and abstract ideals of the Noble, the Beautiful and Cosmic—these form the stuff of early "serious" writing. A concrete realization of the emotional consequences of a new way of life, and the awareness of a strenuous here and now, are among the things missing from the poetry of the nineteenth century.

At the same time, certain characteristics which New Zealanders have come to recognize as part of their national make-up do show themselves in the writing of the early years. New Zealand mores incorporate a substantial inheritance of Nonconformist and puritan attitudes, embodied, for instance, in the country's obsolescent liquor and licensing laws, its guilt-feelings about gambling, its tendency to regard the making of money as a sign of grace, its regard for the value of work for its own sake, its narrow concept of "respectability," its drab Sabbatarianism, and its disapproval of extroverted pleasures. It is true that, in many ways, private practice conflicts with public and official morality; yet the fossilized puritan concepts still dominate official life, especially at the local administrative level, and color much national legislation. The most monolithic school system in the world outside of Soviet Russia, and the barest tolerance of private schools, tend to perpetuate nineteenth-century values. In many ways, New Zealand thinking remains Victorian, as much in the outmoded rationalism surviving in small pockets as in the reluctant allowance of Sunday films.

New Zealand life shows a curious duality—legacies from the pioneering period in the booze party, the segregation of the sexes on social occasions, the addiction to race-horse betting and the passion for Rugby football, the prizing of the practical man and the suspicion of the artist and the intellectual, existing side by side with a puritan disapproval of many of these things. At times, of course, there is concord on certain matters, perhaps most notably in the conviction, possibly less unquestioned today than it was in earlier times, that New Zealand is "God's Own Country," that it has "the highest standard of living in the world," that it "leads the world" in progressive legislation, and that a New Zealander, weight for weight, is *ipso facto* more self-reliant and possesses more initiative than the "Pommy" (Englishman) or the "Yank." For the New Zealander, a "high standard of living" has nothing to do with a gracious way of life or intellectual or artistic accomplishments, but means the possession of a certain minimum quantity of consumer goods.

Yet, if a narrow philistinism and a tendency to measure New Zealand's standing in the world by the success or failure of touring Rugby teams still persist, there have been certain gains arising from the New Zealander's rooted distaste for privilege. As a contemporary historian, Professor Keith Sinclair, puts it: New Zealand "must be more nearly classless than any other society in the world. Some people are richer than others, but wealth carries no great prestige and no prerogative of leadership. . . . New Zealand 'Society' is a middle-class clique in what is, in European terms, a middle-class community—is an anaemic relic of English gentility and an outlet for harmless snobbery." This egalitarian instinct showed itself very early in New Zealand writing. Even though the proclamation of a freer and more independent life in the colony sometimes seems like whistling in the dark, the better poets and novelists on occasion proclaim values that have become central to the New Zealand philosophy—whether it be the celebration of the equality of all men by John Barr, the example of success-through-hard-work in Bathgate's novels, the dry understated Kiwi humor of F. E. Maning, or the visionary political Utopianism of Julius Vogel's novel, *Anno Domini 2000*. But the presence of these elements does not in itself constitute an indigenous literature, especially since the writers themselves were still embedded in the older tradition, and wrote not for a native audience, but for a distant one.

When we seek for the signs of change, then, the watershed that separates the writing of exiles from that of New Zealanders, in which, to quote the poet James K. Baxter, writers write "from the point of view of one who has grown up in entire acceptance of his environment, truly inhabiting the country," there is room for a difference of opinion. For our most distinguished literary historian, Dr. E. H. McCormick, the 1890's was the period of significant change, although he regards it as in some ways a false dawn. This was the first age of native-born writers. "The literature of the nineties," writes Dr. McCormick, "like its legislation, is marked by a spirit of independence, owing something to the Australian national movement, but more often of local origin." But, he adds, "In all the writings of this generation, with the exception of Reeves's prose, there are signs of prematurity, as of people urgently striving to say something but without adequate means of self-expression." On the other hand, Allen Curnow, a prominent poet, finds in the poetry of the 1890's only "a strident falsity," and believes that "in the first decade of the present century, it is still the fresh impact of the country on an English-bred sensibility that produces the better verse."

Whatever the achievement of the writers of this period, few would dispute the suggestion that the really meaningful transformation can be dated from the 1920's, with the best work of Katherine Mansfield and the early poetry of R. A. K. Mason and A. R. D. Fairburn. Here is the first body of work which was a part of New Zealand as nothing earlier had been. These writers, whether they remained in the country or followed Katherine Mansfield to Europe, had, as she herself said, New Zealand in their very bones. Third- and fourth-generation New Zealanders, they were not yet completely free from inherited conflicts or the pull of Europe. Yet they were facing directly for the first time the challenge of their own society and environment, and they saw the writer's task, as, in Fairburn's words, that of being "willing to partake, internally as well as externally, of the anarchy of life in a new place and, by creative energy, give that life form and consciousness." The world they aimed to re-create in their writings was no longer the world of English literature. Their utterances were personal ones; the values they expressed were those of the society in which they lived, values they, in fact, helped to shape. Yet the 1920's was not ready for this kind of statement. The first poems of Mason and Fairburn passed virtually unnoticed; Mason threw the 200 unsold copies of his initial volume, *The Beggar* (1924), into the Waitemata Harbour.

It was not until the 1930's, under the impetus of a new mood generated largely by the Depression, that Mason, Fairburn, and one or two others began to find acceptance and were joined by authors of a similar kind. In a sense, the Depression was a catalyst, in that it brought together poets and audience; it also jolted men into a sharpened awareness of immediate realities and made them realize that, in their lives and circumstances, not in received literary stereotypes, lay the stuff out of which literature is made. During the Depression years, New Zealand writers found their proper subjects, and themselves as well.

The Depression did not create this sensibility; already in the 1920's, perhaps more faintly even earlier, fresh themes had been enunciated. And, of course, the talent had to be there before memorable work could be produced. Yet unquestionably the economic crisis deepened and canalized writers' concerns. Where there had been before scattered, isolated achievements, there was now a substantial and coherent corpus of work, distinctive and individual, which could properly be called a literature. There was also an audience for it, an audience at first by no means large, but increasing as readers found in the writing of their fellow-countrymen not only their own thoughts and feelings given significant shape, but intimations of further growth. During the past thirty years, this body of writing has undergone many transformations; it has had its periods of advance and retreat, its triumphs and its failures. But throughout the past decades, and especially since the end of World War II, it has continued to grow in scope and diversity. The great expansion of New Zealand publishing, the raising of standards of book production under the inspiration of the Caxton Press, Christchurch, and various presses in Auckland, the success of New Zealand writers in the United States and Great Britain, the assistance of the State Literary Fund, the development of literary criticism, the gradual acceptance by an ever wider public of their own writers, the high level of general literacy—these are some of the factors that have aided the growth of a flourishing contemporary New Zealand literature. But, above all, the surprising disclosure of talent among writers, and the willingness of really gifted ones to use their skill to reflect the New Zealand scene and interpret the New Zealander to himself are the chief reasons for the currently healthy state of writing in the country.

2

POETRY

THE POETRY of the first sixty years or so makes depressing reading. Surprisingly large in bulk, its drab Victorian landscape is diversified only occasionally by small outcroppings of individuality. Although outlets for verse were initially limited largely to periodicals, much was written. Newspapers provided space for large quantities of topical verse and sentimental doggerel; small volumes were hopefully issued, as were folders and sheets of verse. Once the labors of breaking-in were ended, a real thirst for poeticizing seemed to prevail. But most of the result is intolerably dull; the critical pan held patiently in the turbid waters of newspaper verse yields not the smallest nugget.

If one early strain of verse was a journalistic one, the other was more ambitious, nothing less than an attempt to supply a literature where none existed, a literature fabricated, of necessity, on English models. Some poets were vaguely aware of the tensions of life in the new society, but they had no way of turning these tensions into poetry. Perhaps those who came closest to catching the spirit of the pioneering period were the entertainer-poets who recited topical verse at a public ceremony or at "socials" rather than those who donned bardic robes and solemnly invoked the Muse of Poetry. Though these early pieces were often vigorous and witty and strongly imbued with a sense of community, their topicality and out-dated colloquialisms have dragged them down to oblivion. Just now and then an odd specimen turns up which can still give pleasure. Most of the verse of this type was written by Scottish settlers, such as William Golder (1810–76), an immensely prolific writer, who struck off some energetic ballads, and in *The Pigeons' Parliament* (1854) produced a lively, if crude, satire on colonial life, and John Barr of Craigielea (1809–89). Barr's *Poems and Songs*, published in Edinburgh in 1861, reveals a tidier and more artistic writer who made forceful use of the Scottish idiom to portray life in the Scottish settlement of Otago, to celebrate New Zealand freedom as contrasted with the restraints of "Home," and to satirize the grasping selfishness of money-grubbing colonists.

These poets were at least concerned with the essential matter of New Zealand living; those who turned to "serious" themes were dominated not only by a stilted poetic diction of a pseudo-Romantic kind, but also by the idea that poetry must be elevating, consoling, awesome, or wrapped around "poetic" subjects. For instance, Sir Charles Christopher Bowen (1830–1917), a very able public man, wrote ambitious, hollow poems on classical themes and Sir Frederick Napier Broome (1842–96), another lively intelligence, found his models, rarely happily, in Swinburne and others of a similar kind. The most ambitious of these poets was Alfred Domett, who became Prime Minister in 1863. Domett, Browning's friend "Waring," spent thirty years in New Zealand, and made numerous contributions to the country's life and culture. But his *Ranolf and Amohia* (1872), an "epic" of Anglo-Maori life, hardly ranks as one of them. A diffuse, highly Romantic work, embarrassingly inflated, and told in a dead diction, it lumbers along in stolid prolixity, trying to shape a poetic New Zealand far removed from the realities of struggling settlements. There are some good things in it, however, notably some of the descriptive passages, and the verbiage does not quite bury the inner yearning for a cultural milieu that can provide some substance for the mind.

Nevertheless, the most characteristic and popular poet of the age was no classical imitator, but Thomas Bracken (1843–98), Irish immigrant, journalist, Member of Parliament, tireless drinker, and kindly Bohemian. There were three different versifiers in Bracken—the snook-cocking writer of topical doggerel and political comment as "Paddy Murphy," the pompous Bard sprinkling the earth with clichés and loftily addressing the heavens with "Hail!" and "Behold!," and the popular rhymster with something of Hood's and Longfellow's ability to poeticize the commonplace and tellingly express homely sentiment. His most ambitious book, *Musings in Maoriland* (1890), sumptuously printed in Leipzig, with a preface by Sir George Grey, the Governor-General, and dedicated to Tennyson, embalms between its ornate covers verse typical of the uninspired mechanical outpourings of the time. In an occasional piece like "The March of Te Rauparaha" Bracken catches some of the vigor of the better Victorian poetry of statement. In "Not Understood," perhaps the most popular poem ever written in the country, he expressed concepts dear to the heart of many humble folk:

> Not understood! We move along asunder,
> Our paths grow wider as the seasons creep
> Along the years; we marvel and we wonder
> Why life is life: and then we fall asleep,
> Not understood.

And in "God Defend New Zealand," he wrote New Zealand's national song. Yet, although his work had a tremendous popularity in the 1880's, none of his books survives in print, and his first editions line specialist library shelves like tombstones.

In the 1890's, as has been suggested, some signs of change were manifest. By this time, the country had moved out of the period of colonizing and gold-rushes. It was attaining something like a balanced economy; the population had grown and with it urban life; and a liberal-minded government was introducing progressive, humanitarian legislation. The second and third generations of native-born New Zealanders began to produce writers formed in the new society, and it seemed as if the time were ripe for a rejection of the exile mentality and for a manifestation of a truly indigenous consciousness and tone in literature, which earlier writers had tried to produce by forced cultivation. Unhappily, the expectation proved premature: for one thing, there was not as yet a wide enough audience for serious poetry; for another, there was no cultural continuity inside the land itself. The South Island, once so productive and vigorous, was left behind in virtual stagnation by the growing economic dominance of the more heavily populated North Island, and fresh beginnings had to be made.

The leading figure at the turn of the century was William Pember Reeves (1857–1932), a New Zealand-born lawyer, statesman, historian, and, as a parliamentarian, shaper of some of the country's experimental legislation. His poetry, though cultivated and dignified, deals fairly heavily in conventional phrases and imagery. Perhaps his most successful poem is "A Colonist in his Garden," written after, finding his colleagues too conservative-minded for him, he left New Zealand for ever in 1896. Here the intimations of new emphases and a more truly indigenous spirit is seen in his dramatizing of the cultural split felt by many of his contemporaries as a debate between his New Zealand self and his English self. For the latter, the country consists of

> Isles nigh as empty as their deep
> Where men but talk of gold and sheep
> And think of sheep and gold.

But the former retorts:

"No art?" Who serve an art more great
Than we, rough architects of State
  With the old Earth at strife?
"No colour?" On the silent waste,
In pigments not to be effaced,
  We paint the hues of life.

Yet, despite one or two happy accomplishments, Reeves's verse is more interesting for its enunciation of themes important to the New Zealand poet than it is for its own sake.

Similarly with Jessie Mackay (1864–1938), the other important versifier of the 1890's. She is typical of her age in her febrile humanitarianism and her energetic supporting of a wide variety of causes—women's rights and prohibition among them. Her poetry also ranged widely, taking themes from the past of her Scottish ancestors, Celtic and Scandinavian legends, classical history, and all types of people who had sacrificed their life for a cause. Her temper is idealistic, and her tone often hectic and hysterical; quite often, too, her selection of parallels to legislative and cultural changes in New Zealand is grotesque and humorlessly inapt. One trouble was that there was not, as yet, enough national consciousness to give authority to such an attitude; another was that Miss Mackay was deficient in poetic sensitivity and seemed unaware of the banality of much of her diction and metrical form. But her fervent trust in the future and the emotional sincerity of her feeling for the oppressed struck a responsive chord in her generation.

Another popular poet of the same period was David McKee Wright (1867–1928), who won a large working-class audience with his jingling ballads of the life of the tramps, shearers, and itinerant workers, his glorification of the vagabond life of the open air, and his Bret Harte-ish sentimentality. Wright imitated the Australian balladeers, but beside their vigorous, if rough, verses, his own too often seem manufactured.

The promise, if promise it was, of the nineties did not find fulfilment in the two following decades. During those years New Zealand verse stubbornly maintained its provinciality. It is true that in the years that straddle the centuries several distinguished historians and sociologists found their feet, and laid the path for more polished successors. But poetry and fiction failed to develop, principally because the writers were unaware that social and scientific changes were sweeping away things they accepted as permanent, and because there was still no established society to write for nor a literary tradition from which they could draw strength.

In fact, instead of a confident assertion of national and literary independence, the opening years of this century saw instead an intensification of the sense of loyalty to Great Britain, partly because of the close association of New Zealand with Britain in the Boer War and World War I, partly because so many gifted writers, finding the still amorphous society and narrow conventions uncongenial, elected to seek more stability, intellectual stimulus, and larger audiences in Europe. A large number of New Zealanders prided themselves on being "more English than the English"; a nostalgic conception of "Home" derived from books and from the recollections of parents meant that the standards and manners of the Old World continued to predominate in poetry. It was inevitable, then, that the New Zealand idiom should have been considered *ipso facto* non-poetic in the poetry of 1900 to 1920. So, too, with images drawn from the local scene, which were self-conscious or decorative rather than an integral part of the poet's imagination. Writers did not so much make poems as "contribute to a literature." Living in an artificial poetic world unrelated to their experience as men and women, they produced shapely, pleasant, empty lyrics, evanescent sonnets, fragile odes.

Yet, although most suffered from the handicap of practices derived from the English Georgians, without the Georgians' awareness of a new direction, one or two managed to point the way to the future. Blanche E. Baughan (1870–1958), for instance, in *Reuben* (1903) and *Shingle Short* (1908) fashioned a formalized style from the New Zealand idiom, which, although still in part manifestly "literary," enabled her to reflect something of the special character of local life. Arnold Wall (1869–1963), university professor, essayist, and prolific poet, achieved a gnomic and often witty expression, technically skilful, Edwardian in tone and English in sentiment, yet pervaded with an awareness of his adopted country that sustains images such as that he uses in respect of Christchurch, the city he has made his home:

> Each of her streets is closed with shining Alps,
> Like Heaven at the end of long plain lives.

Both Blanche Baughan and Arnold Wall were born in England: their better poems record the response of a newcomer to the land. Other poets of this time, born in New Zealand, were attached by still stronger cords to Great Britain. Alan Mulgan (1881–1962), the son of Northern Irish settlers, typifies in his poetry the virtues and weaknesses of writers of his generation. He carried tastes and attitudes formed before World War I into work written in the 1940's and 1950's—a classic case of the overlapping of styles that fortunately defeats neat literary-historical classifications. His generous sympathies allowed him, as a newspaper editor, to give practical encouragement to young talented writers with whose type of utterance he had little temperamental sympathy. Torn between "Home" (the title of one of his books dealing with a journey to Britain) as a cultural norm and a deep love for his native land, he tried to express his response to New Zealand in the forms of traditional English verse. *Golden Wedding* (1932), a long narrative poem in rhymed couplets, reminiscent of Goldsmith and Crabbe, combines, in a genteel, decorous way, kindly portraits, mild satire, and a sense of place and history. It is amiable verse, based upon love of rural New Zealand and sympathy for its "characters." But technically the poem is often feeble, and its language rarely rises above the commonplace. Yet there was much in Mulgan's verse that suggests that, in different circumstances, he might have been a considerable poet. *Aldebaran* (1937), for instance, with its vigorous forms and unexpected penetration, has an individuality and power that seldom show elsewhere in his work.

Eileen Duggan (b. 1900), more clearly a born poet, carries the Georgian manner to perfection in New Zealand poetry, and moves beyond it. Her lyrics have a purity and a refinement rare in local verse. Sensitive rather than strong, and at times barely avoiding sentimentality, her work nevertheless shows the result of a stern self-discipline; a sincere love of the land and a devout Catholic faith charge her poetry with deep feeling. Her verse rests upon a spiritual certainty which possibly robs it of fruitful tensions, but leaves her free to work at an art that refines her experiences to precise utterance. In her early poems a reaction against modern life and a cultivated literary sensibility show themselves in an occasional unassimilated bookish word of a conceit, and several of her poems contain successful lines rather than establish themselves as successful wholes. She shares not at all in the poetic fashions of our times, but has gone on quietly developing her own kind of statement, from her first book, *Poems* (1921), to her fifth, *More Poems* (1951), moving from her earlier lyricism to a metaphysical manner, tauter, less prone to conventional feeling, wise, and compassionate. This remarkable maturing in manner has been accompanied by a move away from the subjects of her earlier work—childhood memories, New Zealand history, Marian religious themes, and so on, to broader topics—the nature of human suffering, God's impact on history, the effects of war, for instance. In her first religious verse she was often content with analogies; in the later, a more mature vision informs the verse with a powerful sense of God's immanence, of that sacrifice that yields wisdom, of the agony of all men. Miss Duggan has been largely ignored by recent critics, with the honorable exception of Dr. E. H. McCormick; her aloofness from internecine critical warfare and from vogues has led her to be classified as belonging to a past period. Yet to others it is clear that, while several recent versifiers have been merely making gestures in the direction of poetry, she has never been anything less than a poet, and her very lapses are those of a poet.

Miss Duggan's achievement is an individual one, although it is quite likely that her work has influenced some younger poets, especially in Wellington, her home town. But it was in the 1920's that the first signs appeared in another city, Auckland, of a distinctive body of indigenous New Zealand verse. The significant date may be taken as 1924, with the publication of R. A. K. Mason's first, still-born volume, *The Beggar,* although the group in which Mason (b. 1905) is an important figure did not develop until the 1930's. Earlier poets had, in the main, been concerned with singing the relationship between the New Zealander and his environment or the nation. In Mason's first work, immature and uneven though it was, there sounded a decisively personal note, the voice of a man determined to make his own private sense out of experience. Here was a proclamation that poetry is a personal concern; here, too, was the presentation of poetry as an art, shaped and ordered by a craftsman.

Mason grew to full stature as a poet in the 1930's, in Depression days. Marxist by conviction, he wrote his poems not, however, about political matters or conditions in society, but out of his own sensibility as it reacted to the condition of his age. Allen Curnow says, "Mason is dramatising, not himself, but a predicament of the human spirit," and calls his poems "rituals of participation." Mason made himself the most notable poet of his generation. He began writing in his teens and had written himself out by his thirties. His first poems, among which are several of his best, show plainly the style, themes, and syntactical characteristics of his subsequent ones. In *No New Thing* (1934) and *This Dark Will Lighten* (1941), the poems exhibit, in their spare language and taut rhythms, the assimilation of the influence of Latin poets, and of Housman and Beddoes, and in their somberness, skepticism, blended pity and anger, and emphasis on human suffering, something of the Georgian reaction from socially directed nineteenth-century poetry. The product of a conscious art, or, as has been suggested by Dr. C. K. Stead, of a spontaneous expression of feeling not always fully understood by the mind that brought it forth, Mason's poetry deals not with New Zealand or New Zealanders, but with what it means to be a man. The voice which speaks of the problems of sex, personal identity, time, and man's pain, is often a harsh one, but, as he says:

> If the drink that satisfied
> the son of Mary when he died
> has not the right smack for you
> leave it for a kindlier brew.
>
> For my bitter verses are
> sponges steeped in vinegar
> useless to the happy-eyed
> but handy for the crucified.

Mason's diction mixes slightly old-fashioned language with direct colloquialisms and classical references with modern realistic detail, usually successfully. His refusal to be discursive provided a salutary example to his contemporaries; and his idiosyncratic vision inspired confidence that true poetry could be made in the country. Since the later 1930's Mason has abandoned lyrics; the little verse he has since produced is inferior work.

A more extroverted poet, A. R. D. Fairburn (1904–57) was also an Auckland writer. *He Shall Not Rise* (1930) revealed a Romantic lyricist, full of nostalgia for the past, of delight in Nature and of a sense of loss and regret; it also showed a firm command of lucid, responsible English. Taken as a whole, however, the volume recorded a rejection of Romantic preoccupations. Elsewhere Fairburn proclaimed his conviction that New Zealand writers must repudiate cultural dependence on Great Britain, and that the local poet must forsake the emotional security of such reliance to immerse himself in the chaos of New Zealand life, and help by his work to impose a new order on it. *Dominion* (1938) is a series of brief poems depicting his reaction to the circumstances of Depression days. More completely than any other New Zealand poet, Fairburn expresses here the whole mass of spiritual and social discontent and the hope for a renewal and rebirth the thirties called forth. The decaying institutions of the land, its shoddy community values and its insensitivity to beauty, are defined in brilliant rhetoric:

> and the night sky, closing over, covers like a hand
> the barbaric yawn of a young and wrinkled land.

It is to the healing forces of Nature that the poet turns for assurance or renewal:

> Fair earth, we have broken our idols:
> and after the days of fire we shall come to you
> for the stones of a new temple.

Other poems by Fairburn record a lyrical response to life and love. He affirms a humanist trust in man's pure fundamental instincts and especially in his capacity for love. No other New Zealand poet has written so much, or so variously, of love, from the wild passion of youthful sexual love to the calm placidity of later married affection. The often explicitly passionate lyrics are underpinned by his constant symbols of beach, sea, tree, cliff—aspects of the New Zealand scenes he loved. Much of his poetry, too, deals with death, the great enemy of love; for all Fairburn's repudiation of the traditional manner of the Romantics, he remained a Romantic to the end, singing of death with mingled fascination and terror, and more than half in love with it. His vitality, his gift for sensuous imagery, his tender response to natural beauty, his humaneness, his virile common sense, as well as his delight in verbal fireworks, link him with the Romantics, too. Another side of Fairburn was his irrepressible talent for light verse, half-mocking, half-serious, and for sharp-edged satirical slashes directed at the publicans and the pharisees.

Fairburn was a deeply patriotic man, often disguising his love for his country under a mocking gibe. "This is my country," he wrote, "and I am very glad to belong to it—in spite of everything. I also claim the right to talk about it—and to talk about it with the bluntness one uses in a family discussion. Flattery can be left to the visitors." In "To a Friend in the Wilderness," a long poem written shortly before his death, and notable for a more pared and direct form than was usual with him, he reaffirmed his faith in man from a more poised and less doctrinaire point of view and meditated movingly on the human dilemma. This poetic statement crowned a restless, active life, in which one consistent strain was a hatred of cant in all its forms.

Walter D'Arcy Cresswell (1896–1960) deserves mention at this point, since his attitudes had something in common with those of Fairburn concerning the deficiencies of life in this "brief miscreant of midnight and bad dreams, / Thou I miscall'd my Country." Isolated first by temperament and later by self-imposed exile from his New Zealand contemporaries, Cresswell never attained the poise, urbanity, or wisdom of Fairburn. Adopting the older Romantic notion of the poet as legislator, Cresswell wrote in a style combining archaisms, rhetoric, and local details. At odds with modern technology, business, and science, he affirmed the healing power of Nature, the primacy of the emotions, the superior wisdom of the poet, and the beauty of homosexual love. Deliberately rejecting current poetic styles, he did his best work in a sequence of sonnets, *Lyttleton Harbour* (1936), in which the anger and the wit almost redeem the shop-soiled diction. But little of his verse has worn well—his later poetry is repetitive and hollow—and he is likely to be remembered chiefly for his prose autobiographies, *A Poet's Progress* (1930) and *Present Without Leave* (1939).

Two women, of very different temperaments, contributed to the new assurance of verse in the 1930's. Mary Ursula Bethell (1874–1945) did not publish poetry until she was in her middle fifties. *From a Garden in the Antipodes* (1929) contains witty, cultivated verse, largely domestic in subject and feeling. But in *Time and Place* (1936) and *Day and Night* (1939) the mood deepens, as she embarks on an attempt to convey the essence of her Canterbury landscape in terms of time and eternity. A deeply religious Anglican, sensitive, highly intelligent, and learned, Miss Bethell worked hard at poetry, avoiding Romantic simplicities, and trying to mould her verses in harmony with her themes. Her ear was not always sure, her mind sometimes outstripped her feelings, and the chisel-marks show on her lines. But she had no peer in such tranquil meditativeness as is shown in "The Long Harbour," in which a vivid impression of the New Zealand scene is transformed through contact with traditions remembered by the poet:

> From far, palm-feathery, ocean-spattered islands
> there rowed hither dark and daring voyagers.

She is, too, capable of a magical power of incantation and of a mystical exaltation like that of the seventeenth-century metaphysical poets.

The poetry of "Robin Hyde" (Iris Wilkinson, 1906–39), gifted novelist and journalist, suffers considerably from the habits of slickness and casualness she picked up from journalism. Her early volumes, *The Conquerors* (1935) and *Persephone in Winter* (1937), contain much Romantic posturing, self-conscious use of classical allusions, and mistaking of the poetic will for the deed, although her religious verses indicate the presence of strong personal anxieties. But in *Houses by the Sea*, published posthumously in 1952, she attained a new depth and seriousness. In these poems, Robin Hyde, like Katherine Mansfield before her, turned in her final years to recall, with insight and tenderness, her childhood in Wellington. Free now from literary affectations and strained rhetoric, these poems use lyric and descriptive styles to re-create the sense of a time and a place, people, the joys and fears of childhood, the simple pleasures of sensation and learning; the details are delicately placed, and the whole book is beautifully evocative of the emotions both of girlhood and of the adolescent on the threshold of womanhood.

More deeply immersed in his time, Denis Glover (b. 1912) began in the 1930's as a literary associate of Mason, Fairburn, and Curnow. A champion university boxer and a gallant sailor awarded the Distinguished Service Cross for his part in the Normandy invasion, Glover has to some extent fostered a public image of a roystering, irreverent, clowning, hard-drinking, practical "Kiwi"; from this character come leg-pulling radio talks, the highly-colored reminiscences, *Hot Water Sailor* (1962), lampoons, epigrams, and outrageous burlesques. But this is the Glover mask; perhaps a New Zealand strategy to divert too much attention from his other personality, the excellent printer and typographer whose work at the Caxton Press, Christchurch (which he founded in the 1930's), did so much to raise the standard of local book-production, the democrat, the sensitive appreciator of Nature, the compassionate singer of misfits, dead-beats, and solitary ones. In the pre-war years, his verse tended to reflect fashionable Leftist concepts of the good life. Although this strain of doctrinaire optimism has gone, he has retained his ability to identify himself with the "ordinary bloke" as no other New Zealand poet has done.

The poems in *The Wind and the Sand* (1945) display irony, pity, tenderness, skepticism, and, at the same time, a sense of those basic human qualities that unite all men. His best work, however, is found in the two collections, *Sings Harry* (1951) and *Arawata Bill* (1953). In both the style is compact, bare, colloquial, the rhythms conversational. Harry, the singer, is a man alone, a philosopher-tramp wryly commenting on man and finding his solace in Nature. Like Arawata Bill, the gold-prospector of the other sequence, Harry embodies one of the country's most durable myths—the solitary eccentric, the man who finds the open spaces more congenial than cities. When Bill dies, the poet writes:

> R.I.P. where no gold lies
> But in your own questing soul
> Rich in faith and a wild surmise.
>
> You should have been told
> Only in you was the gold:
> Mountain and river paid you no fee,
> Mountain melting to the river,
> River to the sea.

Glover's work is rich in a clear-eyed compassion and in a special feeling for New Zealand places: his crisp re-seeing of familiar scenes strikes responsive chords in his readers; the apparent simplicity of his forms is the product of deep feeling skilfully controlled.

Another member of the group who began publishing in the 1930's is Charles Brasch (b. 1909). Brasch spent some years abroad, but returned home to found in 1947 the country's best literary periodical, *Landfall.* In his books of verse published since 1939, he has revealed a talent perhaps less robust than that of his contemporaries, fastidious and sensitive rather than hard-ribbed. His poems early indicated a kind of love-hate relationship to his native land; on the one hand regretting the absence in New Zealand of a sophisticated culture and much aesthetic sensibility, on the other hand enamoured of its scenery and its Polynesian history. One of his themes is the disparity between the land and those who inhabit it, and the absence of a history:

> The plains are nameless and the cities cry for meaning,
> The unproved heart still seeks a vein of speech
> Beside the sprawling rivers, in the stunted township,
> By the pine windbreak where the hot wind bleeds.

He contrasts this condition with the settled culture of older lands where the landscape is tamed, and scene and man are in harmony. He sees sea and land in New Zealand as symbols of isolation and division. In *The Estate* (1957) which, like his earlier work, is marked by a preference for abstract words and quiet understatements, the point of view is less ambivalent, as if the poet has found his own point of resolution and sees it relevant to the community at large. While still preoccupied with the notion of human separateness, he has discovered areas of repose in friendship and art, and, more tranquilly, envisages place and people coming together in harmony.

The most noteworthy figure to emerge from the 1930's is Allen Curnow (b. 1911), who, most of all, has grown in reputation and stature over the years. As a poet of technical resource, variety, intellectual curiosity, and subtlety, he has no contemporary rival; as a critic, he has established one of the orthodoxies of New Zealand poetic analysis; as a writer of light verse, he is an acute critic of his country's mores; as a playwright, he is a tireless experimenter. Some of his first verses were satirical, in the manner of Glover and Fairburn; in these he castigated suburban squalor, petty-mindedness, and "the chemical farmers." But this mood has been retained, with greater urbanity, only in his overtly light verse. More important is his early search for a coherent poetic myth of island and time to make some sort of sense of the New

Zealand fact, in volumes significantly entitled *Not in Narrow Seas* (1939), *Island and Time* (1941), and *Sailing or Drowning* (1943), wherein he considers, among other things,

> a land of settlers
> With never a soul at home.

In these books he plumbs New Zealand history, Pacific exploration, and the march of Empire for subjects, writing, not with the facile patriotism and easy certainties of the nineteenth century, about the paradoxes of the long sea voyage, the hostility of the land, the settlement of the country, and the character of the society established here. These are not historical or descriptive poems, but ones in which mutability, national destiny and character, the nature of time and place, are all re-seen in an almost metaphysical way as an attempt on the part of a New Zealander to fashion a lasting image out of his own experience of his land's history and landscape, finding it "something different, something Nobody counted on." In poems like "House and Land," "The Unhistoric Story," and "Country School," he abstracts an element from his environment and moves through it to a meditation on time and history. One of his persistent themes is the relationship between man and his physical environment; Curnow feels that each interacts with the other, that the land, far from being passive, is an active shaping agent. And as man despoils or abuses the land, it in turn despoils him.

One of his finest poems, "Landfall in Unknown Seas," written in 1942 to celebrate the 300th anniversary of Tasman's discovery of New Zealand, transcends its occasion to examine the New Zealander's spiritual landscape and ponder

> Who navigates us towards what unknown
> But not improbable provinces?

This work and his verse play, *The Axe* (1949), look forward to his more recent poems in *A Small Room with Large Windows* (1961) and elsewhere, in which the preoccupations become more personal, the verse more allusive and gnomic, and the tone wiser, perhaps sadder (although a very high proportion of his verse is pervaded with a melancholy which, indeed, informs a considerable amount of New Zealand poetry), and the themes are often self-understanding, the nature of poetic experience and of art, and the problems of being and becoming. Both Curnow's early and later poetry is at times difficult and obscure; yet his work is always beautifully shaped, rich in intellectual power, and governed by what is possibly the keenest artistic sensibility possessed by any living New Zealand poet. His work has been influenced, first, by his older contemporaries, and later by such American poets as Wallace Stevens, but he is able to assimilate such influences into what is an unmistakable personal manner.

Curnow's practice, and his manifestoes in his prefaces to his two anthologies and elsewhere have, in conjunction with the critical writings of M. H. Holcroft, stressed the nature of New Zealand as a remote island, the animistic implications of the landscape, the importance of the memories of voyagers and explorers, the notion of "sundering seas." "No other people in the world is so surrounded by ocean immensities," he writes; and in another place, "The true poet is more apt to feel underprivileged in his geographical isolation. He is subject to the pressures of an English, a European tradition, which the ocean distances transmit, as they do radio signals, more forcibly than land masses would." It was inevitable that a younger generation of poets should, in some degree, react against this. The reaction came in the 1950's, most articulately from a Wellington poet, Louis Johnson (b. 1925), who in his verse and his criticism has sought to present the concept that New Zealand poetry should treat, not of the problems of being a New Zealander, but of those things that are every man's concern. As editor of the *New Zealand Poetry Year-Book*, which he founded in 1951, Johnson did a good deal to aid and to exhibit this shift of emphasis. His own early poems in *The Sun Among the Ruins* and *Roughshod Among the Lilies* (both 1951) are powerful and rather undisciplined expressions of personal anguish, sexual torment, the loss of innocence, and domestic tensions. He has, however, matured into a poet of mordant satire (*Poems Unpleasant*, 1952) and a poet of urban life (*New Worlds for Old*, 1957). The sexual motif is still present, but controlled and part of a mature vision of the realities of life. As a poet of the responses of men and women to modern everyday living, he has helped to draw the attention of other New Zealand poets to such subject-matter and away from the Nature themes; his poems of love and marriage and parenthood are probably his most successful. He sympathizes with the oppressed and suffering—the aged, the young, the housewife-drudge, and he distrusts the bureaucrats and business-men "with prominent, aggressive eyes," the well-to-do, the social climbers. But he is more than a social commentator and satirist; a rough anger and distaste for New Zealanders' obsession with material possessions and status inform his verse with a vibrant, passionate unrest. His technique lacks subtlety, his syntax is sometimes clumsy, and a certain lack of self-criticism allows him to publish inferior work, but the very absence of the polish found in, say, Curnow imparts a kind of dogged power.

> Oh the heart stood still as I came up out of the bog
> where I burned my bedbug selves by a rotten log,
> and wounded my hands in doing so that the heart
> must stare and weep for the scars of the secret hurt.

Johnson's voice is an individual one; his setting himself against the absorption of New Zealand poets in matters of technique and against the "Curnow-Holcroft" myth, as it has been called, and in favor of less manifestly indigenous poetic statements, has had significant influence on the direction of New Zealand verse.

James K. Baxter (b. 1926) stands aloof from both the Curnow and the Johnson points of view. His talent flowered early, in *Beyond the Palisade* (1944), and has developed steadily, undergoing unpredictable transformations on the way. To a formidable body of verse Baxter has added several plays and much criticism. Basically a lyrical poet, he is also something of a prophet and a rhetor. "We have greater need of prophets than we have of mechanics," he says. His powerful, if often tormented, moral sense issues, not as preaching, but as searing irony, savage satire, as in his "Ballad of Harry Fat," on capital punishment:

> O some will kill in rage and fear
> And some will kill in hate,
> And some will kill in foreign lands
> To serve the master State.
> Justice walks heavy through the land
> She bears a rope and shroud.
> "We will not change our policy,"
> Says Harry Fat the Proud.

or as a fierce concern with integrity, truth and goodness. Among his themes, perhaps the most frequent are those of the Fall, the loss of innocence seen as a personal and as a cosmic thing, the attempt of man to regain Eden, the contrast between the City of God and the City of Man, the demon of sex, the agonies of a world that has deviated from its real end.

As a young poet, Baxter showed the impress of other writers—Bunyan, Blake, and Burns among them; throughout his career, he has submitted to others—Dylan Thomas and Robert Lowell, for instance—yet always his imagery and his tone remain unmistakably his. His poetry often takes its point of origin from an aspect of local landscape, but only to pass from this to problems proper to the human condition. He has a rare gift for domesticating alien traditions, with greater success than, for instance, Jessie Mackay, as when, in "The Homecoming," he assimilates the return of a New Zealand soldier from Greece to the return of Odysseus. Baxter's unusual eloquence, his ability to strike out memorable images, his metaphysical sense, his realistically religious vision, his almost surrealistic angles of seeing, and his corrosive wit have been widely praised, while some have also seen in him a dangerous taste for the rhetorical gesture, a lack of precision, diffuseness, and an adolescent delight in shocking. As a center of controversy and a poetic chameleon, he remains one of the most complex, exciting, and unclassifiable of New Zealand poets. Not the least of his talents is one for burlesque and parody, which has embraced several of his contemporaries, for rollicking ballads and for impishly debunking humor.

Both Johnson and Baxter are Wellington poets, whose example and precepts have helped to make the capital a vital contemporary center of poetry. Some critics assert the existence of a "Wellington School," characterized by the cultivation of an "international style," by such subject-matter as suburban life and domestic occasions, by a refinement of New Zealand Romanticism; others, while acknowledging several common factors, deny the existence of a "School," and emphasize the differences between the Wellington poets. In fact, attempts to define specific regional characteristics in New Zealand poetry remain inconclusive.

Other notable Wellington poets include Alistair Campbell (b. 1925), Hubert Witheford (b. 1921), Pat Wilson (b. 1926), Ruth Gilbert (b. 1917), and W. H. Oliver (b. 1925). Campbell's *Mine Eyes Dazzle* (1950 and several revised editions) showed a forceful rhetoric, strongly controlled rhythms, and a sharply real experience of beauty and compassion. Campbell's lyrical and elegiac tones blend in a delicate, yet firm, celebration of place. But he has had little to say since his first book. Hubert Witheford in successive volumes also shows little development of a rather rarified sensibility. For almost all his work he draws heavily upon Asiatic and Steiner-ish philosophies in a consideration of flux, emptiness, and the material world, blending in his utterance ritual and esoteric philosophizing. Pat Wilson's *The Bright Sea* (1951) contains calm, symbolic poetry, adept in rhythm, often moving from abstract ideas to a vivid concreteness. Ruth Gilbert in *Lazarus* (1949), *The Sunlit Hour* (1955), and *The Luthier* (1968) makes delicate, rather fragile poetry out of domestic happenings, writing most movingly, perhaps, on religion and motherhood. W. H. Oliver, a scholar-poet, has a tough mind, a dry wit, a sense of history, and a tightly-reined sensibility that allow him to explore the inner heart of his land in taut, unemphatic verse in *Fire Without Phoenix* (1957).

Charles Doyle (b. 1928), an Irishman who grew up in New Zealand, published first in Wellington, later in Auckland. *A Splinter of Glass* (1956) is somewhat imitative poetry in the modern anonymous, cryptic manner, although now and then it shows a real eloquence and a keen sense of rhythm. Doyle has matured considerably as a poet. *Distances* (1963) and later books, in which his style is more direct and personal and his themes more various, repress the poetic gesture and the self-heightening in favor of humble submission to experience. Doyle acknowledges the influence on his work of such young Americans as W. D. Snodgrass, Galway Kinnell, and James Wright.

Of recent years, Christchurch, once (in the days of the Caxton Press) the center of poetic production, has lost its precedence. One older poet for whom the city is "my holy land of childhood" is Basil Dowling (b. 1910). His first poems, in *A Day's Journey* (1941) and *Signs and Wonders* (1944), were in the Georgian tradition, often overly sentimental and formal. But *Canterbury* (1949) reveals a more sanguine spirit, a skilful use of speech rhythm, and a frank confronting of moral and religious experience. Dowling's verse is lit with an awareness of the physical features of the South Island; its great rivers, mountains, and plains (and few people) press more heavily upon the consciousness of the South Islander than does the environment of the North Island upon its inhabitants. Other poets associated with Christchurch are Charles Spear (b. 1910), William Hart-Smith (b. 1911), "Paul Henderson" (b. 1913), and J. R. Hervey (1889–1958). Charles Spear's single book, *Twopence Coloured* (1951), has fewer obvious connections with the local scene than any work since Mason's. Taking his subjects from European history, personal experiences overseas, foreign literature, Continental scenery, he writes elusively, preciously at times, with a faint smell of the British 1890's, subtly exploiting symbolism in the interest of wise acceptance and stoical resignation, and an adult vision of pain, sacrifice, and mutability. His exquisitely shaped little poems are things self-sufficiently made, standing absolutely like Chinese vases. William Hart-Smith, who has divided his literary life between Australia and New Zealand, produced in *Christopher Columbus* (1948) an interesting, if only intermittently successful, sequence of poems on the main events of Columbus's voyage. A later New Zealand volume, *On the Land* (1950), exploits Canterbury subjects in meters derived from loose Australian ballad-type poems; the pieces, slackly colloquial, often tail off into near-prose. "Paul Henderson" (Ruth France, the novelist) in *Unwilling Pilgrim* (1955) is less tied to the local scene. Absorbed in man and his pattern of living, she uses Nature as a means of searching out his aspirations. Her poems sometimes lack economy of statement, but provide insights that make her a sophisticated descendent of earlier more overtly Wordsworthian poets.

Particularly interesting is the accomplishment of J. R. Hervey, an Anglican parson whose first book, *Selected Poems*, appeared in 1940, when he was 50, yet which showed a contemporary awareness and skill equal to that of much younger poets. Although his themes are mainly age, death, the changes time brings, and man's destiny, he is never morbid, but charged with meditative joy and peace, acceptance, and humble love. Sparing of images, his poems arise nobly from the hard-won simplicities of feeling. His finest achievement is *She Was My Spring* (1954), a sequence in varying forms dedicated to his dead wife, which is marked with a rare elegiac dignity, often shading to true poignancy and reflecting the tranquility of a mature, wise personality:

> For growing old, my joy is held
> From time in never-yielding hand;
> I sing where songs have fluttered down,
> I sing my love through autumn land.

The southernmost poet of all, Ruth Dallas (b. 1919), of Invercargill, in *Country Road* (1953) and *The Turning Wheel* (1962), wrings from her knowledge of the Southern landscape and life itself gravely graceful and strong-pinned poetry that seeks no consolation from Nature nor looks for man's image there, but accepts the rhythms of the seasons and bows to the transitoriness of all things.

Finally, in Auckland, the country's largest and most cosmopolitan city, a substantial body of poetry has been produced since World War II. It is no more possible to speak of an "Auckland School" than of a Wellington one, but, tentatively, one may suggest that, whereas in the capital, poetry tends to be concerned with urban life and social contexts, or to exhibit a new romanticism, the dominant tone in Auckland poetry is academic or metaphysical. In general, Auckland poets write a more cerebral verse; they are deeply involved in problems of form in the larger sense. Allen Curnow's residence in the city since 1951 has had some effect in these directions on younger Auckland poets.

M. K. Joseph (b. 1914), a university professor, draws in his two collections, *Imaginary Islands* (1950) and *The Living Countries* (1959), upon a wide range of reading and an interest in philosophy and art for starting points for poems about the eternal verities, religious faith, time, change, and the nature of being. He is much concerned with the problems of spiritual reality and the relationship between time and eternity. His sequence, "The Lovers and the City," based upon characters from *Romeo and Juliet,* shows brilliant psychological insight and a Gothic imagination, while his "Mercury Bay Eclogue" is about love and reality caught in an instant of timeless vision. Joseph's poetry reveals a curious and subtle mind rather than a whole personality. He is also a gifted parodist and satirist, and his "Secular Litany," ironically observing New Zealand materialism and stodginess, is one of the best-known of New Zealand poems. Another professor-poet, Keith Sinclair (b. 1922), in three volumes magnificently imprisons the distinctive character of the national landscape, writes vigorously of love and marriage, and gives rein to a quirky and freakish imagination, but is perhaps most successful when he writes about his country's past. Also a distinguished historian, Sinclair is able in his poetry not only to recapture the emotions of men in past times, but to erect upon history lyrical and intellectual structures of true beauty.

By contrast, Kendrick Smithyman (b. 1922) owes comparatively little to the New Zealand scene. Complex and cryptic in much of his work, which is academic in its intellectual playing with ontological concepts and with questions of identity and identification, he has assimilated some elements from modern American verse. His habit of leaving out one term of his poetic syllogisms, and his packed, elliptical style, make him possibly less readily accessible than any of his Auckland contemporaries. But the reward of this strenuous wrestling with the outer reaches of experience, and with problems of artistic form, result in a poetry deserving to be fought through and conveying general human experience. Between *The Blind Mountain* (1950), *Inheritance* (1963), and *Flying to Palmerston* (1968), there is an advance towards greater clarity, less indulgence in ellipses and syntactical obscurities, and a corresponding gain in individuality and emotional power. Smithyman is a dedicated poet and a meticulous craftsman, intensely self-critical, and his haunting, austerely conceived poems are among the most sophisticated productions of the past twenty years.

Two Auckland women poets deserve mention as well. Gloria Rawlinson (b. 1918), who began as a child poet, writing fey and sentimental verse, has steadily developed into a writer with a grace, strength, and insight of which her first poems gave little hint. Her latest book, *Of Clouds and Pebbles* (1963), illuminates New Zealand themes with sharp imagery and clean diction. Mary Stanley (b. 1919), in *Starveling Year* (1952), writes mainly as wife and mother;

avoiding facile sentiment and domestic clichés, her vision comprehends both passion and wry affection.

For the size of its population, New Zealand has produced an unexpected number of good poets, not all of whom have been mentioned here. New and interesting ones are continually appearing: recently, Gordon Challis; Peter Bland; Vincent O'Sullivan; Alan Roddick; C. K. Stead, with his sardonic humour, his humaneness, and his reanimation of traditional forms; Hone Tuwhare, whose integration of Maori and pakeha traditions marks a fruitful new development; and Fleur Adcock, with her frank treatment of sexual love. At the same time, New Zealand publishers have become increasingly wary of poetry, even with Literary Fund assistance. A new poet is lucky if his book sells two hundred copies.

The major poetic achievement seems to belong to the 1930's. There is perhaps, less force and urgency in New Zealand poetry today, although a handful of poets—Baxter, Smithyman, and Joseph among them—have maintained the artistic integrity of our poetry. The present poetic scene shows a fruitful diversity of style and philosophy, yet there is much versifying and mistaking of the form for the substance, and there is a predominating tone of sobriety and melancholy in the verse.

3

THE NOVEL

THE EARLIEST NOVELS written in New Zealand were inevitably produced almost wholly for a British audience and shared with pioneering guidebooks and journals the aim of describing and interpreting the new land. When the early novelist departed from this purpose, it was to select material from New Zealand, especially Maori life, for exotic adventure tales paralleling the Red Indian romances of Fenimore Cooper. Naturally, too, several novels, based upon personal experience, take the form of a first-person account beginning in England, recording the long voyage out, and plunging into varied pioneer adventures. By comparison with the great novels being written in England at this time, the New Zealand fiction of 1860 to 1890 is usually crude, melodramatic, and sub-literary. New Zealand life was as yet amorphous and divided: despite the presence of some educated and sensitive settlers who tried to depict a life of quality in the new environment, most novelists reflected the concern of the majority to acquire material security, to win a home from a primitive land. Hence they produced clumsy yarns which merely skimmed across the surface of the contemporary society.

The first New Zealand novel was *Taranaki: A Tale of the War* (1861) by Major H. B. Stoney (1816–94). This was the prototype for several novels exploiting the wars between the Europeans and the Maoris; it did not deal with the moral or social issues involved, nor even with the human values, but with the thrilling possibilities inherent in Maori "witch-doctors" and cannibalism, and in the appeal of stage-cloth Antipodean backgrounds. Major Stoney's singularly naive tale, which tries to fuse portions from actual military despatches with a vapid love interest and an adventure yarn, has its full quota of shrieking Maoris, inaccurate native lore, tender European heroines, and bloody conflicts. It was followed by similar books in which the Maori is shown with neither understanding nor sympathy, such as Emilia Marryatt's *Amongst the Maoris* (1874), R. P. Whitworth's *Hine-Ra, or The Maori Scout* (1887) and H. B. Marriott Watson's *The Web of the Spider*

(1891). Writers in other countries—G. A. Henty, Jules Verne, and Rolf Boldrewood among them—further garbling the confused information found in these novels and in guidebooks, set sensational tales of adventure among the savage, predatory Maoris.

Only one or two writers made some attempt to get inside the Maori mind and seriously represent his culture and his personality—notably John White (1826–91), a scholar who wrote a useful ancient history of the Maori, in his novel, *Te Rou, or The Maori at Home* (1874). But though the novel is accurate in detail and very well intentioned, *Te Rou* and its successor, *Revenge,* published posthumously in 1940, are stodgy, overly didactic, and virtually unreadable. Much more fun is *Mihawhenua* (1888), by R. M. Chapman, a diverting story written with some gusto about a party of travellers who, behind the mountains of Western Otago, find a Shangri-la valley where a lost Maori tribe dwells idyllically, even to the possession of tame moas! It was hardly to be expected that nineteenth-century popular writers would be able to transpose Maori life and customs into fiction without strain and the need for elaborate explanations; but the generally low level of novels about the Maoris indicates the limited sensitivity of those using the theme. It was not until towards the end of the century that anything like a faithful picture of the Maori began to be given in fiction. But that the older crude simplifications have not yet vanished on the popular level is seen by the appearance in 1960 of *Mary Bravender,* by Olga Stringfellow, which, save for some sophistication of language and emotion, might have been produced eighty years before.

Another early fictional pattern was established by Mrs. Isabella Aylmer, the first local woman novelist, in her *Distant Homes: Or the Graham Family in New Zealand* (1862). Closely modelled on *The Swiss Family Robinson,* this naive novel, which entertains today in a different way from that intended by the author, is loaded with didacticisms, inaccuracies, sentimentality, and implausible plot elements. Yet it provided the model for the pioneer-emigrant novels which ran from the setting out in England to the final stages of settling-in in "Maoriland." An able children's novel, Helen Sandall's *The Immigrants,* published a century later, in 1962, has precisely the same pattern.

In the hands of women writers, the pioneer-emigrant novel tended to center on the experiences of a family, but most men novelists who used the migrant framework preferred to deal with the varied adventures of a lone hand. W. M. Baines (d. 1912) in *The Narrative of Edward Crewe* (1874), obviously autobiographical at base, crudely yokes together miscellaneous experiences as trader, bushman, and gold-miner. Dugald Ferguson (1833–1920), in *Bush Life in Australia and New Zealand* (1893), gives more plot, but a melodramatic one set among the shearers, stockmen, and miners. Perhaps the best of the group is *Waitaruna* (1881), by Alexander Bathgate (1845–1930). The Presbyterian ethic of the author sustains a variation on the good and bad apprentices theme; by his industry, the hero rises to become a sheep-station manager, while his opposite number sinks into alcoholism. For all its ingenuousness, *Waitaruna* projects much of the atmosphere of early sheep-station life.

Another group of novels, the smallest, was prompted by the gold rushes of the 1860's and 1870's in the South Island. The pioneer in this vein was B. L. Farjeon (1838–1903), whose *Shadows on the Snow* (1865), dedicated to Charles Dickens, imitates Dicken's sentiment without his saving humor and imagination. Farjeon later went to England, where he founded a distinguished literary family. Much livelier were the novels of the versatile Vincent Pyke (1827–94) who, in 1862, became Government Secretary to the Otago Goldfields and later a Member of Parliament. Pyke wrote valuable factual books on early Otago and on the gold discoveries. His *Wild Will Enderby* (1873) and *The Adventures of George Washington Pratt* (1874) are still readable; their style is stilted, lumberingly jocose, and larded with the more hackneyed Shakespearean quotations; the heroes are "tall and shapely as an Adonis, and as muscular as a Hercules," and the plots combine Bret Harte-style sentiment with knockabout farce and melodrama. Yet these things are largely compensated for by Pyke's verve, economy, and sense of detail. The character of the drawling, slangy American, Pratt, full of country shrewdness and wise saws, is an attractive one and reminds us that the goldfields attracted men from all over the world. *Wild Will Enderby*, the first novel to be both written and published in New Zealand, went into three editions in its first year. Several later books dealt with, or touched on, gold-diggings life, such as Henry Lapham's *We Four* (1880) and W. Davidson's *Stories of New Zealand Life* (1889), but none equalled Pyke's in popularity.

No novel of this age has the least claim to be regarded as literature. Although there are occasional incidents and characters to be enjoyed, and the books have some documentary value, this fiction, almost without exception, offers the stock characters of Victorian circulating-library popular tales. The construction is clumsy and the style usually combines declamatory dialogue, periphrastic humor, and rhetorical description with sledge-hammer sentimentality. By 1910, however, the pioneering period had been succeeded by a period of consolidation. The new mood of confidence is reflected in fiction. New Zealand novelists began to feel that the country had a character of its own, and that the expression of that character was not just a matter of depicting settings and customs different from those in the Old World. Attempts were made to come closer to reality, which meant, of course, some modification of the old popular fiction conventions. It was, in fact, some decades before these aims were to be fulfilled, but in the 1890's, the first signs of this new attitude are seen. The pioneer-immigrant novel virtually disappears.

At the beginning of the new period a remarkable book appeared, George Chamier's *Philosopher Dick* (1891). This novel has been variously valued. Professor Joan Stevens calls it "the most mature of our novels before the turn of the century," while E. H. McCormick points to its resemblance to the early pioneer novels and says, "it is even more amateurishly contrived than many of its kind," but praises it for its critical view of New Zealand life and for Chamier's "approach to serious themes barely recognized by his predecessors." *Philosopher Dick* shows its hero, a young, idealistic immigrant, gradually becoming disillusioned with New Zealand life, sardonically re-appraising it, and coming in the end to at least a partial acceptance of its underlying assumptions.

The novel is oddly formless, over-detailed, inconsistent, and sometimes dull. Yet for all its faults of form and style, it does try to come to terms with New Zealand life and to explain its unevenness; intuitively, too, Chamier prefigures certain themes that were later to become part of the stock ones of our fiction—"the outsider," the need for mateship, the pettiness of small town life, national materialism, and a mannered pessimism worn like an apprentice artist's beard. Chamier's later novel, *A South Sea Siren* (1895), is also interesting, especially for its satire on the attempts of well-to-do farmers to ape the life of Englishmen.

One kind of local society Chamier attacked was depicted admiringly in the novels of Charlotte Evans (1842–82). In *A Strange Friendship* and *Over the Hills and Far Away* (both 1874) class-conscious gentlefolk, impervious to colonial values, and placed—seemingly by Divine decree—in an unshakeable position of social superiority, try to re-create in exile the conditions of English middle-class living, ignoring (as far as compatible with physical necessity) the exigencies of rough colonial society, and escaping (whenever opportunity offers) back to the security of "real" life in Britain.

A different feminine viewpoint from Mrs. Evans' and a form of criticism different from Chamier's are found in other novels of the nineties. A high proportion of the early novelists were women, and one characteristic common to most of them was their militancy in such social questions as women's suffrage, temperance, and marriage laws. That there was need for temperance reform there can be little doubt, even if the form it ultimately took, under Nonconformist pressure, led to liquor laws of a narrow and illiberal kind from which the country is just beginning to break free. But in early days, as Keith Sinclair writes,

> in a society in which the men tended to spend their leisure in the pubs, grog shops, or gambling dens, it is scarcely possible to exaggerate the importance of the women as a civilizing influence. The excessive drinking explains the tremendous fervour and strength of the Women's Christian Temperance Union in the century. To the women, drinking was the greatest of sins. 'Temperance' was the strongest moral—almost religious—movement of the century.

The agitation for women's suffrage was begun in 1869 by Mrs. Mary Muller ("Femina") in her pamphlets. Her work was taken up by the Women's Christian Temperance Union in 1890, whose main interest in the matter was the belief that women voters would hasten Prohibition. Determined agitation under the leadership of the remarkable Kate Sheppard led to women's suffrage being achieved in 1893, so that the New Zealand woman was the first in the world after the Wyoming woman to be given the vote. Prohibition remained as far off as ever, but "local option" polls were introduced.

The associated feminist and prohibition movements inspired several novels. Most militant of all were those of Edith Searle Grossmann (1863–1931) who luridly used fiction to propagandize for women's rights, social reform, honesty in sex matters, and equal opportunities for the sexes. *Angela: A Messenger* (1890) and her later books, *In Revolt* (1893) and *Hermione, a Knight of the Holy Ghost* (1907), are unquestionably sincere and vigorous, but marred by shallow characterization and her inability to find an objective correlative for her indignation. Her last book, *The Heart of the Bush* (1910), which pleads for greater understanding in marriage, is more successful, because quieter in tone. Among the many feminist pamphlets and novels, none reaches the intellectual level of Mrs. Grossmann's works; most, in fact, are deplorably written. But Kathleen Inglewood's *Patmos* (1905), denouncing the evil "Grog Trade" but enlivened by pleasing touches of humor, and Susan Mactier's *The Hills of Hauraki* (1908), with its grim depiction of the life of a woman with a drunken husband, have some quality. All of these novels, with their burning concern for social issues, look forward to the work of later women writers, such as Jane Mander, Jean Devanny, and "Robin Hyde."

Less aggressive women writers of this time either recorded the values of local polite society or tentatively explored other fields. The prolific "Alien" (Louisa Baker, 1858–1926) wrote agreeable light novels, such as *Wheat in the Ear* (1898) which blends conventionally romantic elements with religious and feminist ones. Jessie Weston's *Ko Meri, or A Cycle of Cathay* (1890) and Lady Anne Glenny Wilson's *Alice Lauder* (1893) deal, in different ways, with the relationship between the new colonial society, at the genteel suburban level, and English society. Timid though their approach was, they were aware of the clash between the values of the Old World and the New, which later writers were to depict more expertly. The heroine of *Ko Meri* is a half-caste Maori princess living in the Auckland society of the nineties, and in part assimilated to its outlook, but who, after her English husband is killed, returns to life among the Maoris. Like the author, the princess is haunted by the idea that the Maori race faces impending destruction. This view was common at the turn of the century, and is reflected in several novels. Perhaps the most interesting is *A Maori Maid* (1898) by Harry Benjamin Vogel (1868–1947), which tells—rather novelettishly, it is true, but with some insight—of the attempt of the white hero and a half-caste Maori girl to come to terms with each other's cultural background.

Another group of novels which gives more indication of New Zealand's social and political concerns than of literary skill or imagination are the utopias of the last part of the century. Although Samuel Butler's *Erewhon,* which had its roots in New Zealand during the author's sojourn here, is a "dystopia," it probably helped to establish a local precedent; there were, too, enough visions of a glorious future being produced in Victorian England for New Zealanders to copy. The Victorian doctrine of Progress and the liberal and reformist spirit of local politicians acted as a stimulus to books like *Anno Domini 2000* (1889) by Sir Julius Vogel (1835–99). Vogel, who was Prime Minister from 1873 to 1876, used the novel to present his notions of progress through financial wizardry, the rights of women, and the future of the British Empire. His book is crammed with absurdities and unintentional humor, and the style is execrable; but it is the fruit of a genuinely liberal spirit and contains much political sense. Closer to modern science-fiction are two novels by "Godfrey Sweven" (Professor Macmillan Brown, 1846–1935). *Rialloro* (1901) and *Limanora* (1903) use a thin framework of fiction to sustain, in the first book, a rather cumbersome satire on modern ways, and, in the second, a rationalist utopia based upon "scientific humanism." Actually long speculative discussions in novel guise, they are more literate and intellectual than Vogel's novel, but much less entertaining. The liveliest of the bunch is *Hedged with Divinities* (1895), by Edward Tregear (1846–1931), a satirical utopia mocking the excesses of the feminist movement, in which the hero, the sole male survivor of a world cataclysm, becomes king of the women of New Zealand. The comic and satirical possibilities of the theme are brightly exploited.

Yet, despite interesting individual achievements, up to World War I the country had produced hardly any fiction of abiding interest. Technically, even the better books were often amateurish and without art or style. But, for all the poverty of imagination revealed and the reliance on second-rate models, the fact remains that a surprising number of novels was published. Some of the really basic themes of an indigenous fiction had been enunciated, and the habit of writing novels had been well and truly established. Whatever the faults of the pioneer novelists, when New Zealand fiction came to maturity, its writers owed some of their success to the forerunners who cleared the ground for them.

The first New Zealand novelist with a claim to be taken seriously is William Satchell (1860–1942), whose books appeared in the first decades of this century. Satchell was an Englishman who settled in the country when he was twenty-six, and produced *The Land of The Lost* (1902), *The Toll of the Bush* (1905), *The Elixir of Life* (1907), and *The Greenstone Door* (1914). *The Elixir of Life,* set on shipboard, is the least interesting. But in his first two novels, despite Satchell's creaking dialogue and his poor ear for local speech, despite melodrama and stock characters, he caught the true atmosphere of the bush country and of the kauri-gum lands. Imperfectly realized, but unmistakably there, is a sense of the power and presence of Nature, which Satchell saw, with something of Hardy's vision, as malign, of the lonely open spaces of New Zealand and of the kind of society that had grown up in such places. His carefully observed details of country life imprison the real character of a male society. His novels are genuine New Zealand novels in that these elements are not superimposed, but essential parts of the very substance of the books. Satchell's major achievement, a book still widely read, is his last, *The Greenstone Door* (1914), which skilfully reconstructs the 1830–60 period of the Maori Wars. There had been only one or two historical novels written before in the country, such as R. N. Adams's *The Counterfeit Seal* (1897), a not uninteresting, but stodgily informative tale of the founding of Otago. Satchell broke new ground not only in his painstaking research into Maori life, but also in distancing his material by making the tale the experiences of childhood as remembered by a mature man. The plot concerns a boy who grows up among the Maoris and who is involved in conflicting loyalties when, as an adult, he finds himself fighting against them. Admirably mixing real and fictional characters, *The Greenstone Door* remains a rattling good story, enjoyed by readers of all ages.

After Satchell, the novel limped along in pedestrian lanes for some years. A great advance was made in fiction by Katherine Mansfield, but her achievement lies in the field of the short story, which is discussed later. World War I acted as a line of division. The effects of this conflict, which involved thousands of New Zealanders, were manifested in the younger generation, as in Britain, by a revolt against the social and moral values of their elders, and a rejection of the Victorian attitudes that lingered on in New Zealand longer than in other places. The most mature of the writers who questioned inherited values was Jane Mander (1877–1949). Like the writers of the nineties, Miss Mander is concerned with social issues, but, in her case, they become an integral part of her novels and not mere propagandist accretions. She combined a keen sensitivity to the intellectual currents of her time with a sense of place and background like that of Satchell. Both of these qualities are seen at their best in *The Story of a New Zealand River* (1920), which is set in the Kaipara district of the North Island in the days of the busy timber-mills. It tells of the gradual, painful readjustment of a genteel Englishwoman, with English Victorian prejudices on sex, class, and religion, who is married to an uncultured New Zealand husband, to the mores and attitudes of her new environment, and, in the process, her awakening to a sense of the fulness of life. Contrasted with her is her daughter, Asia, typifying the new "emancipated" generation. As a picture of the intellectual and cultural problems of women of the new post-war generation, and as a reflection of the new ideas—in part from Shaw and Wells—that were shaping their outlook, the novel has some merit. Hailed in its time as "the great New Zealand novel," it has not worn well in other respects. Today its preachments appear old-fashioned, its "advanced" ideas shallow, and its melodrama and its plot clumsy; yet it retains a certain force and was obviously a sincere attempt to make some sense out of the facts of New Zealand life. Jane Mander's other novels are less interesting, although *Allen Adair* (1925) gets beyond melodrama to treat in some depth the problems of an Oxford-educated New

Zealander with an urban-minded wife trying to readjust himself to rural life.

On a much lower and cruder level, Jean Devanny (b. 1894) in a series of lurid novels beginning with the sensational *The Butcher Shop* (1926), proclaimed a Socialist humanitarianism with all the hectic emotion of a Sunday newspaper feature story.

In a sense, fiction marked time in the 1920's. It was not until the next decade that it found its feet and began to acquire sophistication and a sense of form which enabled a new seriousness to be made manifest. Not only was there a multiplication of writers and a development of different levels of fiction, but the whole temper of the novel changed under the impact of the Depression. As the economic crisis destroyed the Edwardian temper of gentility in fiction, it focused attention on living, contemporary issues and made English subjects and attitudes appear unreal. Typical of this new mood were the novels of John A. Lee (b. 1891), a Member of Parliament and also of the first Labour Government, elected in 1935. Violent, bitter, frank, his *Children of the Poor* (1934) and his *The Hunted* (1936) are based upon his own childhood as a ward of the State and a fugitive from a correctional school. The first novel forcefully denounces social conditions in the Dunedin of the 1890's and a society that ignored its under-privileged. Clearly reflecting a study of Jack London and Upton Sinclair, it shares the crudities of these writers and belongs to the same socialist-propagandist tradition; at the same time, its gaucheries and lack of control do not dampen its considerable power.

The sequel, *The Hunted,* is perhaps the better book, telling of the hero's experiences at training school, his escape, and his recapture. In no sense are these novels works of art. Lee's style is that of the political pamphleteer he was, in fact, for his party; the books are emotional to a fault, over-simplified, over-emphatic, over-colored. But Lee's bull-like charge against the conventions of polite New Zealand fiction left them in ruins. *Civilian into Soldier* (1937), based upon his experiences in the First World War, is also crude and ill-shaped, but contains some compelling pictures of the savagery of war. Two volumes of short stories dealing with "The Shiner," a colorful real-life "gentleman of the roads," recreate the days of the itinerants and are often very funny.

Another novelist who helped to change the direction of fiction in the 1930's was "Robin Hyde" (Iris Wilkinson, 1906–39), poet, journalist, novelist, and a more complex writer than John Lee. Her five novels are uneven, yet show an increasing artistry. Cursed, as she realized, with stylistic habits acquired while working on newspapers, she nevertheless had something of true genius. Two novels based upon the life of James Douglas Stark, war-hero, misfit, and outcast, *Passport to Hell* (1936) and *Nor the Years Condemn* (1938), show a remarkable ability to identify herself with this unusual character and to reconstruct imaginatively the world of tough soldiers. "Starkie," the New Zealand-born son of an American Indian and a Spanish woman, passed through a corrective school, deserted from a ship, went to prison, enlisted at the age of sixteen in the army, and had an extraordinary war-career during which several courts-martial decisions against him were cancelled because of his deeds of bravery. Aged twenty, he returned to New Zealand to fight his way through the age of forgotten heroes and the gray days of the Depression. Robin Hyde transforms these facts into something between documentary and fiction. Coarse-grained in style, yet full of startling detail and exact in their evocation of battlefield, pub, prison, and slum, these novels are still alive. *Wednesday's Children* (1937), a whimsical work, blending wry satire, humor, fancy, and philosophizing, gives a likeable picture of Auckland but is only a partial success. She was at her best in her novels when a sub-stratum of fact sustained her. In *The Godwits Fly* (1938), her last novel, she sympathetically depicts the life of a middle-class Wellington family, probably her own, and in a delicate prose, refined now of many of her earlier crudities, dramatizes the pull of the Old World on New Zealanders, which the migratory birds of the title symbolize.

However, Robin Hyde's major achievement is *Check to Your King* (1936). Based upon a careful study of the historical documents, some of which are woven into its texture, it tells the story of the Baron Charles de Thierry, a well-meaning French eccentric who tried to establish himself as Sovereign Chief of New Zealand in the 1830's. Part novel, part an experiment in biography, this curiously shaped and original book, fusing fact and imagination, delights in its subject, which it makes a likeable human being, silly yet courageous, comic yet pathetic, and with his own shabby dignity. The mixture of poetry and journalism, the playfulness, the half-loving, half-mocking asides, all combine to draw the reader intimately into the story and bring the Baron and his circle vividly alive. In this book, as in the "Starkie" novels, Robin Hyde showed a deep personal sympathy for the offbeat character.

While Lee and Hyde were breaking new ground, older, more polite conventions of the novel still found their champions. Alan Mulgan (1881–1962), in *Spur of Morning* (1934), kept close to the middle-brow manner in his presentation of pre-1914 life and the conflicting attitudes of young New Zealanders towards the concept of "Home." Nelle Scanlan (b. 1881) won a large public with her *Pencarrow* series (1932–39) which, on a light level, attempted with much success the saga of an ordinary New Zealand family over a century; the characters are stock ones and the developments romantically predictable, yet the books are professionally written and a useful amount of social history is caught in their pages. Ngaio Marsh (b. 1899) began in 1934 to produce her literate and skilfully constructed detective stories. Only three of them, however, have New Zealand settings, and she seems more at home in the world of the English theatre and middle-class.

Although he never quite fulfilled his early promise, "John Guthrie" (John Brodie, 1905–55) tapped a new vein of good-natured national satire in *The Little Country* (1935). In this witty send-up of many of the pretensions of New Zealand life, Brodie inaugurated a healthy tradition. In general, the book's social observation is shallow, but it has a Kiwi exuberance and a jauntily comic common-sense that have not faded. His other novels are commonplace, although *Paradise Bay* (1952), a return to the manner of *The Little Country*, pleases with some sharp satirical portraits. Somewhat more ambitious were the historical romances of "G. B. Lancaster" (Edith Lyttleton, 1873–1945). Her *Promenade* (1938) courageously essayed the story of three families from colonial days to the Boer War. Skilful and inventive, and based upon close historical research, this, like her other novels, just lacks that extra something of imagination and style that might have made it into first-class historical fiction.

With such novelists as these, clear signs of professionalism began to be seen in local fiction. For some, novel-writing became a serious occupation and not just a leisure-time activity. Care in construction, the awareness of a more fully literate audience, attention to matters of style—things which in the past had too often been left to look after themselves—now concerned more and more novelists. Most conspicuously, in the 1930's a fresh approach was made to language. The major advances in style were, of course, related to new subject-matter and attitudes and came originally in the short story and partly through the example of Katherine Mansfield. The work of the short story writers is discussed below. One of these, Frank Sargeson, made a literary instrument out of a sophisticated variant of New Zealand colloquial speech, but the significance of this was not realized until the 1940's.

As the thirties were drawing to a close, a novel appeared which is of special importance, since, while it looked back to former socially conscious fiction, it both reflected the Leftist outlook of several contemporary writers and looked forward to a new type of fiction. This was *Man Alone* (1939) by John Mulgan (1911–45). In a laconically understated style reminiscent of Hemingway, Mulgan depicted the experiences of a tough, rootless, nonconformist in Depression times. His Johnson is perhaps the best fictional embodiment of a New Zealand literary stereotype—the solitary, self-reliant individualist—as he moves from job to job, becomes involved in the Auckland unemployed riots, kills a man by accident, hides in the back country, and finally leaves New Zealand to fight in the Spanish Civil War, which was the Leftist "Cause" in New Zealand as elsewhere. Without direct propaganda, *Man Alone,* by its emphasis, expresses the predominant political sentiments of the time, dramatizes modern man's dilemma in a bewilderingly divided society, and embodies Mulgan's idea of the human situation. It is very much a novel of its period, and suffers from this today, but its expert handling of incident and detail, its humaneness and its skillful story-telling keep it readable, and it is still, in part, relevant.

The "Man Alone" theme recurs in such later books as *Outlaw's Progress* (1943) by R. M. Burdon (b. 1896), *The Huntsman in His Career* (1949) by Erik de Mauny (b. 1918), *Strip Jack Naked* (1957) by Guthrie Wilson (b. 1914), and *A Gun in My Hand* (1959) by Gordon Slatter (b. 1922). Both Burdon's and de Mauny's books were inspired by a real-life case in which a murderer who went berserk was hunted down in the bush. Burdon's novel attempts to explore the springs of his central character's actions—he is a returned soldier driven to crime by economic circumstances—but the book lacks depth and conviction. De Mauny's more complex novel presents the situation from three points of view (those of the murderer, his victim, and a young liberal pacifist about to go on war service), and by so doing considers questions of responsibility, will, violence, and pacifism. Despite some youthful overwriting and a rather ambivalent philosophy, this is a thoughtful novel, but its author has produced no successor.

Although twenty years separate Mulgan's and Slatter's books, the subject-matter is in many ways similar; a lone wolf views his society with disillusioned eyes, violence is a major element, women are traps for men. Slatter, however, suffuses his story with irony, rejects violence as a solution, and sees the "man alone" as a destructive social force.

In the serious novels after the 1930's, writers were able to take their country largely for granted, in the sense that they no longer needed, as their local audience grew, to splash on so much local color, although they manifested an increasing concern for questions of national and personal identity and just what kind of reality life in this land amounted to. Political themes died away with the advent of the Second World War and with the general movement away from the easy ideological nostrums of the previous decade. Newer and more diverse subjects presented themselves to writers who had lived through significant national experiences. The community, too, was now big enough and the society stable enough for novelists to be able to treat of specific social or professional groups or to exploit regionalism.

For instance, Dan Davin (b. 1913) has set three novels in the Irish Catholic community of Southland. He made his debut in 1945 with the rather imitative *Cliffs of Fall,* echoing Joyce's *Portrait of the Artist,* and showing a university student in violent and calamitous revolt against the values of his Irish Catholic parents. His later novels are both more sensitive and sympathetic in using similar material. In the moving *Roads from Home* (1949), the conflict between generations is again taken up; this time there are two sons, one of whom (a student for the priesthood) rejects his vocation, his mother's desire. But there is no loading of the dice, and both attitudes are seen with understanding. Despite a tendency to rhetoric, the style is alive and the book is unified by its imagery as well as by its plot. *The Sullen Bell* (1956), set in England, is less assured in its exploration of the restricted society of expatriate New Zealanders, conscious of their displacement. *No Remittance* (1959), a more ambitious work, with a glance at Joyce Cary, has as its central character a raffish scoundrel who surveys the Irish Catholic family into which he marries with a mixture of scorn and self-pity. Davin is never short of wit or intelligence, although at times his characters seem subservient to ideas. There is in his best novels a not unsympathetic re-creation of an organic community with integrated values combined with a half-regretful, yet realistic, acceptance of inevitable change.

Another view of the Irish in New Zealand is found in *Moonshine* (1944) by Helen Wilson (1874–1957), which recreates an isolated community of "bog Irish" in the 1890's. While the treatment is old-fashioned and the plot ingenuous, the book is spiritedly true to the Irish character and more successful than the later *Land of My Children* (1955), a stiff, shambling historical saga.

In the 1940's, the influence of Frank Sargeson is strong, both stylistically and in the repudiation of second-hand puritan values. One striking novel, *The Cunninghams* (1948) by David Ballantyne (b. 1924), which was first published in New York, combines Sargeson's influence with that of James T. Farrell. It was about this time that American writing began to have a more evident effect in several areas of New Zealand literature. Ballantyne's picture of a working-class family, compassionate, yet unsentimental, realistic in its approach, with its almost-prototypal Mum and sensitive, rebellious son, scores both by its honesty and by its pinpointing of inadequacies in the New Zealand way of life. With its documentary drabness and dismal sobriety, it lacks the animating quality of a tragic sense or the imaginative lift that would imply hope or transformation; Ballantyne seems to see few deeper implications in what he conscientiously records. *The Last Pioneer* (1963) also shows a small town—lifeless, debilitated, dreary—an ironical relic of a once-vital pioneering settlement, and so de-energized as to communicate this effect to the book as a whole. In *A Friend of the Family* (1966), the debilitation of spirit has been replaced by a frantic energy in its farcical-cum-satirical view of the urban business milieu, and, while there does not yet appear to be a positive side to Ballantyne's attitude to life, there is some force in the comic treatment of misdirected endeavor.

By the time New Zealand became involved in the Second World War, fiction was flourishing. To some extent the war marked the end of Depression-inspired concerns and also of the dominance of the early Sargeson manner and attitudes. Increased prosperity after the war; a new sense of community; a sense, too, of a shared history, however short; a more ready acceptance by New Zealanders of their own fiction—these, and, of course, the presence of talented writers, helped to produce an explosion of novels. In quality, the new New Zealand fiction overtook poetry and the short story which had hitherto been the more artistically superior forms.

Out of the New Zealander's experience of war in Greece, the Middle East, Europe, and the Pacific came several war novels. Without the resentful anger of the American war fiction or the sophistication of the British variety, the New Zealand ones set themselves to examine not so much the nature of combat itself, as, in general, moral problems in relation to war or arising out of it. Dan Davin's *For the Rest of Our Lives* (1947) is perhaps the angriest. An episodic, seemingly unintegrated book, it scarifyingly depicts the waste of war through the experiences of three members of the Second New Zealand Expeditionary Force in the Middle East. Often stridently emotional, it is noteworthy for its fine battle scenes, and for its endeavor to come to terms with questions of loyalty, courage, time, and life's changes and disappointments. Somewhat firmer in characterization, if more conventional, is *Brave Company* (1951) by Guthrie Wilson, which achieves a unified impression by concentrating on a small company of New Zealanders involved in a raid in Northern Italy. Unlike Davin's novel, which is written from the officer's point of view, Wilson sees things from that of the ranker, and his laconic prose reflects the typical responses of the Kiwi soldier. Almost impersonal in tone and not emphasizing the horror of war, the book shows fighting as a job—if a dirty one—to be done, and comes closer to realities of combat than the more hysterical or more philosophically analytical war novels do. At the same time, *Brave Company* tends, like some of Wilson's later novels, to reproduce stereotypes of the novel of action and violence.

I'll Soldier no More (1958), by M. K. Joseph (b. 1914), treats of yet another aspect of war—the lengthy training period in England, with its corrosive boredom, and the occupation of Germany. The novel dramatizes effectively the strains of army life and the reactions of diverse personalities to the demands of soul-destroying routine rather than to the "shooting war." It also gives a superb impression of Germany in defeat. In the ultimate, the characters seem manipulated and predestined rather than "free," but the novel is a welcome antidote to the type of novel which exploits war, since it is mature in outlook, ironical without skepticism, true to the facts of most soldiers' experience, and informed with a balanced philosophy of life.

Gordon Slatter's *A Gun in My Hand,* already mentioned, captures much of the post-war malaise of a man for whom combat has been a satisfying substitute for a drab civilian existence. The central character is a returned soldier determined to revenge himself on the cheating girl he left behind in Christchurch. It is perhaps most notable for its sardonic appraisal of New Zealand mores and for its vigorous use of the local vernacular, some elements of which appeared in print for the first time in this book.

War is a continuing concern of Errol Brathwaite (b. 1924). *Fear in the Night* (1959), dealing with the attempt of the crew of a bomber forced down in Japanese territory to repair their plane and escape, makes a taut, exciting story; but Brathwaite is at least equally committed to presenting the differing reactions of the men to their situation. *Long Way Home* (1964), about a search and rescue operation in the mountains, is similar in its organization. A more subtle work, *An Affair of Men* (1961), which won a literary prize, has no European characters, but centers on a clash of wills and ideologies between a Japanese officer in pursuit of a group of white airmen in Bougainville and a Christian-educated native headman. The conflict between two sets of disparate values is boldly handled, and the plot leads to a convincing resolution in terms of the psychology of the antagonists. Brathwaite has further pursued his investigation of the moral dilemmas presented by and in war in an ambitious historical trilogy about the Maori Wars: *The Flying Fish* (1964), *The Needle's Eye* come closest to achieving this, but, even here, the characters shift at times from a concrete reality to a semi-symbolization of abstract qualities.

Several writers who made an impact in the 1950's have gone on to develop their skill. Guthrie Wilson, for instance, has moved beyond the war subject. His *Julian Ware* (1952) is a somewhat stolid story of snobbery among the wealthy Canterbury sheep-farmers. Among his other novels, some of which rather too aggressively exploit brute violence, his best are *Sweet White Wine* (1956), dealing with a successful novelist, which has sub-acid observations on New Zealand provincialism and a maturely ironical style; and *The Incorruptibles* (1960) which, centering on the appointment of a principal of a Sydney school, dissects the tangled motives of those who tread the corridors of power. Wilson, who is now principal of an Australian school, has become a highly competent professional writer with a wide range of subject, an assured style, and still-unused reserves of power.

James Courage (1903–63), a long-time expatriate, set most of his novels in his native land, drawing his subject-matter from often shadowy memories of his childhood in Canterbury before the First World War. His work has a curiously unreal and slightly repulsive flavor; it is at times almost Gothic in its blend of melodrama and sentimentality and its unusual number of odd, neurotic, and frustrated characters. With its tenuous backgrounds and its restricted milieu, his fiction seems projected from inside a neurotic personality rather than made from observed and felt experience. Courage is at his best when he is able to suggest something of the strange poetry of living and loving and to express his sympathy with abnormal people. *Desire Without Content* (1950), his second novel, has at its center a mother's possessive love for a mentally defective son. *Fires in the Distance* (1952) is a would-be tragic four-way bisexual love story; *A Way of Love* (1958) is a homosexual love story rich in unintentional comedy. His most satisfactory novel is *The Young Have Secrets* (1954), in which the Christchurch of 1914 is re-created through the experiences of a sensitive ten-year old viewing adult relationships with bewilderment. Here the greater concreteness of place and time help to discipline the story and the point of view is sustained with skillful irony.

A more successful venture into the same territory is *The God Boy* (1958) by Ian Cross (b. 1925). Owing a little, possibly, to Salinger, but with an individual tone blending pathos with gentle understanding, it tells of a tough little Catholic eleven-year old who believes himself "a God Boy," but who is buffeted cruelly by a fate he cannot fight back against. With sure technical mastery, Cross shows the same child, at thirteen, re-living his earlier tragedy, with the complexity and limitation of attitude this double vision calls for. In the process, adult feelings and behavior are submitted to the analysis of the innocent eye. The presentation of Jimmy's personal dilemmas is rather more successful than the more general theological implications about belief that the novel seems ready to bear. *The Backward Sex* (1960), also seen through an adolescent's eye, is less original and rather predictable in its handling of the young hero's introduction to sex. More ambitiously, in *After Anzac Day* (1961), Ian Cross tried to convey an impression of New Zealand's essential character, especially its social and political values and its history as a community, through the consciousness of a household of four involved in seemingly private relationships. Many New Zealand themes—race relations, the appeal of "Home," puritan traditions, for instance, as well as the national significance of Anzac Day, inherited political clichés, and the Kiwi's idea of his own virility—are probed to illuminate the role of the dominant male in our society. A mature and subtle technique and a complex and delicate sensibility are evident in this novel, yet somehow the situations and characters seem at once almost too slender and too contrived to bear the weight of significance that rests upon them. This consideration does not prevent *After Anzac Day* from being the most interesting near-success of its decade.

The God Boy is but one of a number of novels which deal with the process of growing up or the child's view of reality—a persistent New Zealand subject. These include Roderick Finlayson's *Tidal Creek* (1948), Maurice Shadbolt's *Among the Cinders* (1965), Norman Harvey's *One Magpie for Sorrow* (1967), and, most delicately, Noel Hilliard's *Power of Joy* (1965), in which a young man comes to a realization of the significance of the influences, especially of Nature, upon his personality and outlook which, as a child, he uncomprehendingly accepted. It may be that, lacking rewarding and various experiences, some novelists find that their childhood is the one separable part of their lives they can exploit with some detachment or that therein they discover the identity that eludes them in the suburbs of their maturity or that, consciously or unconsciously, the process of maturation offers them an image of the New Zealander's quest for his own identity as an individual and as part of a new society.

While most of the writers who use childhood experience as the stuff of fiction are men, most of those who deal with abnormal states of mind are women. The most gifted and idiosyncratic of these to appear since the war is Janet Frame (b. 1924). *Owls Do Cry* (1957), her first novel, is a truly remarkable one, which organizes—if that is the word—her intuitions about loneliness, spiritual exile, and emotional insecurity through the intricately told story of a family in a small New Zealand town. On the realistic level, the characters—insane, undeveloped, or epileptic—and their experiences are incredible. But Miss Frame makes them imaginatively real by her graphic detail and types of humanity by an elaborate pattern of symbols, poetic devices, interior monologues, and iterated images, which shifts from the poetic to the realistic with sometimes perplexing but often illuminating results, and implies a criticism of the intellectual and spiritual aridity of life in small towns. The quasi-Joycean devices are not always successful and it is hard at times to decide whether certain passages are semantically subtle and complex or merely confused, or even whether they belong to character or author. Yet, as a whole, *Owls Do Cry* is an unforgettably individual work with a poetic character new to our fiction and conveying a powerful sense of the tragic dimension of being.

Miss Frame's next novel, *Faces in the Water* (1961), set in a mental hospital, has so little plot as to be almost a documentary, but painfully and cumulatively evokes the physical atmosphere of the hospital, as well as the nightmare world between madness and sanity, often in passages of moving poetic realization. Her four later novels, from *The Edge of the Alphabet* (1962) to *A State of Seige* (1967), likewise deal mainly with abnormal, introverted, or unbalanced characters searching for a handhold on identity or communication with others. Despite much powerful writing, they are less satisfying than her first two books, since they strain credulity too far, they appear to be insufficiently distanced, and they are capricious and uncritical in their use of the author's intuitions. This comment may only mean, of course, that this reader finds her uncomfortable in her blurring of the line of normality and in the amount of free-flow consciousness that seems to seep into her novels. A partial exception may be made of *A State of Seige*, an obsessive novel of fear and hallucination. Reminiscent of Carson McCullers in the nature of her preoccupations and her identification with human oddities, and in the thin-skinned awareness of the disparity between the world of the mind and the world of things and of "the others," Janet Frame is nevertheless a distinctive writer, concerned with ultimates, with life and death, normality and abnormality, with the search for what is truly valuable in the past and the present of the individual, with "the genuine treasure," as she calls it, and capable of not only acute social comment, but also of a freakish comedy.

In 1957, Sylvia Ashton-Warner's *Spinster* was widely acclaimed in Britain and the United States, where it was made into a mediocre film, and greeted with mixed feelings in New Zealand. A strange book, the product of a hectic imagination, it retails the career of a dedicated teacher, Anna Vorontosov, a brandy-tippling spinster who introduces into her class-room revolutionary methods designed to liberate the sensibilities of her Maori youngsters, but which bring her into conflict with authority. Through a well-sustained first-person narrative, Anna emerges as a vital, if highly emotional and neurotic person. The most vivid parts of the novel are the class-room episodes, which illustrate those theories of the education of the artistic impulses and creative living instincts which Miss Ashton-Warner has presented, without fictional sugar-coating, in *Teacher* (1963). The male characters of *Spinster*, however, including a highly-strung teacher who commits suicide, are not far from women's magazine stereotypes. Yet, exasperating, cranky, and self-indulgent though it is, this novel is joltingly different and often stimulating.

Miss Ashton-Warner's second novel, *Incense to Idols* (1960), has all of *Spinster's* faults with few of its virtues. Again we are plunged into the consciousness of a neurotic female; this time, most improbably, a French concert pianist in a minor New Zealand town, and we share her infatuation with a thundering Evangelical preacher. The author's ostensible themes—the problems of conversion, the aesthetic sensibility, and the nature of sanctity—defeat her, and in the hysterical prose, the turgid pseudo-poetic rhetoric, and the pretentious philosophizings, the figure of Marie Corelli seems terrifyingly close. *Bell Call* (1964) has its moments of truth as it shows its heroine reacting against soul-destroying institutions, conventions, and restrictions and as it depicts the singularly odd, yet not unreal Pracket family; but the shapelessness of the book and its rattling feminine style—as well as its chip-on-the-shoulder feminism—are high prices to pay for these. *Greenstone* (1967), aiming at fantasy, falls into romantic day-dream and is unconvincing, even on its own level, in its treatment of racial attitudes and social distinctions. Miss Ashton-Warner is an eccentric writer, largely undisciplined, prone to indulge in fanciful romantic excursions and to abandon reality in the interests of wilful fantasy; at the same time, she does possess valuable intuitions and a conviction that the New Zealand milieu represses and distorts artistic and spiritual impulses; these come through, if fitfully and confusedly, in all her books.

Of the three novels of Marilyn Duckworth (b. 1935) only the first, *A Gap in the Spectrum* (1959), is of particular interest. Its subject-matter is not dissimilar to that characteristic of Janet Frame, but the treatment is very different. The fantasies of a girl in London who loses her memory and tries to rebuild her personality, it has some perceptive observations on mental states and interesting, if occasionally strained, hallucination sequences. The novel hints at an intriguing talent not yet confirmed by the later novels, which try too hard for knowingness and sophistication.

In various ways recent novelists have commented critically on aspects of the national life with an assurance rarely found in their pre-war predecessors. Several satirical works in a light vein, for instance, have refined on the efforts of John Guthrie. One of the best is *Voyagers in Aspic* (1954), by John Gillies, a clever anatomizing of New Zealand snobberies which scores its hits chiefly by placing social-climbing New Zealanders on a visit "Home" in the midst of masterfully rude English people. Robin Muir's *Word for Word* (1960) surveys the hazards of local publishing and the uncertain cultural values of the country. R. Casey's *So Short a Spring* (1963), a shade reminiscent of *Billy Liar,* amusingly deals with a university student who tries to escape from his unsuccessful life by adopting a series of outrageous personae.

On a quite different plane Frank Sargeson's *Memoirs of a Peon* (1965) develops the criticism implied in his short stories, of the philistine provincial society, its crudities, its drab functionalism, and its puritanism, in a very funny first-person narrative notable for its suave imitation of eighteenth-century picaresque styles, its keen sense of place and period, and its pompous narrator whose limited self-awareness produces some delicious ironies. *The Hangover* (1967) surrounds its adolescent hero, a misfit in a spiritually bankrupt urban society, with realistic detail of city life and beatnik habits and with a complex set of literary and mythical images and symbols, and by doing so aims at expressing an attitude towards not only New Zealand life, but modern life in general. If the vision of youth and academic values appears lop-sided, out-dated, and grossly partial, and if the narrative appears too simple for the grand implications, the novel is nevertheless impressive in its density of reference, its genuine sophistication, and its lack of triviality.

In other novels the community's values and its flattering image of itself are criticized with various degrees of skill. Bill Pearson's *Coal Flat* (1963) is rather more successful in its painstaking evocation of a small-town world than in its rendering of human feelings; its achievement as sociology is superior to its achievement as fiction. Maurice Gee's *The Big Season* (1962), in which the hero's revolt against New Zealand mores is partly, and rather confusedly, fulfilled by his selecting as a model of rebellion a convicted burglar; *Footsteps in the Sea* (1964), by Pat Booth, and his later *Sprint to the Bell* (1966), commenting on small-town small-mindedness and sham amateurism in sport respectively; Redmond Wallis's *Point of Origin* (1962), concerned with snobbery in Christchurch; Gordon Dryland's *An Absence of Angels* (1915), which squints disenchantedly at local intellectual phonies and pseudo-Bohemians—all of these find cause for mirth or disquiet in the New Zealand way of life.

A not uncommon cause of the novelists' unease is the scant room for the artist, the eccentric, the nonconformist, or the individualist in a lower-middle-class, puritan-based welfare state. Maurice Shadbolt (b. 1932) deals with these and similar problems, but with a larger reference, most sensitively in his group of three novellas *The Presence of Music* (1967). M. K. Joseph, in *A Pound of Saffron* (1962), a civilized study of power politics played out in the University of Auckland, comments only incidentally on attitudes peculiar to New Zealand. The book, which suffers somewhat from its organization for the purpose of its thesis, and its subsequent conditioning of its characters and also from some melodrama, is nevertheless sharply perceptive on moral and academic values. In the course of laying bare the character of a university Machiavelli, Joseph catches the common-room atmosphere admirably and ironically conveys the shallow intellectualism of conventional academic positivists.

The widening of subject-matter by such novelists and their more mature evaluation of their own society are signs of vigor and health. Unhappily, some critical attitudes have hardened into clichés. The freshness and the novelty have gone from snipings at obsolescent liquor laws, the worship of sport, the unhappy lot of creative artists, the limited sensibilities of government officials, the admiration for the overseas expert, the male fear of women, petty suburban snobberies, the expense-account vulgarian, the pathetic imitations of English middle-class customs. There is not, often enough, much urbanity in the New Zealand novelist's treatment of the defects in New Zealand mores or a point of view sustained by a positive philosophy rather than by near-adolescent grouches. And frequently the novel seems to be concerned less with re-creating human experience and expressing a vision of the human condition than with using fiction for marginal sociological comment of a fairly shop-worn kind. Even in such an interesting novel as Maurice Gee's *A Special Flower* (1965), with its unusually thoughtful treatment of married sex and family tensions, the novelistic stereotype of the oafish football player intrudes.

Contemporary writers make a much more earnest attempt to understand the Maori than their predecessors did. *Maori Girl* (1960), by Noel Hilliard (b. 1929), treats with genuine understanding the only-too-common fate of the Maori uprooted from tribal life and subjected to urban pressures. In summary, the plot may read like a Victorian tale of Jennie's fate in the Big City, but Hilliard's insight into the Maori temperament, his ability to see the world from the Maori point of view, his presentation of racial discrimination, and his unsentimental realism makes his book both moving and disturbing. Charles Frances's *Johnny Rapana* (1964) less successfully tries to do the same for a Maori man. In *The Outcasts* (1965) Phillip Wilson, whose two earlier novels fall somewhere between popular fiction, with melodrama and stock plots, and serious novels dealing with men finding fulfilment in activities and environments away from urban complexes, has produced a telling story of action and violent death which dramatizes the plight of a half-caste Maori crushed between the two cultures he shares.

For all the realism and sympathy of such novels, other novelists and short story writers are tending to sentimentalize the Maori, from the best of motives, no doubt, with an over-emphasis on his virtues of courtesy, personal generosity, and community feeling, using him as a liberal stick with which to beat the modern technological culture to which the authors themselves are unable to adjust, and at the same time ignoring the need to accept the Maori as a human being without patronizing, idealizing, or leaning over backwards. Sometimes recent New Zealand fiction appears in danger of substituting an over-compensating romanticized twentieth-century Maori stereotype for the nineteenth-century one.

An indication of popular preferences in home-grown fiction is given by the commercial success of Barry Crump (b. 1935), a former deer-culler. In *A Good Keen Man* (1961), which sold over 60,000 copies in New Zealand, Crump tells a loosely-linked series of expanded anecdotes in the life of a deer-culler, including several well-known folk stories and men's yarns which had never seen print before, in dinkum colloquial speech. He followed this with other books of a similar kind. Largely unsubtle and comparatively artless, these novels embody many basic male Kiwi attitudes, with the emphasis on beer, the traps of domesticity, mateship, action in the bush or on a farm, the outdoor life, resourcefulness, and casualness. They have their roots in the past century's novels of the diggings and in bushmen's camp-fire yarns, although the author, one feels certain, is largely innocent of literary ancestries. Mary Scott (b. 1888), whose books have been translated into several languages and who has a large following in Germany, has produced several pleasant, innocuous novels of rural and family life which have a special appeal to young women. Ruth Park, an efficient professional novelist, gained her greatest popular success with *A Harp in the South* (1948), set in a Sydney slum. Other popular novelists with several books to their credit include Frank Kenyon, Dorothy Eden, Barbara Cooper, Frank Bruno, Arthur E. Jones, Arthur Manning, Ken Sanford, George Joseph, Bruce Beaver, Margaret Jeffrey, and R. L. Bacon.

The books of these writers range from detective stories and historical romances to stories of family life and racial tension. There is considerable diversity in quality, but because the New Zealand publisher, catering for a small audience, cannot afford to take risks, especially since the relatively recent advent of television in New Zealand, and because the local writer who achieves publication abroad does so in competition with hundreds of writers physically closer to the publishing world, the general professional standard of New Zealand popular fiction is high.

More serious New Zealand novels suggest that our writers find it very hard to write meaningfully about sex. The emphasis is often on mateship, and a good number of novels and short stories have either a latent or an explicit homosexual strain. Heterosexual relations, when they are plumbed at all, are seen in terms of adolescent excitement or in fictional clichés. R. H. Morrieson's story of a necrophilic killer in a small town, *The Scarecrow* (1963), or Janet Frame's mixture of incest and violence in *The Adaptable Man* (1965) seem more characteristic of New Zealand fiction than any treatment of mature sex, love, and marriage with insight and sensitivity.

In the main, the novelists are technically conservative, even when they tackle new subject-matter. Few pursue their art with the assiduity and adaptability of a Frank Sargeson. It is something of a relief to turn to the complex imagination, literary sophistication, and fabular dimension of M. K. Joseph's superior science-fiction novel, *The Hole in the Zero* (1967). Apart from such sports, there is a certain predictability in recent New Zealand fiction—solid craftsmanship, competent writing, some sensitivity expended on a restricted range of themes, most likely one with a sociological bias, and a nagging dissatisfaction with aspects, sometimes central, perhaps more often peripheral, of life in this land.

4

THE SHORT STORY

It was in the 1860's and 1870's that the short story began to take shape as a distinct form in New Zealand writing. Lady Barker, for instance, in *A Christmas Cake in Four Quarters* (1872), told attractive tales. One in particular, "Christmas Day in New Zealand," put into the mouth of an old shepherd, catches much of the flavor of contemporary colloquial speech. Most of the early stories were, in fact, "yarns," often based upon actual happenings or popular anecdotes of mining days. Henry Lapham's *We Four* (1880) and W. Davidson's *Stories of New Zealand Life* (1889) collect typical examples of this kind and give some idea of the lusty masculine fun and simple sentiments of those days.

The Maori was another popular subject for early short story writers, as shown in the books by two sons of missionaries: Alfred A. Grace's *Tales of a Dying Race* (1901), and William Baucke's *Where the White Man Treads* (1905). Both authors make earnest endeavors to understand and be fair to the Maori, but neither ventures very far beyond stereotypes of characterization. Grace (1867–1942) is rather the better writer of the two.

Early in the new century, two women brought art and sensitivity to a form that had usually been regarded as a condensed novel or a refuse-bin for odd fictional ideas. Alice F. Webb (b. 1876), whose stories were written mainly in the first decade of the century but collected in *Miss Peter's Special* (1926), are gentle, perceptive tales of life in a country community, seasoned with a delicate, unfolksy humor. Blanche E. Baughan (1870–1958), who likewise wrote of rural life, shows in *Brown Bread from a Colonial Oven* (1912) a tougher mind and a sharp eye for the colonial character; in some of her stories she makes a tentative stab at a native colloquial style.

But it was "Katherine Mansfield" (Kathleen Beauchamp, 1888–1923) who not only raised the New Zealand short story to the level of an art, but who became the country's first writer to achieve an international reputation. In 1908, when she was twenty, she left New Zealand to seek wider horizons in England. Her life in Europe, and her early death, as well as her assiduous dedication to her art, have been definitively discussed by her fellow-countryman, Antony Alpers, in *Katherine Mansfield* (1954). Always somewhat immature and chaotic as a personality, she was a perfectionist in her work and sought tirelessly for precision and clarity. "Lord," she wrote, "make me crystal clear for Thy light to shine through." Beginning as an imitator of Chekhov, she steadily developed her own individuality, until shortly before her death, she wrought, as Arthur Sewell has said, "a new texture out of English prose." In general, her stories are presentations of a swift penetrating look at a character or a situation. They rely hardly at all on plot, but greatly on the creation of atmosphere: the method is impressionistic, catching the innerness of life in the slight things of everyday. Concentrating the time-span of her stories, she explores the sensations of her characters in depth and miraculously imprisons the transient mood or stir of evanescent memory. For her "the truth is in minutes rather than in years." It is this fineness of truth to the more elusive movements of the soul, and to the inexpressible apprehensions, notably of children, as in the splendid "The Doll's House," that make her outstanding. Although her range is comparatively narrow, few before her had handled her kind of material with such subtle art.

One of her greatest gifts was her ability to relate moods to outward signs by an exact use of imagery that sets her characters firmly in the world of things. Her style, refined in her mature work to an exceptional purity, became a beautifully supple instrument, poetic yet firm, delicate yet strong, which no other New Zealand short story writer has since matched. As her health failed and she became more and more overwhelmed by depression, it was her memories of her early life in New Zealand that gave her a center of repose and refuge from the burdens of living. She set herself to recapture her awareness of Wellington at the end of the nineteenth century, and this she did with an incomparable skill, evoking the physical sense of the city she had known, the life of a Wellington family, and the response of children to an adult world. It is all pervaded, in E. H. McCormick's words, with a "certain languorous serenity." Stories like "Prelude" and "At the Bay," with their intense visualization, their sensitive understanding, and their exquisite texture of language, remain the country's highest achievement in the short story.

Shortly after Katherine Mansfield died, a young returned sailor, who had also been a dairy farmer, Frank S. Anthony (1891–1925), contributed something new to the short story. Before his early death as a delayed result of war injuries, Anthony wrote several stories for newspapers. These were collected in 1938 as *Me and Gus,* but met with little success. However, when reissued in 1951, together with a further volume, and broadcast, the "Gus" stories became widely popular. The tales are broadly comic, drawing upon Anthony's experiences as a farmer, and go back to pioneering times in their simple characterization and physical humor. Yet they distill many of the qualities typical of the Kiwi farmer, they are told in a vivacious variant of the New Zealand vernacular, and, in the inept, know-all, good-natured Gus they provide one of our fiction's best-known and most likeable comic characters.

A much more sophisticated writer using the New Zealand idiom, Frank Sargeson (b. 1903), has refined it for a conscious artistic purpose. In his early stories, Sargeson took as his characters the men of Depression days, the misfit, the stray, the failure; the general attitude his work conveys is a distaste for the conventions of a bourgeois society, a special emphasis on male relationships, an assertion of the superior quality of life lived true to natural instincts, and a powerful sympathy for has-beens, drifters, and those who have opted out of socially conforming routines. His first collection, *Conservations with My Uncle* (1936), led to *A Man and His Wife* (1940) and *That Summer* (1946), which show a marked increase in subtlety and craft. There are times when he seems to exploit his characters to make a point against New Zealand smugness, but more often, in his mature stories, he identifies himself humanely with those whose instincts are defined or frustrated by their environment and, notably, with children. A conte, *I for One* (1954), unexpectedly extended his range by telling in the first person a completely convincing account of a spinster who moves from hope to disillusion; it is a tragi-comic love story in which the narrator's self-explorations comment obliquely on the type of suburban life in which she is involved.

Two of Sargeson's novels have already been mentioned: in his first novel, *I Saw in My Dream* (1949), a study in "growing up," the main character wrestles with himself and his conventional environment's values in search of freedom and fullness. This book, broken-backed and in some ways episodic and disordered, gave indications of a broadening of subject-matter, an enrichment of technique, and a thickening out of significance by literary allusions and parallels.

Influenced early by the style and matter of Sherwood Anderson and Hemingway, especially the former, Sargeson gradually evolved his own special manner and vision. Many of his stories are first-person narratives; others seem as if they should be so. His quest for what is fundamental in language is allied to his quest for what is fundamental in human behavior. Using as a foundation the flat, uninflected New Zealand colloquial speech, he forged a style through which the hopes, fears, disappointments, and cravings of largely inarticulate people find expression. Simple only in appearance, his language is both flexible and subtle, brilliantly adapted to individual characters, retaining the rhythms of everyday speech, yet making apparent the finer shades of feeling.

All his work—novels, novellas, and short stories—is concerned with the problems of identity in the New Zealand context, and the society's mediocrity, lingering puritanism, materialism, timidity before new ideas, conditioned reflexes masquerading as moral assertions. In the novels and later stories, some as yet uncollected, his style has undergone a progressive refinement in the direction of more complexity, at times approaching a Jamesian manner. His vocabulary remains basically simple, but is now more extensive, while his sentences are more involuted and sinuous. This change seems the result of the conscious development of a stylist seeking further nuances of expression for richer insights, of a shift in subject-matter from working-class characters to middle-class ones, of a concern with several levels of meaning, and of the emergence of a more complex vision of human beings.

It is, however, Sargeson's earlier style and view of life which have had the more immediate effect upon younger writers. In a sense, he summed up in prose many of the attitudes of restlessness, revolt, and the new egalitarianism that the poets of the 1930's also expressed. But his work has a relevance beyond this decade; those who were influenced by him shared his reaction against bourgeois values and a critical attitude towards New Zealand's Victorian heritage. Among those short story writers owing something to his example are G. R. Gilbert, whose stories in *Free to Laugh and Dance* (1942), often slight and wispy, seek for an elusive truth behind everyday life's "reality"; A. P. Gaskell, in *The Big Game* (1947), which is shrewdly observant of New Zealand male society, speech, and behavior; David Ballantyne, in *And the Glory* (1963), which reveals the suffocating life in suburbia, and O. E. Middleton, in *The Stone* (1959) and *A Walk on the Beach* (1964). Middleton's understated stories deal with ordinary people, usually of the working-class, in their everyday environment and coping with the business of living. They precisely catch the New Zealand mood, with its egalitarian basis, and the country's physical background, while their unadorned realism, if sometimes seemingly more "documentary" than re-created, in its skillful averageness of tone records selected responses of the ordinary "joker."

In Sargeson's early period, Roderick Finlayson (b. 1904) brought sympathy and knowledge to his portrayal of the Maori. In *Brown Man's Burden* (1938) and *Sweet Beulah Land* (1942) he contrasts what he deems to be the decadence of white society with the simplicity and dignity of the Maori. Underlying this attitude is a romantic anarchism which results in a tendency to glamorize the Maori—at least in his earlier stories. However, he is an alert observer of Maori customs and few have better comprehended the tensions beneath the Maori's placid exterior. Some of Finlayson's stories dramatize the conflict between the customs of the old people and the European ways of their children; others deal with the Maori's difficulty in adjusting himself to European morality; still others tell of the frequent degradation he suffers in a white man's society. Pity, gentleness, and humor season the stories which, though sometimes clumsy in structure, have the merit of a direct, perhaps ingenuous, honesty. In his later work—the loosely linked episodes that make up *Tidal Creek* (1948) and a novel set on a Pacific island, *The Schooner Came to Atia* (1952)—he has, with somewhat less success, used European characters to express his criticism of "unnatural" modern materialism and to point up problems of race relations.

In his single volume, *It Was So Late* (1949), John Reece Cole (b. 1916) wrote a notable series of stories dealing with the impact of war and its aftermath in which the tensions, fears, and sense of isolation and abandonment of the participants are most feelingly transmitted. Dan Davin, in *The Gorse Blooms Pale* (1947), also writes with humane understanding of war-time strains and revaluations and also of his Southland childhood. James Courage's short stories likewise plunder his youthful memories.

In three volumes of short stories, of which the best are collected as *The Reservoir* (1965), Janet Frame uses the same range of themes as appear in her novels. Sometimes fragmentary and tentative in the early stories, but increasingly firmer and more controlled in the later phases, these briefer works frequently achieve a more unified impression and more coherent statement than her novels do. Her method of placing a single dominant image at the center of the story, as in "The Reservoir" itself, or of counterpointing the story with a series of related images, is an artistic strategy which produces an effect of symbolic depth and haunting beauty. Helen Shaw (b. 1913), in *The Orange Tree* (1957), reveals a precise, fastidious sensibility fascinated by old and strange things, especially houses and people. Like Katherine Mansfield, she manages her atmosphere exquisitely and conjures up a sense of melancholy decay touched with grotesque comedy.

Difficulties of finding publishers for novels in New Zealand in the 1930's and 1940's and the existence of outlets for short stories in local and Australian magazines helped to make the short story a popular form with talented writers in these decades. With more opportunities for novel-publishing and with the increasing reluctance of publishers to handle volumes of short stories, fewer new writers specializing in the shorter form have appeared of recent years. But two writers have made a special impact by creating distinctive worlds of their own in the short story.

Maurice Duggan (b. 1922), in *Immanuel's Land* (1957) and *Summer in the Gravel Pit* (1956), offers rigorously disciplined stories, sometimes impressionistic, sometimes subtly realistic, sometimes slightly precious in style, but usually economically exact. He is mainly concerned with such topics as the narrow, drab, and emotionally phoney life of Irish people and the fretful adolescence of boys at a Catholic boarding-school. The general effect is of a sad and deprived world, lacking love or meaningful connections and greyed with indifference, betrayal, and sensual itches. Lost, faithless, disturbed, Duggan's lonely characters inhabit what is perhaps the most melancholy emotional landscape the modern New Zealand short story has to offer.

Maurice Shadbolt (b. 1932) shows in *The New Zealanders* (1959) and *Summer Fires and Winter Country* (1963) a wider range than Maurice Duggan and a more sanguine outlook. He, too, deals with people faced with emotional difficulties, but they are explored more intimately and in more complex terms. His stories cover a broad area of New Zealand experience and settings, so much at times in his earlier work as to leave the impression that the characters are slightly less meaningful in themselves than as they embody aspects of the national sensibility. Shadbolt is especially responsive to the country's landscape and, in depicting man in relation to it, shares something of the primitivistic and romantic philosophy of Sargeson and Finlayson. A particular concern with the relationship of the artist to a still largely undeveloped society is given special emphasis in the three novellas which make up his most impressive book, *The Presence of Music* (1967). Shadbolt is always extremely readable; his style, if infrequently economical and if not as manifestly self-conscious as that of several of his contemporaries, is forceful, yet capable of subtle effects. He is clearly a writer with more still to say.

5

DRAMA

DRAMATIC writing in New Zealand has been hampered by the absence of native professional theatre. Overseas companies have visited the country regularly since early days and there have been valiant attempts at forming professional companies, but in the main the problems of geography and of small and dispersed audiences have frustrated these efforts. It is only very recently that fully or partly professional theatre has begun to take shape in some of the main cities. Most New Zealand theatre is amateur, and often reaches a more than respectable standard in the performance of a diversity of types of play, from Shakespeare to Pinter and from Sophocles to Beckett.

Because of the lack of professional outlets, in the past at least, dramatists determined to make their mark have gone abroad to become absorbed into British or American milieux; such has been the case with Merton Hodge, Bruce Stewart, and Ted Kavanagh, who wrote the BBC's popular program, *It's That Man Again,* in the war years. Those who remain content themselves with writing plays performed only by amateur groups—and that infrequently—or else turn to writing radio and television dramas. Despite this a considerable number of interesting plays have seen the light since the war, although New Zealand has not yet found a play equal in dramatic force and popular appeal to the Australian plays of Ray Lawler, Alan Seymour, and Richard Benyon.

Early theatre, if artless, was vigorous enough, and popular melodramas or adaptations of novels and farces were written and produced, though few of them ever found their way into print. The occasional published examples show a close following of the broad conventions of English barnstorming. It was not until the 1920's that plays began to be both written and published in noticeable numbers. For much the same reason that short stories rather than novels were written in New Zealand, most of these plays were one-acters, in general no better and no worse than those which are the staple vehicle for Drama League Festivals in Britain. But in the 1930's J. A. S. Coppard (b. 1899) broke away from convention with a batch of experimental one-act dramas owing something to contemporary German expressionism and using symbolism and poetic language in a variety of original dramatic techniques. Such plays as *Sordid Story,* which takes place entirely inside a character's mind, with his emotions embodied as characters, *Machine Song,* which turns machinery into people, and *The Axe and the Oak,* which personifies aspects of nature, were published and performed in New Zealand and overseas. He has had few successors as daring, but in the one-act field Isobel Andrews, Eric Bradwell, Jean Lawrence, Marie Bullock, Bruce Mason, Joseph Musaphia, Warren Dibble, and Wayne Torelle have done work above the average.

Poetic drama has attracted the greater number of writers of full-length drama. The earliest and one of the most successful practitioners was the poet Douglas Stewart, whose *The Golden Lover,* a Maori legend, and *The Fire in the Snow,* about Scott's Antarctic expedition, are plays of genuine power and with real dramatic shape. But *Ned Kelly* (1943) a much-performed drama about the notorious Australian bushranger, is his outstanding achievement, as much for its genuinely tragic sense as for its transformation of colloquial speech into moving dramatic poetry. Also in the poetic tradition is Allen Curnow's *The Axe* (1949), dealing with the clash between two cultures, Christian and pagan, on a Pacific island. James K. Baxter, in *Jack Winter's Dream* (1959), is a shade too close to Dylan Thomas, but in *The Wide Open Cage* (1959) he essays a contemporary tragedy with considerable success. Both show Baxter's flair for jolting poetic symbolism and his preoccupation with the dark places of the mind. Like Allen Curnow, he has written other plays which have been performed by amateur groups or on radio but not published. W. D'Arcy Cresswell's *The Forest* (1952) is a virtually unplayable closet drama, mixing didacticism, farce, old-fashioned Romanticism, and homosexual views of women and love. Frank Sargeson has also experimented with drama. *A Time for Sowing,* which is based upon the fall from grace of the real-life missionary, Thomas Kendall, has considerable power; *The Cradle and the Egg,* a symbolic cosmic drama, dense with a rather private philosophy of generation and rebirth, is considerably less interesting. Indeed, a significant number of New Zealand plays show the writers' remoteness from the realities of the stage for which they are presumably writing and an ignorance of what makes a play "go" in the theatre. A certain amount of closet drama is inevitable in a country where theatre is not yet a normal part of its life.

In a more orthodox mode, the half-dozen published plays of Claude Evans (b. 1905) have a sound theatrical sense, but are conventional in characterization and situation. His best play, *Overtime* (1953), plausibly dramatizes the decline of old values of craftsmanship in modern industrial society. Stella Jones's *The Tree* (1960) is psychologically acute in its portrayal of family tensions; its seemingly orthodox plot is given depth by an ingenious time-scheme and an analytical eye for the unpredictable element in human beings. In *The Pohutukawa Tree* (1960), one of the best constructed and most playable of recent plays, Bruce Mason (b. 1921) courageously and sympathetically tackles the theme of race relations. His "monodrama" *The End of the Golden Weather* (1962) transfers a common literary theme to the stage as it surveys adult life through the eyes of a growing boy. Ngaio Marsh has written the libretto for a fantasy-opera, *A Unicorn for Christmas* (1962), with music by the New Zealand composer, David Farquhar.

It is radio which has given New Zealand dramatists their greatest opportunities and greatest challenge. On local noncommercial channels full-length plays are regularly performed without the encumberances of commercials or the procrustean rigors of restricted time. The enlightened policy of the New Zealand Broadcasting Corporation, especially of recent years, is encouraging local dramatists to write for radio (television drama is still in its tottering infancy) and to be venturesome in experimentation, has brought to light a number of new talents. Apart from writers already named, successful radio writers of serious drama include John Gundry, John Monteith, and Ivan de la Chaumette. Few of their works have been published. In the absence of a well-established commercial theatre, New Zealand is almost knee-deep in unpublished and unperformed plays, some of them winners of playwriting competitions.

6

GENERAL PROSE

Only a handful of general prose works stand out from the first eighty years or so of New Zealand writing. In the main, like the novels, they are much to a pattern—either personal narratives, journals, diaries, or guidebooks designed for intending settlers. The last were usually dauntingly dull, uninspired hack-work crammed with useful information. The others, although untidy and slapdash, are usually the more interesting, since they are based upon personal experience; apart from their historical interest, they often engage the attention of the modern student with their enthusiasm for the potentialities of the new land and with their generous pioneering spirit.

Typical of the "tract-and-water" brand of early journal, is W. B. Marshall's *A Personal Narrative of Two Visits to New Zealand in His Majesty's Ship Alligator, A. D. 1834* (1836), a flat, grayly impersonal work which even the sincere Christian interest shown in the Maoris fails to animate. Typical of the early guidebook is E. B. Fitton's *New Zealand, Its Present Condition, Prospects and Resources* (1856), a heavy-handed compilation aiming to persuade Englishmen of the wonders of the New Zealand climate, scenery, and agricultural possibilities. Much more alive is *A Narrative of a Voyage to New Zealand* (1817), by John Liddiard Nicholas, who accompanied the first missionary, Samuel Marsden, when he arrived in the land. Nicholas, pompous and self-consciously literary in the eighteenth-century manner, intersperses his often valuable accounts of Maori life with philosophizings about the nature of civilization. Augustus Earle (1798–?) wrote the more agreeable *Narrative of a Nine Months' Residence in New Zealand* (1832). Earle sailed from Australia to New Zealand with some members of the Wesleyan Mission. He was an artist of considerable quality, and his *Sketches Illustrative of the Native Inhabitants and Islands of New Zealand* (1838) remains one of the most prized of early books for the excellence of its colored lithographs. Earle's smooth, humane account of pioneering times and his artist's-eye descriptions of the Maoris make his *Narrative* a most engaging work. The *Letters and Journals of Samuel Marsden* (published in 1932 by Professor J. R. Elder) are also attractive. Marsden, a man of strong and complex character, had a direct style which never aims at literary effects, and it serves him well to convey his genuine solicitude for the natives, and to present cogently the tribulations of early missionaries and the effect of the established missions on the life of the New Zealander.

Possibly the most idiosyncratic of the early writers was J. S. Polack (1807–82), a picturesque Jewish trader, author, artist, and store-keeper. His *New Zealand: Being a Narrative of Travels and Adventures* (1838) combines his own experiences with matter from written and spoken sources to produce a history of the founding and growth of the new settlement, and a plea to Great Britain to colonize the islands. Lurid, especially in its descriptions of cannibalism, vivid in its anecdotes, vivacious in its puns and its blustering, Polack's book has no stylistic grace, but a boisterously compelling tone that gives it a rude appeal. After leaving the country, he returned later and wrote his *Manners and Customs of the New Zealanders* (1840), giving further lurid details of Maori life.

The Polynesian inhabitants inevitably attracted attention from pioneering writers. *Savage Life and Scenes in Australia and New Zealand* (1847), by George French Angas (1822–86), is a descriptive text supplementing Angas's *The New Zealanders Illustrated* (1847), a magnificent production of colored lithographs in which Angas portrays the Maori in the formal poses of Greek warriors. In his prose, Angas, a young traveller of wealth, gives a much more exact and realistic impression of the natives, recording their bravery, dignity, hospitality, and sense of humor. So, too, *Traditions and Superstitions of the New Zealanders* (1854), by Edward Shortland (1812–93), and his later *Maori Religion and Mythology* (1882), as well as Richard Taylor's *Te Ika a Maui* (1855) marked the beginning of a more serious and scientific appraisal of Maori life and traditions. Sir George Grey (1812–98), Governor-General of New Zealand, reinforced the work of these pioneers by collecting the legends, poems, and traditional chants of the natives in three volumes issued between 1854 and 1858, and thus preserving these remarkably imaginative blends of legend and tradition before they became too blurred by contact with the white man's culture.

The most ebullient of the early records is that of Edward Jerningham Wakefield (1820–79), *Adventures in New Zealand from 1839 to 1844* (1845). E. J. Wakefield, son of Edward Gibbon Wakefield, founder of the British immigrant organization known as the New Zealand Company, gives a fascinating impression of the colony in its infant days, and of the troubled period when it passed under British protection. As a boy of nineteen he came to New Zealand in the *Tory* in 1839 and kept a diary from which *Adventures in New Zealand* was elaborated. Leaving in 1844, he returned in 1851 to play an important part in the country's development as explorer and Member of Parliament. While his book is highly colored by New Zealand Company prejudices against the government and the missionaries and often bogs down in complex details of land transactions, it is kept lively by its warm enthusiasm for the new land and its able sketches of men and women. With much more exuberance and gusto than the novelists who were to venture into the same territory, Wakefield captures for us the dress, conversations, and habits of the whalers, the flax-dressers, the bullock-drivers, the soldiers, the Maoris, and the self-important government officials. His book is much more readable than *Travels in New Zealand* (1843) by Dr. Ernst Dieffenbach (1811–55), naturalist to the New Zealand Company, a work full of useful scientific information but ploddingly written, and *New Zealand and its Colonisation* (1859), by William Swainson, the country's first Attorney-General.

The year 1859 saw the publication of the first large-scale history, *The Story of New Zealand, Past and Present—Savage and Civilised,* by Dr. A. S. Thomson (1816–60), Surgeon-General of the 58th Regiment, who spent eleven years in the land. This still interesting work is a comprehensive, systematic, and intelligently selective history of the Colony from early Maori times to the later 1850's. Thomson is especially good on the Maoris, among whom he lived, and the Maori Wars, in which he served. An adept and shrewd recorder of colonial society, he also had a profitable interest in natural history; he writes of both with dignity and charm. His bibliography of some 1,600 items demonstrates both his own thoroughness and the great amount of commentary the country had produced in about three decades.

The Maori Wars, which disturbed New Zealand intermittently from 1845 to 1872, inspired much fiction, documentary material, and written history. Perhaps the most durable of these records is *The Maori King* (1864) by J. E. (later Sir John) Gorst (1835–1916), who was Civil Commissioner of the Waikato district during one of the most difficult phases of the conflict. Gorst's analysis of the causes of the wars is unusually perceptive, and shows his deep sympathy with the problems of the natives; he also draws the chief actors in the drama on both sides with fluent skill. Not only is the work an important historical document, it is also widely accepted as one of the best nineteenth-century accounts of life among the

Maoris. Gorst returned to England convinced that the Maori race was doomed to extinction. He became Solicitor-General in England and a Privy Councillor, and, many years afterwards, returned to New Zealand to find the Maoris regenerated and harmony established between the two races. His *New Zealand Revisited* (1908) records his later impressions. Many other eye-witness accounts of the wars survive, such as *Principal Causes of the Present War* (1859), by Lieutenant Colonel I. McDonnell, who won the Victoria Cross in the campaign, and William Fox's *The War in New Zealand* (1866). The most spirited piece of reporting from the militiaman's point of view is Lieutenant T. W. Gudgeon's *Reminiscences of the War in New Zealand* (1879), a comparatively dispassionate survey, with intimate details of the various campaigns and an honest sympathy for the enemy.

The Maori Wars have continued to provide material for research and controversy. James Cowan (1870–1943), who produced many books on the Maori, was commissioned by the Government to write his massive *The New Zealand Wars and the Pioneering Period* (1922–23) but this has been superseded by Professor Keith Sinclair's *The Origins of the Maori Wars* (1957), a work of fine scholarship now accepted as the definitive study of a tangled area of our history in which the white man shows up by no means uniformly well.

In the Maori Wars period, the opening up of the pastoral provinces found its chroniclers. By the 1860's, the era of the first settlers had been succeeded by that of a new generation, many of whom had become, by hard work, people of wealth and influence. In this group two important writers belong–Samuel Butler (1835–1902) and Lady Mary Anne Barker (1831–1911). Butler came to New Zealand in 1860 to try his hand at sheep-farming. He spent five years in the Canterbury area, where he did well, leaving the country with his initial capital of 4,000 pounds doubled. His letters and some notes sent to his parents in England were edited by his father and issued as *A First Year in the Canterbury Settlement* (1863). This is undoubtedly one of the best of early New Zealand books, catching the authentic atmosphere of sheep-farming in the 1860's and much of the temper of the country in a relaxed, racy style. In these pages there is the freshness of a lively young personality and little of the acerbity, perverseness, and self-conscious smartness of the elder Butler. Some of his comments on New Zealand mores have become celebrated; for instance, "There is much nonsense in the old country from which the people here are free. There is little conventionalism, little formality, and much liberality of sentiment; very little sectarianism, and, as a general rule, a healthy sensible tone in conversation which I like much."

While in New Zealand Butler conceived what was to be the germ of his celebrated *Erewhon*. In 1863 he published an article, "Darwin Among the Machines," in the *Christchurch Press*. When he returned to England, he developed this into "The Book of the Machines," which became the basis of *Erewhon*. His hero's journey to the land of Erewhon, "beyond the range," is based upon Butler's own travels through the Canterbury Plains to the headwaters of the Rangitata in the Southern Alps. Professor I. A. Gordon has also suggested that *Erewhon* owes much more than its scenery to New Zealand, in that the impressionable young Cambridge man found the country a land of upside-down, a society very different from the rigidly class-stratified Victorian England, one in which many of the British social values were reversed, and that this helped to shape the fundamental idea of the topsy-turvey *Erewhon*.

The other notable writer of the pastoral period, Lady Barker, came to New Zealand in the 1860's with her second husband, F. N. Broome, to live on his Canterbury sheep-station. She adjusted herself quickly to her new life and came to love the country and its people. There is no more charming recorder of early New Zealand manners than this gifted and likeable English lady who so completely assumed the cares and responsibilities of a station-owner's wife. Although she sees the colony's life from the point of view of a genteel aristocrat, she does so with unpatronizing understanding. She describes the weather—her description of the snowstorm of 1867 is magnificent—the routine of station life, pig-hunting, servant problems, burning off, picnics, lambing, riding and visiting, and gives us shepherds' stories in their original idiom. Apart from her books of short stories, her most important works are *Station Life in New Zealand* (1870), *Station Amusements in New Zealand* (1873), and *Colonial Memories* (1904).

About the same time Lady Barker was absorbing her impressions, there appeared two books by F. E. Maning (1811–83), one of which, *Old New Zealand* (1862), is the most animated and original prose work of New Zealand's nineteenth century. Maning was an interesting character who came to know the Maoris well as husband to a Maori woman, and later as a Judge in the Native Land Court; he was a "pakeha-Maori," the contemporary phrase for a white man who associated with Maoris, and this he used as his *nom de plume*. Taking his cue from earlier memoirs, Maning welds together burlesque, yarning, mock philosophizing, and horrific anecdotes into a clever style, half-comic, half-serious, and largely ironical, through which he gives a highly individual appraisal of Maori life and customs. The thesis of *Old New Zealand* is the decadence of modern times as compared with those of the past, a tongue-in-cheek attitude which he illustrates by ripely comic descriptions of such customs as *tapu* and *muru*. Nobody would go to this book for an accurate picture of native life, any more than one would go to *Tristram Shandy* for details of the strategy of Malplaquet, but as an idiosyncratic and lusty piece of writing with an impish quality all its own, it has no rival in its age. A different aspect of Maning's personality is seen in *History of the War in the North* (1863), a monologue put into the mouth of an old chief of the Ngapuhi tribe. The tone of this book is quite different from that of *Old New Zealand*. Without ridicule or condescension, Maning gives us the Maori viewpoint on the European, with dignified artistry and a knowledge of Maori oratory that imparts a noble seriousness and rhythm to his prose.

As the pioneering and opening-up periods receded into the past, much of the energy that had gone into the making of "journals," "adventures," and "travels" was diverted into fiction. Reminiscences and guidebooks diminished in number as exotic elements of interest to an overseas audience were replaced by the familiar patterns of Western civilization. With such developments, too, the rude vigor and rough individuality of early memoirs gave place to a more formal and genteel style, substituting the shapely yet lifeless for the shapeless yet dynamic. Thus, only a handful of memoirs of any interest were written between the 1860's and the 1890's. *Rambles with a Philosopher* (1867), by Otago's first surveyor, J. T. Thomson (1821–84), has some appeal as an oddity, one of the freakish, near-crackpot books New Zealand has never been short of. It outlines a curious theory of "contraries," discourses on a multitude of scientific, philosophical, and social topics, and deals lavishly in tart comments on the state of "Mudedin." In 1879 John Barr (1809–89) published the best of the nostalgic recollections of the pioneers, *The Old Identities*, a spirited account of the "great men" and personalities of early Otago. In the same year the remarkable Captain W. J. Barry (1819–1907) issued his *Up and Down: or Fifty Years' Colonial Experiences*, the last true example of the artless, directionless, extroverted compendium of pioneering anecdotes and reminiscences. Born in England, Barry had run away on a whaling ship and visited New Zealand, where he saw cannibalism. He survived two shipwrecks and in 1840 joined the British Navy in Calcutta, serving in the first China War. After farming in Australia and gold-mining in

California, he returned to New Zealand in 1862 to prospect for gold in Gabriel's Gully. He was in turn miner, farmer, butcher, auctioneer, and Mayor of Cromwell in 1864. Later he went to England and became involved in the famous Tichborne case. Back in New Zealand again, he lectured on his adventurous life and explored the uncharted King country. A picturesque, dynamic, hard-living character, a tireless wanderer and a man who made fortunes quickly and lost them as quickly, Barry wrote memoirs uncontaminated by literary flourishes, set down in a torrential style, and doubtless highly colored by his imagination. Yet, for all this, it is an absorbing book, catching in its artlessness more of the true spirit of the times and the character of the adventurers attracted to New Zealand than most laborious historical re-creations.

With Barry's book, we say farewell to the characteristic type of pioneering record, although to the present time octogenarians publish recollections of the later opening-up era and newly-discovered diaries of earlier days are issued almost as soon as they are found. In a land with little history, every scrap of information is deemed to have its value. After the 1880's, prose broadens out to encompass more diverse types of expression, and at the same time becomes progressively refined.

In the 1890's the new national spirit manifested itself in the beginnings of an indigenous literature. The effects of this change in poetry and fiction have already been discussed. Typical of the times is the *New Zealand Illustrated Magazine*, founded in 1899, which set out to fulfil the object of being "a Magazine with a distinctive New Zealand colouring, one which will have for its aim the encouragement of the best Literary and Artistic Talent which we have in our midst," and which confidently sought to educate the public to accept creative treatment of specifically local themes. Some sixty years later, it is hard to detect any basic difference between most of the work printed in the *Illustrated* and earlier writing. But, despite its provinciality and its rather ingenuous concept of the nature of an indigenous culture, the magazine was a portent of the future, and in its pages appeared the earliest work, not so much of significant creative writers, as of historians and anthropologists who were later to make valuable contributions to New Zealand life and thought, such as G. H. Scholefield (1877–1963), Sir James Hight (1872–1958), James Cowan (1870–1943), and Elsdon Best (1856–1931).

The major personality of the 1890's was W. Pember Reeves, who has already been discussed as a poet. A state socialist whose contributions to New Zealand progressive legislation were considerable, Reeves left his native land in 1896 for London where he became Agent-General and identified himself fully with English life. More enduring than his verse is *The Long White Cloud* (1898–the title translates the Maori name for New Zealand, "Ao-tea-roa"). This essay-history, of great charm, polished and thoughtful, has gone into many editions, and, although its historical judgments are dated and colored by Reeves's radical bias, it is still admired for its perception and intellectual liveliness. Reeves had the wit and much of the civilized urbanity of the eighteenth-century essayists. The whole tone of the work marks a remarkable advance upon that of earlier historians; it is cultured, scholarly, and placidly witty; it is not only history, but an affectionate description of the land Reeves loved. His later work, *State Experiments in Australia and New Zealand* (1902), recording the legislation in which he took a hand, is more restricted in interest, but shows a gift for style and a conscious craftsmanship that mark it off from its predecessors.

Writing about the Maori continued on several levels. One important work of this kind is *Where the White Man Treads* (1905), by William Baucke (1848–1931). Although this is a somewhat untidy collection of reprinted newspaper articles and stories, it largely achieves its object which is "to enter into the inner life of the Maori, and coincidentally entertain his readers with a series of incidents, impressions and word pictures, painted with such skill as an amateur may possess, and a lifelong intimacy with the Maoris has given him command of." At times journalistically written, Baucke's book remains thoroughly readable and contains much of interest to modern anthropologists. Other important writers on the Maori at this time include Elsdon Best, James Cowan, and Johannes Andersen (1973–1962). But the finest flower of the age is *Tutira* (1921), by W. H. Guthrie-Smith (1861–1940), which is a classic of our writing. Guthrie-Smith wrote several other books, such as the admirable *Sorrows and Joys of a New Zealand Naturalist* (1936), but *Tutira* remains his main achievement. Born in Scotland, he came to New Zealand in the 1880's to work on a Canterbury farm. Later he bought a large sheep-station named Tutira, in Hawkes Bay, where he lived until his death. He was a naturalist, an antiquarian, a scholar with a most inquisitive mind, and a writer gifted with a wry, occasionally sardonic, humor. *Tutira* was planned simply as "The Story of a New Zealand Sheep Station," which is its sub-title, but by the time it was finished, Guthrie-Smith had expanded his original plan to include geology, anthropology, natural history, ethnology, and meteorology. He gives us the physical and human history of his own section of New Zealand from the earliest geological times right up to and through his own occupancy. By this intensive study of Tutira over countless centuries, he not only says almost as much as it is possible to say about any place, but makes us aware of all that is characteristic of New Zealand as a land and as a community. The unique character of *Tutira* is the result of the unique combination in its author of poet, artist, philosopher, scientist, and inquiring mind. Above all, he is a humanist, always conscious of his fellowmen. He saw his station in relation to the larger world of things and was keenly aware of the potentialities of his "dear adopted land." The section dealing with the Maoris, a combination of imagination and shrewd observation, is one of the most balanced appraisals of Maori culture ever penned.

With Guthrie-Smith, we reach the beginning of the modern period of New Zealand writing. From the 1920's to the present day, there has been a great growth of books of all kinds which reveal an intensified interest in varying aspects of the national life and a closer attention to things of the mind. Many are of purely local and ephemeral interest, but a considerable number have found audiences abroad, and have some literary value.

The past forty years have witnessed many advances in the writing of New Zealand history, in great part as a result of the growth of historical and anthropological studies in the universities. There is still much work to be done in the study of documents and in political history: some early papers still await publication. But the older kind of appreciative history has given way to a more scientific scrutiny of materials and considerable revaluation of earlier concepts, especially of the causes of the Maori Wars and the planned settlement of New Zealand. While some early histories may have been more colorful than recent ones, several modern historians are able to marshal facts with literary skill and a sense of drama.

Some valuable work was done, if rather haphazardly and in an unscholarly way, by T. Lindsay Buick (1866–1938) and Robert McNab (1864–1917). Buick, a journalist and Member of Parliament who wrote well but neglected to document his work, left two useful histories in *Old Marlborough* (1900) and *Old Manawatu* (1903). McNab, Minister for Lands in the First World War Government, searched old sailing records throughout the world to compile a fascinating collection of data concerning the sealing and whaling trades, in *Murihiku* (1904) and *The Old Whaling Days* (1914) among other books, all of which contain most valuable historical material.

The writing of historical biography is of fairly recent development. J. R. Elder's edition of Samuel Marsden's *Letters and Journals* (1932) has already been mentioned. The life of William Colenso, missionary, botanist, and the country's first printer, has been well written by A. G. Bagnell and G. C. Petersen (1948); Lillian G. Keys has ably recorded the life of Bishop Pompallier, the first Catholic missionary (1957); *Letters from New Zealand, 1850–53* by Charlotte Godley, wife of the "Father of Canterbury," edited by J. R. Godley in 1951, gives a clear picture of beginnings in the settlement, and A. J. Harrop's *The Amazing Career of Edward Gibbon Wakefield* (1928) sets out the chequered career of the founder of the New Zealand Company.

A great impetus to historical studies was given by the development of a first-rate library service by Dr. G. H. Scholefield, who, in his twenty-two years as Parliamentary Librarian, not only greatly enlarged the library's collection of manuscripts, but also established a national archives system. In 1918, the Alexander Turnbull Library in Wellington, with its magnificent Pacific collections, passed into government hands. With these facilities, and efficient development of the Country Library Service and the comprehensive inter-loan service, contemporary historians have material at hand far superior to that available to their predecessors.

New Zealand's leading historian, Professor J. C. Beaglehole (b. 1901) has set a high example of scholarly thoroughness combined with a most literate style and a gift for illustrative imagery, which is not surprising, since he is also a poet. His best-known books are *The Discovery of New Zealand* (1939) and *The Exploration of the Pacific* (1947), but his crowning achievement is his magnificent edition of Captain Cook's *Journals* (1955–). J. B. Condliffe's *New Zealand in the Making* (1930) is the nearest thing to a comprehensive treatment of our history to that date, but concentrates largely on the country's economic development. Professor Keith Sinclair's *Pelican History of New Zealand* (1959) is the broadest, liveliest, and best-written general survey of recent years, full of provocative judgments and given depth by the author's range of extra-historical interests; like Dr. Beaglehole, Dr. Sinclair is a noted poet. Also worthy of attention are Harold Miller's *New Zealand* (1951), and *A Short History of New Zealand* (revised, 1953) by J. B. Condliffe and W. T. G. Airey.

There is still room for good historical biographies in New Zealand. The standard work of reference remains G. H. Scholefield's two-volume *Dictionary of New Zealand Biography* (1940), the fruit of patient scholarship. Among the best recent biographies is *King Dick* (1955) by R. M. Burdon (b. 1896), who has written several other biographies and volumes of "brief lives." *King Dick* is a brilliant study of Richard John Seddon, Prime Minister from 1892 to his death in 1906, a self-made man and Liberal under whose benevolent despotism New Zealand developed its radical legislation. Another biography is *Sir George Grey* (1961) by Professor James Rutherford (1906–1963), a massive two-volume work giving the definitive picture of the colonial administrator whose period as Governor of New Zealand formed only part of a long life in the service of the Commonwealth.

A further sign of recent change is the writing by educated Maoris on their own history and myths. Sir Maui Pomare (1876–1930), a physician, joined with James Cowan to produce the two volumes of *Legends of the Maori* (1930). The most distinguished of this group was Sir Peter Buck (Te Rangi Hiroa, 1880–1951), a Maori anthropologist who became director of the Bishop Museum at Honolulu, and for a time visiting professor of anthropology at Yale University. His most celebrated books, *Vikings of the Sunrise* (1938) and *The Coming of the Maori* (1949), advance theories about the long voyages of his ancestors from the legendary home of Hawaiki in the Pacific, which have been called into doubt by Andrew Sharp's *Ancient Voyagers in the Pacific* (1956). Other notable works on the Maori and his culture have been written by Johannes Andersen, Roger Duff, Raymond Firth, Ernest Beaglehole, and Sir Gilbert Archey.

The fields of general biography and memoirs have been well tilled of recent years. Four autobiographies may be selected from the mass as representative of major trends, and as superior to the many garrulous and self-laudatory and often inaccurate memoirs of later pioneering days. These are *Cheerful Yesterdays* (1928) by O. J. T. Alpers (1867–1927), *The Poet's Progress* (1930) by W. D'Arcy Cresswell (1896–1961), *My First Eighty Years* (1951) by Helen Wilson (1874–1957), and *The Making of a New Zealander* (1960) by Alan Mulgan (1881–1962).

Oscar Alpers' autobiography tells of a poor Copenhagen boy who came to New Zealand in 1875 at the age of eight, and by hard study, determination, and talent, became an eminent lawyer and, in 1925, a Supreme Court judge. His story is of permanent interest because of its kindly humanity, gentle humor, and absence of egotism, as well as for its graceful style. Antony Alpers, his son, has written the best biography of Katherine Mansfield. W. D'Arcy Cresswell, poet, wanderer, and eccentric individualist, wrote two books describing his Bohemian life in New Zealand and Britain, *The Poet's Progress* and *Present without Leave* (1939), in a stylized prose, archaic and informal by turns. A consistent, uncompromising and distinctive personality, who mixed common sense with crackpottery, Cresswell was hostile to the main trends of modern civilization, bourgeois values, and the Western world's worship of science.

Mrs. Helen Wilson's account of her long life of varied activity and community service provides invaluable pictures of country life during the previous seventy years; her book, full of revealing details, is sustained by a robust philosophy of life. Alan Mulgan's autobiography covers the same period, but from a different standpoint. Perhaps the last of our "men of letters" in the old sense, Mr. Mulgan, poet, essayist, novelist, historian, journalist, biographer, and social commentator, tells, in *The Making of a New Zealander,* of the gradual process whereby he, a son of Ulster settlers at Katikati, moved from a nostalgia for "Home" to a total acceptance of New Zealand as his spiritual ground. Mulgan summed up the virtues of his generation of literary men and left a lasting impression on New Zealand letters.

Only a few biographies need be mentioned to give some idea of the scope of recent work. Dr. E. H. McCormick (b. 1905), in *The Expatriate* (1953), has produced an invaluable study, done with impeccable scholarship and taste, of Frances Hodgkins, the country's most celebrated painter, who won a considerable reputation in Europe. John Pascoe (b. 1908), in his fine *Mr. Explorer Douglas* (1957), both delineates a remarkable figure in our history and gives a real-life example of that archetypal character, the "man alone." Perhaps the best of the personal stories produced by New Zealanders during World War II was *Infantry Brigadier* (1948), by Major-General Howard Kippenberger (1897–1957), who, after a very distinguished war career in which he was severely wounded, became editor-in-chief of the Official War Histories. Sir Howard's unusual gifts as both soldier and scholar make his book a unique personal record of the war in Crete. It combines exemplary observation with imaginative presentation in a clear prose salted with gently reserved humor. *Infantry Brigadier* will be read long after the war becomes distant history for its literary qualities and for its incidental revelation of a man of exceptional talents.

Volumes of general essays find small favor in New Zealand these days. A generation or so ago, however, there was a steady market for collections of this kind in the tradition of Lamb, E. V. Lucas, G. K. Chesterton, and others, often reprinted from the columns of newspapers. This type of occasional writing flourished in the earliest days of the colony, and even today an infrequent volume makes its appearance. A recent amiable example is *A Shepherd's Calendar* (1962), by Oliver Duff (1883–1966). This selection from a regular feature contributed to the *New Zealand Listener* by its former editor, who had also written a social history of the country, is distinguished by a lively, pungent style and provocative observations on often unchronicled aspects of life on the land.

Among earlier essayists of some note were Alan Mulgan, whose *Home* (1939) and *First with the Sun* (1947) typify his activity as a journalist; Professor F. Sinclaire with his *Lend Me Your Ears* (1942) and *A Time to Laugh* (1951); and J. H. E. Schroder (b. 1895), with his *Remembering Things* (1938). These volumes are the work of men of an older generation, and belong to that meditative or personal kind of essay which seems to have had its last flash of quality in Edwardian times. Among exceptions to the tradition are the essays of A. R. D. Fairburn, a Roman candle of a writer, who, in addition to his varied verse, wrote much trenchant, calculatedly provocative prose and has left in *We New Zealanders* (1944), a frank, hard-hitting piece of national self-criticism. Another essayist of true distinction is M. H. Holcroft, whose *The Eye of the Lizard* (1960) collects his editorials in the *New Zealand Listener*. But Mr. Holcroft has made his most enduring mark as a critic of our literature and its values.

Literary criticism, in the strict sense, is a comparatively late development in New Zealand. Much useful work was done in a tentative way in the several magazines issued from the nineties to the eve of World War II—the *New Zealand Illustrated Magazine*, the *New Triad, Tomorrow*, the *New Zealand Artists Annual, Art in New Zealand*, and others, for the country has been as prolific as other lands in "little magazines," many of them enjoying the briefest of lives. Serious criticism came as a consequence of the development of New Zealand writing in the 1930's; there had, in fact, been little worthy of consideration before that. The greatest initial stimulus was given by M. H. Holcroft, who won the essay section of the 1940 State Centennial Literary Competitions with his book *The Deepening Stream*. This was followed by *The Waiting Hills* (1943) and *Encircling Seas* (1945), the three later published together under the collective title of *Discovered Isles* (1950).

In this epoch-making trilogy, Holcroft set himself, as no earlier critic had done, to examine the nature of critical problems in New Zealand. He gives at once an anatomizing of national culture, pointing to its pragmatic basis, its ingrained materialism and its failure to develop the highest instincts of its citizens, a discussion of leading themes in New Zealand writing and their significance, and a fruitful examination of particular writers—Ursula Bethell, Eileen Duggan, and D'Arcy Cresswell among them. He emphasizes the themes of exile, loneliness, and frustration in our literature, and stresses the effect on this writing and our culture of the "bush" (the forest) and the memory of the immigrants' long voyage from Britain, and finds in them both basic drives and conditioning factors. A Wordsworthian vision of the character of literature and of the forces of Nature operating on the poet is the source of both the strength and the weakness of Holcroft's criticism. While his work has been criticized and in part rejected, and its intuitions condemned as vague and pseudo-mystical, and while it is true that parts of his work are suffused with an irritatingly tenuous pantheism, there can be no doubt as to the originality of the mind it reveals, the fine sensibility of its aperçus, and the dynamic effect of Holcroft's example on his successors.

Also of outstanding importance in this field was the publication, in 1940, of E. H. McCormick's *Letters and Art in New Zealand,* a work of painstaking scholarship, written with grace and lucidity, the first historical survey of our literature and our painting, which examined the development of local literature in close relation to the growth of the community. A revised edition of the book, *New Zealand Literature,* appeared in 1959.

The foundations laid by Holcroft and McCormick were rapidly built upon in the post-war years. Allen Curnow prefaced his anthology, *A Book of New Zealand Verse, 1923–1945* (1945) with a long, discerning essay, expressing a well-argued personal assessment of poetic growth, having some affinity with Holcroft's essays in its stress upon indigenous elements and on the role of landscape in poetry. Curnow's later anthology, *The Penguin Book of New Zealand Verse* (1960) contains a longer preface, which plumbs the characteristics of New Zealand verse still deeper. This essay is tendentious, provocative, and based upon a firmly individual notion of poetic values; yet, as an appraisal of the achievements of New Zealand poets, it remains unrivalled. Other books and booklets dealing with various aspects of the national literature are E. M. Smith's *A History of New Zealand Fiction* (1939), Alan Mulgan's *Literature and Authorship in New Zealand* (1943), J. C. Reid's *Creative Writing in New Zealand* (1946), James K. Baxter's *Recent Trends in New Zealand Poetry* (1951) and *The Fire and the Anvil* (1955), Ormond Burton's *Spring Fires* (1955), and Joan Stevens's *The New Zealand Novel* (1961, revised 1966).

Of special significance, too, has been the development of the periodical *Landfall*; by setting high standards, it has done much for critical writing. Some of the most acute analyses of our literature, as well as of our society, are to be found in its pages, or in the collections made from the journals. *Arena,* founded in 1943, prints mainly creative writing, while *Mate* and *Comment* (which casts its net wider for subject-matter) have given interesting appraisals of individual writers.

Another source of critical writing was the *New Zealand Poetry Year-Book,* a hard-backed annual founded in 1951 by Louis Johnson and appearing sporadically for some years. In general, this selection of current verse shows in its editorials and incidental critical articles a hostility to the "myth" of New Zealand literature it attributes to Curnow and Holcroft of "a lonely island-desert, discovered by navigators and developed by baffled explorers," and emphasizes the value of poetry dealing with urban realities or with values common to all modern societies.

Much critical work is still to be done, especially in the direction of full-length assessments of particular writers, although this is beginning to emerge in reconsiderations of the poets of the 1930's which are appearing in journals like *Landfall* and *Comment.* Among the handful of books that have so far been published are W. A. Sewell's brilliant monograph, *Katherine Mansfield* (1936), Airini Woodhouse's study of *Guthrie-Smith* (1959), Phillip Wilson's books on W. A. Satchell, *The Maorilander* (1961) and *William Satchell* (1968), and Paul Day's *John Mulgan* (1969).

A concern for locating and defining national identity has been, as the preceding pages indicate, a feature of New Zealand writing from early times. The first nineteenth-century writers saw New Zealand as a British province with a provincial culture distinctly different in character from what they felt was the brash, independent colonialism of Australia. They recognized, of course, the differences between the social conditions of the new land and those of Britain and they suffered some strain in reconciling the two, in imagining the smooth lawns, stately homes, and social customs of "Home" as re-created in clearings in the New Zealand bush. But, secure in the imperial context, they were sure that their country's destiny was as a cultural province, especially distinctive for its noble Maoris, its fertile lands, and the taste, intelligence, and earnestness of its people. All communities, particularly developing ones, need such myths to sustain them.

Whatever might be distinctive to the new land, the nineteenth-century settlers trusted to literature to demonstrate, and, to begin with, the distinctiveness was mainly topographical. But in the 1880's anxious doubts began to creep in as to whether, in fact, such a thing as a national New Zealand character did exist. The economic depression of that decade gave a sharp jolt to the dream of a British Pacific Utopia and some topical satire and disillusioned verse appeared to dilute the bland provinciality.

The 1890's, with their progressive legislation, produced another swing of the pendulum—a fresh examination of the possibilities of life in this land and of cultural dependency. Could New Zealand remain a cultural province and yet be the source of a new, more enlightened way of life? Was the choice between a raw, restricted New Zealand and a remote, idealized Britain? Pember Reeves chose to sponsor an aggressive colonialism; yet the narrowness of New Zealand society finally drove him to England. So another change of mood followed. The most favored line until after the First World War was a renewed attempt to retain in literature and life the best of two worlds—to preserve the more "civilized" British values and combine them with the best that could be distilled from the New Zealand experience.

A strong awareness of her national identity produced by New Zealand's part in the First World War, paradoxically through rallying to the aid of Mother England, and accentuated by the realities of the economic depression of the 1920's and 1930's, was reflected, as has been pointed out, in a body of literature which, if only from the character of its concerns, seems to have a new distinctiveness. Yet, in retrospect, the creative writing of those days is seen to deal, at bottom, with ideas and themes which had long been a part of the New Zealand consciousness. The dominant mood of the 1930's was a prolongation of Reeves's colonialism, with a strong emphasis on severance from domination by received British values and traditions, especially in literature, and on the importance of the New Zealand thing.

The reaction in the 1950's and 1960's by younger writers was inevitable. They repudiate both the colonial impulse, however rationalized, and, with the decay of Empire, the provincial sensibility as well. Both in theory and in practice, they stress the internationality of literature, the common experience of city living throughout the world, the impossibility of maintaining a myth of exile in an age of jet-flight and the ubiquitousness of certain literary influences. Their aim is not to abolish landscape poetry as such, but to question its centrality, and to write, not of the problems of being a New Zealander, but of those things that are every man's concern.

Questions of identity have become personal, not national—not that, in the best literature, they have not always been. But for younger writers all subject-matter is New Zealand subject-matter; literature, for them, is written by men and women about men and women, not by New Zealanders about New Zealanders. At the same time, they recognize that only by response to a specific environment is it possible for a writer validly to report a human reality. The contemporary scene shows an overlapping of provincial, colonial, and international attitudes, with the emphasis perhaps on the latter and with the colonial sensibility revealing itself with more subtlety and art.

The fresh developments in literary criticism suggest that a new phase has been reached in New Zealand's struggle toward some kind of literary maturity. Most earlier criticism had, necessarily, a sociological or historical bias; writing tended to be valued to the degree to which it revealed or interpreted New Zealand or New Zealanders or reflected the curve of social change. There is now a decided move towards a more rigidly literary criticism, in which judgments are made in a context wider than the national one, and attempts made to evaluate works by the kind of human experience they present and how skilfully they do this.

The present situation is one of healthy diversity, with writers side by side who have passed through all, or remained fixed in one of the various theoretical positions of the last forty or fifty years—or who have accepted none. During this time New Zealand literature has acquired technical skill, sophistication, and a measure of self-confidence. New Zealand readers, once justifiably suspicious of the local product, have come to accept New Zealand books, when they amount to anything. Much that is published in the country would be of very little interest to the world at large. New Zealanders, like other people, see a value in works that interpret them to themselves, that provide criticism of national values, that articulate submerged feelings of insecurity or unrest beneath the Welfare State façade of "all's-well." But it is generally accepted that the true quality of our writing is to be determined not by the presence or absence of patently indigenous elements, but by the vision and talent of its writers.

On the whole, the achievement of these writers is modest enough, but the work and the continued presence of Frank Sargeson, Janet Frame, James K. Baxter, Allen Curnow, and others gives confidence to younger writers that this land can spin literature of quality out of its own resources. More writers than was the case a quarter of a century ago are prepared to be accepted simply as poets, novelists, and dramatists without the national modifier. And there is a widening awareness of the fact that a healthy national literature depends upon the participation, at various levels of enjoyment and understanding, of reader and critic as well as of writer.

INDEX